National Congress on Languages in Education

Language awareness

NCLE Papers and Reports 6

Edited by B Gillian Donmall

Sponsors of the activities of the Language Awareness Working Party:

The Bell Educational Trust
The Centre for British Teachers Limited
The Hilden Charitable Fund

Centre for Information on Language Teaching and Research

First published 1985

Copyright © 1985 Centre for Information on Language Teaching
and Research
ISBN 0 903466 99 6

Printed in Great Britain by Multiplex Techniques Ltd

Published by Centre for Information on Language Teaching and
Research, Regent's College, Inner Circle, Regent's Park, London
NW1 4NS

CONTENTS

INTRODUCTION

The National Congress on Languages in Education is a body which consists of professional associations for languages of all kinds including, although it is not always fully appreciated, English (as mother-tongue, second and foreign language) as well as minority community languages and foreign languages. Among the activities carried out under its remit prior to 1981 had been a number relating to specific language areas but its responsibility for all languages had engendered much useful work in establishing not only areas of common concern but also in setting out those aspects of language which underpin every kind of language teaching and learning. The setting up of this working party was a quasi natural development following the work already done for NCLE and elsewhere, from insights expressed in the Bullock Report of 1976 and recommendations made by its authors, and from individual initiatives taken by schools which were not widely co-ordinated and lacked a solid foundation of coherence and defined purpose.

It was important for the working party to draw up a definition of that area of Applied Linguistics called Language Awareness both to indicate its nature and to point to its intention and also to avoid misunderstandings. In particular it had been thought by some to mean a reversion to past practices in language teaching which had been experienced as unsuccessful in their own right and inappropriate in view of the present-day emphasis on the communicative purposes of language learning. It was important, too, to establish its place in the curriculum especially in view of the vital role language has to play in the teaching and learning of all subjects. All this is carried out in The Report.

The development of work in Language Awareness has had the considerable advantage that it has arisen from experienced needs. Content, syllabus and methodology are not hide-bound by previously determined examining requirements. Nonetheless, in the instance of the Oratory School whose course does lead to an A/O qualification, it has been shown that it is possible to match assessment criteria to the criteria already established for the teaching programme.

The working party has become a focal point for contact, and for dissemination of information as well as an agent for stimulus to new initiatives. It has sought to respond to and incorporate work carried out by others external to the group. Much interest has been shown nationally. Local education authorities have been involved in several ways and a meeting took place at Elizabeth House between the working party members and the Senior Chief Inspector of HM Inspectorate, Mr E Bolton, together with Staff Inspectors for English, Modern Languages and the Primary Sector. Interest has also been shown abroad.

Recommendations put by the working party to NCLE and considered at the Assembly at York in July received wide-spread support. Standing Committee of the NCLE 1984-1986 cycle has responded by ensuring the continuation of Language Awareness activities under its remit as a Language Awareness Continuation Project. Gillian Donmall and John Sinclair are the co-ordinators of developments. The particular undertakings for the members of the continuation project to carry out are the production of a module for initial and in-service teacher training and of a monitoring scheme for use by schools for the purposes of evaluating the effectiveness of their own Language Awareness programmes. Further Newsletters will be produced and the bibliography will be updated.

It has been a feature of the working party that it has worked closely with schools, endeavouring to ensure a useful combination of theory and practice, and this will undoubtedly continue to be the case. The descriptions of school activities, some already advanced and sophisticated, others still at the exploratory stage of early learning, form an important part of this publication. Work in Language Awareness is still in its infancy. It is surely right that it should grow to maturity in response to the needs and experiences of those active in the field.

Gillian Donmall

Section A

THE REPORT

THE REPORT OF THE LANGUAGE AWARENESS WORKING PARTY

I. ORIGINS AND TERMS OF REFERENCE

Since the inception of NCLE in 1976 each successive Standing
Committee has instigated investigations into areas identified as
important to any one or several of the full range of language
interests encompassed within the NCLE framework. Hitherto these have
taken the form of working parties which have submitted an account of
their work and findings in the form of a Report plus additional
papers which have been submitted to constituent organizations and
presented at a bi-ennial Assembly together with recommendation for
implementation, action or further work. Subsequently CILT[1] has
published a compendium of their findings in the form of NCLE Reports
and Papers. Whilst interests specific to one or other language group
have been pursued according to their needs, determined by the
existing Standing Committee (e.g. foreign language teaching examinations) increasingly interest has been shown in the development of
work in language as it relates to all language areas (EFL, ESL,
MCLs, FLs, EMT)[2] and the progression is reflected in the reports
and papers, from E.W. Hawkins' The Linguistic Needs of Pupils in
Reports and Papers No.1 through V. Cook, J. Long and S. McDonough's
First and Second Language Learning and E.W. Hawkins' Language as a
Curriculum Study in Report and Papers No.2 to several papers under
the general heading Language Policies in Schools in Reports and
Papers No.3.

At the 1982 Assembly there was a strong body of opinion emanating
from representatives of the range of language interests that this
work should be furthered. CILT took the first active step in
organising a conference on Language Awareness which was held in
Birmingham in January 1981 and to which there was a very good
response which showed that a considerable number of schools were
introducing courses in 'language', at different levels and for
different age groups. This served to underline the importance
attached to this developing area in many sectors and took work a
useful stage further. Schools which had started to take their own
initiatives in the field began to look for support from outside,

---

1. CILT - Centre for Information on Language Teaching & Research,
   Regent's College, Inner Circle, Regent's Park, London NW1 4NS
2. EFL - English as Foreign Language, ESL - English as Second
   Language, MCLs - Minority Community Languages, FLs - Foreign
   Languages, EMT - English as Mother Tongue

notably from CILT, and it was under the chairmanship of J.L.M. Trim, Director of CILT, that an NCLE Working Party was eventually set up (the Language Awareness Working Party or LAWP), by now well into the two-year NCLE cycle. However, during the remaining period of that cycle an enquiry was carried out nationally with the assistance of local authority Chief Education Officers and Advisers, to establish where Language Awareness initiatives had been taken and a map indicating these areas was drawn up. In addition, a small network of schools engaged in the development of Language Awareness programmes was established which was to feature as the main focus of the Working Party's attention. It was the expressed view of participants at the Assembly as well as of the next Standing Committee that the activities of this Working Party should continue for the next cycle.

The Working Party

In the setting up of the Working Party care was taken to ensure as full representation as possible of language interests and of education sectors. Membership included three practising teachers and sectors ranged from Primary to Higher Education and included Secondary schools and Teacher Training. The full range of language interests was ascertained as far as possible; a number of individuals wore several hats in this respect. Usefully, too, one or two members had served on previous working parties which had helped to bring developments to this point. During the next stage of its operations in the second cycle activities continued under the chairmanship of Professor J.M. Sinclair.

Membership of the Working Party

T.R.W. Aplin, Head of Dept. of Modern Languages, Henry Box School, Witney, Oxon.

Ms. J. Brewster, School of Language Studies, Ealing College of Higher Education, London.

Dr. M.S. Byram, School of Education, University of Durham.

Mrs. F.I. Davies, Department of English Language & Literature, University of Birmingham.

C.E. Dawson, King Alfred's College, Winchester, Hampshire.

Ms. B.G. Donmall, Department of Education, King's College, University of London (Secretary).

P.J. Downes, Headmaster, Hinchingbrooke School, Huntingdon, Cambs.

Professor E.W. Hawkins, Emeritus Professor, York University.

Ms. S. McDonough, Department of Language & Linguistics, University of Essex.

Ms. A. Piper, School of Language Studies, Ealing College of Higher Education, London.

Professor J.M. Sinclair, Department of English Language & Literature, University of Birmingham (Chairman).

A.J. Tinkel, The Oratory School, Woodcote, Berkshire.

J.L.M. Trim, Director, Centre for Information on Language Teaching and Research, London.

Sponsorship

NCLE receives a small sum of money from the Department of Education and Science towards its expenses. This is barely adequate to cover even minimal Standing Committee expenses, however, and it has been necessary for working parties to seek financial support for their operations elsewhere. This Working Party was indebted for this essential support to:

The Bell Educational Trust, 1 Red Cross Lane, Cambridge.

The Hilden Charitable Fund, Gort Lodge, Sudbrook Lane, Petersham, Richmond, Surrey.

The Centre for British Teachers Limited, Quality House, Quality Court, Chancery Lane, London WC1.

Terms of Reference

The activities of this Working Party were seen as the next logical step in the course of developments in the sphere of language both within NCLE and without. A major external influence was the report of the Bullock Committee, A Language for Life of 1975. This report gave a detailed analysis of the situation with regard to school pupils' language competence, not only in the sphere of English as mother tongue but in all other curricular areas (except, surprisingly, foreign languages) and made recommendations for amendments, correction and innovation in order to improve the situation, including the drawing up and implementation of school language policies. Largely as a result of this report, which received an appreciative response nationally, many schools sought to find an appropriate response to suit their circumstances. Whilst much credit is due for useful work carried out, a number of initiatives foundered owing inter alia to lack of clarity of detail with regard to translation of the recommendations into practice (e.g., what precisely was meant by 'policy', what was intended in the classroom). The means for achieving the desirable end, viz pupils' improved performance in and via language in all curricular areas, remained somewhat uncertain.

In addition, the work of the Norfolk County Council Education Department in producing ALPINE materials (A Language Project in Norfolk Education) for use in Language Awareness work in Upper Middle or Lower Secondary schools had given impetus at the school operational level.

The primary intention of the Working Party has been to monitor, co-ordinate, support and guide Language Awareness activities in schools, to draw together strings from work carried out in the realm of theory and to bring theory and practice beneficially together. The focus has been on the schools themselves, the emphasis on the realities of language use.

The Working Party has interest in the eventual effect of Language Awareness work on all subjects, also, for example, on courses in study skills, but given the constraints on its operations, has paid particular attention to courses/programmes specifically in Awareness of Language, since it might be anticipated that expertise arising from this area (for teachers as well as pupils) will have application subsequently to the other fields. It is important to add, however, that the Working Party is still hereby addressing teachers of all curricular subjects, since development of their own language awareness per se and subsequently that of the pupils is a necessary preliminary stage en route to the continued beneficial teaching/learning via language in their subject-specific classrooms as well as the conscious and purposeful fostering of the pupils' personal development via language.

Working Method

By the Assembly of 1984 some 13 meetings of the Language Awareness Working Party had taken place, at which a considerable amount of productive work has been carried out, for example, on definitions, conference planning, content of papers, newsletters, etc and at which the result of external activities have been discussed and next stages planned and prepared. Several of the Working Party members had responsibility for the monitoring and development of work in individual schools, others for particular Working Party activities e.g. the production of a bibliography, conference preparation, etc. The Working Party has tried as far as possible not to be an inward-looking group but to take account of theoretical and practical work carried out nationally and internationally and to disseminate information as widely as possible. There has been useful association with a group in Holland and a summary of Language Awareness work in Australia forms part of these papers.

II. THE TERM "LANGUAGE AWARENESS"

It was an essential first concern for the Working Party to establish in precise terms what they understand by the term 'Language Awareness'. The following simple definition was agreed:

> Language Awareness is a person's sensitivity to and conscious awareness of the nature of language and its role in human life.

The teaching of Language Awareness in schools involves both making explicit and conscious the knowledge and skills pupils have themselves built up in the course of their experience of language, and developing powers of observation and purposeful analysis of language in their immediate environment and more widely in the world.

In different ways and to a greater or lesser extent, Language Awareness programmes will have a cognitive aspect (developing awareness of pattern, contrast, system, units, categories, rules of language in use and the ability to reflect upon them, to make pertinent interpretative judgements and to convey meaning appropriately and effectively) and an affective aspect (forming attitudes, awakening and developing attention, sensitivity, curiosity, interest and aesthetic response). They may deal with the nature of linguistic forms and their realization, the variety of language (language families, languages, dialects, ideolects, modes, registers, styles) and its use, particularly as a mode of communication, by the individual and the group. Heightened awareness may be expected to bring pupils to increase the language resources available to them and to foster their mastery of them, to develop the sensitivity and level of consciousness they bring to their experience of language in everyday school and social contexts and eventually to improve their effectiveness as, for example, citizens, or as consumers and in their working life.

Language Awareness courses may take a variety of forms, serving a variety of objectives, such as:

1. to make explicit and conscious the pupils' intuitive knowledge of their mother tongue.

2. to strengthen study skills for the learning of the mother tongue and foreign languages, also other curricular subjects.

3. to bring about a perception and understanding of the nature and functions of language with a view to increasing the effectiveness of communication in the mother tongue or in foreign languages.

4. to reveal to pupils the richness of linguistic variety

7

represented in the class by speakers of different dialects or by speakers of a range of mother tongues and to show the relation of that variety to standard written and spoken English without arousing feelings of antagonism or inferiority.

5. to foster better relations between all ethnic groups by arousing pupils' awareness of the origins and characteristics of their own language and dialect and their place in the wider map of languages and dialects used in the world beyond.

6. to help pupils overcome the discrepancy between the language of the home or neighbourhood and the school language of secondary education and of the text book.

7. to introduce pupils, mainly at sixth form level, to the concepts and techniques of linguistics and to consolidate what has been learned about language in an unsystematic way in the course of studying English and other languages (modern and classical).

8. to improve the reading skills of the verbally less able.

9. to impart an understanding of the value of language as part of human life.

It is vitally important to be clear as to what we exclude when using the term Language Awareness. Fears have already been expressed about developments based on a misunderstanding of this area of activity.

1. This is no reversion to 'grammar grind' in the learning of foreign languages. Firstly, the language in use is the point of commencement. Thus, the authentic language as setting-off point is underlined. It is the functional operations of language on which Language Awareness work focuses and heightened awareness of the same is intended to improve functional performance in the language. The necessity for use of terms of categorization at all in this area is doubtful, except as carried out in the target foreign language itself.

2. Similarly, vis-à-vis English or other mother tongues, this is no reversion to 'purposeless parsing'.

3. There is no intention that full courses in English (or other mother tongues) or foreign languages leading to C.S.E./O level should be replaced by Language Awareness courses. It will be seen from core school reports that most courses at present in existence are of short duration. Their efficacy should be felt in all curricular areas, including those mentioned above. In instances where time for Language Awareness is taken from other language teaching, despite time loss, hitherto schools have

felt that they have gained by rather than lost as a result of the Language Awareness input (see core school reports).

4. This work is decidedly not intended as a 'sop' for the less able pupils, the latest alternative to European Studies in foreign language teaching time. It should be clear from the reports and papers that this work should be of benefit for every child.

The term 'language across the curriculum' was brought to public notice in the Bullock Report. Generally, 'language across the curriculum' is used to refer to all aspects of the use of language as a tool for the study of all curricular subjects. There is a complex relationship between a school subject and its linguistic expression in educational contexts.

a. The communication of content through language calls on specialized conventions of language structure and language-in-context. If these are used by teachers or pupils without understanding of their significance, the pupil is disadvantaged.
b. The interaction in the classroom, which enables education to take place, has been described in general terms but there are very few studies of subject-specific classroom discourse. All indications are that individual subjects give rise to individual discourse types.

What is the relationship between Language Awareness courses and work in the area of 'language across the curriculum'? The Language Awareness course is directed at the learner and study of language is the content of the teaching/learning programme. Work carried out in the area of 'language across the curriculum' involves teacher, pupils and materials and the focus is on language as a factor in the techniques of teaching/learning in order to effect learning of subject-specific content. Courses in Language Awareness may usefully serve as a basis for developments in 'language across the curriculum', and for study skills.

III. ACTIVITIES

'Core' Schools

Firstly, a network of 'core' schools with whose Language Awareness initiatives the Working Party would be particularly concerned, was established, viz

Farringdon School, Sunderland.
Hambrough School, Ealing.
The Henry Box School, Witney, Oxfordshire.
North Westminster Community School, London.
The Oratory School, Woodcote, Berkshire.
The Priory School, Barnsley, Yorkshire.
Villiers High School, Ealing.

The next stage was the drawing up of a questionnaire for completion by staff of the school together with representatives of the Working Party in order to find out as much as possible with regard to the Language Awareness initiatives and the contexts in which they were operative. The information sought concerned:

a.   The school (number of pupils, age range, nature, structure, school population).

b.   Policy for English and foreign language provision.

c.   Policy for minority community languages.

d.   Cross-curricular language policies.

e.   Language Awareness courses (rationale/objectives, organization, teachers, materials, methods, observable outcome).

As the core school descriptions which form a part of these papers show, objectives outlined earlier are common to most, but there is considerable variation in course design and organizational features between the core schools' activities.

The following may serve to give an example of this diversity:

Language Awareness courses as a 1st or 2nd year introduction either to all kinds of language learning or to specific kinds in secondary schools.
Primary/secondary co-ordinated projects in the Language Awareness field.
Language Awareness as an aspect of teaching in primary Schools.
Sixth form Language Awareness courses.
Language Awareness as an element of a preparation for parenthood course.
Language Awareness as a module in an over-all modular approach to language learning.
Language Awareness as a particular feature in 'language across the curriculum' programmes, including study skills.

The core schools saw the following as some of the ways in which they might benefit from association with the NCLE Working Party:

- by contacts with other schools operating in the same area,

- by further clarification of the rationale of courses,
- by access to annotated reading lists,
- by access to other teaching materials,
- by attendance at conferences or in-service training courses,
- by dialogue with teachers in other education sectors,
- by closer contacts with university specialists,
- by receipt of further information, e.g. through a newsletter.

The Working Party set out to respond to these largely anticipated responses as fully as possible.

The National Scene

Whilst this was taking place, a simple questionnaire was sent out to all chief education officers asking for their co-operation in indicating either themselves or via their advisory staff, in which schools in their locality Language Awareness activities were being carried out. There was a good response giving evidence of many undertakings in individual schools, (Hereford and Worcester were particularly busy already), although often in a small way and rather tentatively. On the basis of these responses a map indicating areas of activity was drawn up.

Language Awareness Conference at Leeds University

The Working Party organized a two-day conference on Language Awareness at Leeds University from 7th-8th January 1983 which was attended by just under 100 people, more than half of whom were practising teachers; amongst the remainder were advisers, teacher trainers, examination board representatives, publishers, representatives of university subject departments, materials writers and others from the full range of language interests. In its broad frame-work the format of the conference was a familiar one - plenary input followed by dicussion in groups - but a particular feature, in accordance with the intentions of the Working Party, was the focus on activities in schools. Teachers from six 'core' schools spoke on the aims and objectives, syllabus, course content, methodology and any observable outcomes of their work.

Other plenary input from people outside schools was given by Professor John Sinclair of Birmingham University, Chairman of the Working Party, Mr. Ron Hardie of Brighton Polytechnic and Mr. Peter Gannon HMI. In addition Mr. Dennis Freeborn spoke for the University of London Examination Board about the new 'A' level examination Varieties of English, representatives of Cambridge University Press spoke on a series of books on Language Awareness in process of publication under the editorship of Prof. E.W. Hawkins, and Ms. Amanda Gray demonstrated material produced by the ILEA Learning Materials Service. The Educational Publishers Council made available a book display.

The principal purposes of the conference were as follows:

a.   to demonstrate the fruits of work in a number of schools.

b.   to clarify further the notion of Language Awareness.

c.   to identify underlying, unresolved issues in language study and language skills, e.g. distinctions between conscious and unconscious knowledge, and between skills and knowledge and the possibility of transfer and interrelationships between them.

d.   to inform concerning developments in higher education, examinations and materials.

e.   to facilitate consultation and co-operation between those operating in the field.

f.   to discover in what ways participants felt the Working Party might usefully respond to their needs (despite only modest funding).

A handout giving background information concerning the core schools was distributed in advance enabling the teachers who spoke to concentrate specifically on their courses including details of classroom activities, materials and methods used and pupils' responses. Their graphic contributions underlined the emphasis placed by J.L.M. Trim on the value of the explorational and experiential components of work done in schools.

In a brief contribution to the clarification of the term language Awareness, Professor Sinclair referred to dictionary definitions of 'awareness', identifying two senses:

-    a semi-technical use suggesting knowledge, competence, consciousness.
-    the sense of being "informed of current developments".

Professor Sinclair suggested that the main point in Language Awareness work should be:

whatever the ultimate goal - e.g. better language learning or improved social integration for the individual - there should be a preliminary concentration on language in its own terms and for its own sake.

(This emphasis would then distinguish Language Awareness work from other curricular activity, such as basic literacy work, where an awareness of language is also involved.)

Professor Sinclair indicated the need for further penetration of the

12

issue of conscious versus unconscious knowledge and the study of language for its own sake. A consideration of the problem of the adjectival forms of the words 'language' and 'linguistics' may serve as a useful starting point when endeavouring to overcome the inadequacies of our language in use. He pointed out the special nature of the study of language in schools; it is a topic dominated by the pupils' resources, viz their operational skills in one or more languages.

Mr. Peter Gannon expressed the opinion that the work the schools are carrying out falls clearly in the category 'linguistics', which has had an unfortunate history with regard to understanding of the term and the work of the experts. He suggested that teachers should not be afraid of the metalanguage of their subjects. Theoretical description and pedagogical presentation should not be confused.

The degree course in Applied Language at Brighton Polytechnic, described by the course director, Mr. Ron Hardie, must be of special interest to those sixth formers who enjoy the study of language and languages and would like to continue at a higher level but who do not wish to pursue in-depth study of literature. The course is a study of 'one area of human behaviour summed up in language'. Among its aims are:

- to develop the students' interest in the structure, learning and use of language,

- to equip the students with a descriptive and theoretical frame-work in terms of which language can be understood,

- to promote critical modes of thought in the study of linguistics and of languages,

- to enhance the students' knowledge of language through studies in their first language and both a familiar and an initially unfamiliar second language.

Students on the course bring to it a knowledge of their mother tongue, some knowledge of a second language (e.g. French or German learnt at school) which they develop, and are introduced to the study of Russian. They therefore operate at three different stages of language learning during the course and monitor their own progress. It is not intended that these second languages are pursued to degree standard in themselves, which raises questions concerning further training or employment, but French is used also as a means of instruction in several parts of the course.

Group discussions were of two kinds. In the first the intention was to promote discussion of the content of plenary talks and for these a wide range of representation from among conference participants was sought to encourage cross-fertilization of ideas. The second grouping reflected the participants' choice from among the following topic areas:

1. Assessment
2. Syllabus design
3. The role of Language Awareness courses in relation to 'language across the curriculum' programmes.
4. Post-sixteen work other than introduction to linguistics.
5. The implications of Language Awareness courses for further language learning (mother tongue or foreign languages).
6. Practical issues of implementation of Languages Awareness courses in the school curriculum.

Members of the Working Party chaired the discussions and representatives of the core schools were spread among the groups. A number of useful proposals for further Working Party activities were made and subsequent initiatives attempted to respond to them appropriately.

Newsletter

In response to suggestions from conference participants who wished to continue to receive information on activities in the field themselves and felt that there was a wider interested readership which should be reached, and in response to the Working Party's view that we should be a part of the wider field, editions 1, 2 and 3 of a newsletter were sent out in October 1983, January and April 1984 respectively and no. 4. was ready for the July Assembly. Ms. A. Piper edited and produced these on behalf of the Working Party and they were distributed by CILT. Initially they were sent to Leeds Conference participants, representatives of HMI, advisers and member organizations of NCLE but further requests from individuals and organizations made for a very wide distribution area by July 1984.

It was possible to make the newsletter available free of charge owing to the generosity of the sponsors.

List of Speakers

In response to a further conference suggestion, the Working Party compiled a list of speakers together with topics within Language Awareness on which they would be willing to speak. The initial list consisted of Working Party members, teachers from core schools plus one or two others who kindly offered their services. The list was published in the 1st edition of the newsletter.

Bibliography

An interim bibliography was compiled and produced in autumn 1983 to fill an immediate need for information about publications on Language Awareness. Suggestions for additions and comments for use as annotations were sought and an up-dated version, most of which is annotated to assist the recipient in selection, was presented to NCLE at the July Assembly. It is divided into four categories with sub-sections, as follows:

A.   Sources of materials for use by pupils.
B.   Sources of materials for use by teachers.
C.   Works of reference for teachers.
    1.   General education and language teaching.
    2.   Language and linguistic theory.
    3.   Journal and newspaper articles.

D.   Class reference books.

The Working Party was grateful to CILT for preparing an initial bibliography, to Mr. T.R.W. Aplin for editing and to Mr. P.J. Downes for production and sales. (The latter was a non-profit making exercise.)

Materials Bank

Schools have drawn up syllabuses for their Language Awareness courses and produced a quantity of materials to support their activities. It was hoped that we might be able to establish a place where such materials may be catalogued, stored and made available for consultation and loan and indeed CILT expressed willingness to help. It is now possible for schools to submit syllabuses and materials, although as yet it is only possible to consult them when visiting CILT. A lending service is not as yet possible since it entails areas of some difficulty concerning cost, copyright and staff time. It may still be a possibility for the future, however.

Papers

In addition to the Report and core school descriptions, a number of papers on aspects of Language Awareness work have been written by members of the Working Party. Also, Dr. T.J. Quinn of the University of Melbourne has written a digest of Language Awareness work in Australia.

A number of papers were produced in addition to those included in this publication. Notable contributions by E.W. Hawkins and J.L.M. Trim have been subsumed in the main body of this Report.

As a result of its work the Working Party has drawn up a list of recommendations for consideration not only by constituent member organizations and the next Standing Committee of NCLE but also by representatives of all interested sectors of education. These have been made as appropriate, within the main body of the Report, but are also listed at the end of the Report on page 27.

Other Activities

a. Members of the Working Party have been asked to talk about Language Awareness on many occasions and requests to do so increase. The following may serve to indicate the range of interest shown: members have spoken on in-service training courses of a variety of kinds, to post-graduate students in training, to the Council of Subject Teaching Associations, at a regional conference of the National Association of Language Advisers, at a meeting of polytechnic staff and students in conjunction with the Commission for Racial Equality, to staff from Birmingham University Arts subject departments at a conference on New Developments in Language Teaching, to the Association for Special Education in Northern Ireland, to a session of a Northern Ireland Speech and Language Forum at the conference of the Joint Council of Language Associations, to deputy head teachers and to doctors.

b. Mr. Downes is working to bring together a group of people from different professional backgrounds to discuss the formulation of a Language Awareness policy for Huntingdon.

c. Mrs. Davies was consulted on Language Awareness as part of a Local Education Authority curriculum review.

d. Ms. Donmall presented a paper entitled "Form and Function of Language in Pluralist Societies: The Developing Role of Language Awareness as a Response to Problems Posed by Linguistic Diversity", at a Conference of European Comparative Education Societies held in Würzburg, West Germany, in July 1983, and gave a guest lecture on "Das Konzept Sprachbewusstheit und ihre Rolle in der multikulturellen Erziehung".

e. Working Party members have been requested to write articles on a number of topics.

f. Details of the following have been received: Brighton Polytechnic degree course in Applied Language; King Alfred College Winchester Part-time Diploma in Professional Studies - Language in Education; University of London 'A' level examination in Varieties of English; Oxford and Cambridge Schools Examination Board's A/O examination Principles of Language (the exam taken by pupils at the Oratory School, see Reports of Courses and Initiatives in Core Schools 7); a pack of materials in course of production by the Open University entitled Language Diversity in the class-room, intended to help teachers of children aged 4-12 yrs; activities of the National Language Unit of Wales, and papers relating to a Language Awareness undertaking in Holland. A paper produced by Prof. H. Rosen of the London Institute of Education has also been received and A National Directory of LEA Literacy Research and Curriculum Develoment: Reading and Language Projects in LEAs.

16

g. A number of schools have written to the Working Party and sent details of their syllabuses and teaching materials.

IV. THE ARGUMENT

1   The Need for Language Awareness in the Curriculum

1.1 Support for language teaching

If it can be accepted that work in Language Awareness supports other forms of language teaching, then we must demonstrate that such support is needed. Some arguments against the promotion of Language Awareness work are discussed in 3. below; teachers will have to be convinced that Language Awareness work is a good use of valuable time, an efficient use of it, and, more keenly still, that it is even preferable to plunging into "direct" teaching of specific languages (including the native language) without the background provided by Language Awareness.

In this section we shall briefly establish that the two principal forms of language teaching in British education badly need support.

1.1.1 English as a mother tongue

Despite the enlightened, progressive and experimental attitudes of the post-war years, the results in terms of basic skills are disappointing. Competence in the written form of the school language is regularly achieved only by those who bring from home the required tools for verbal learning.

Class I children (administrative)   1 in 12 a poor reader at 7
Class V children (unskilled manual) 1 in 2 a poor reader at 7 (48%)

                    – R. Davie et al, National Child Development
                              Study (1958 cohort). Longman, 1972.

This position "worsens as the children grow older, there being a progressive decline in the performance of the lower socio-economic groups between the ages of 7 and 11"
                                                    – Bullock 2.24

The gap between the 'two nations' of fluent readers and poor readers begins to open up in the pre-school period, and schools have been shown to be powerless to prevent it widening by conventional remedial teaching.

The position is even more serious for a sub-group of class V, pupils of West Indian origin. At age 8, according to the ILEA literary survey, they are 10 points behind their white contemporaries, and this gap widens every succeeding year that they stay at school. The consequences of this are indicated by the Rampton Committee's survey (1979) in six large urban areas:

Number of Pupils scoring good passes in English Language at 16+

INDIGENOUS	ASIAN	WEST INDIAN ORIGIN
29%	21%	9%

For many of the Asian pupils, the writing is in a foreign or second language.

Number of pupils scoring 5 good passes in GCE/CSE

INDIGENOUS	ASIAN	WEST INDIAN ORIGIN
16%	18%	3%

These trends make it clear that English mother-tongue teaching as a whole is not teaching enough pupils to a high enough standard. There has been no substantial shift of policy for many years – even the Bullock Report caused little change of direction.

1.1.2 Foreign languages

Failure to master foreign languages, like failure to read in the infant school, correlates closely with parental occupation (c. Burstall et al, Primary French in the Balance. NFER, 1974). 90% of school pupils embark on French at age 11+, but two thirds abandon it at the earliest opportunity. Only 1 in 10 makes the modest target of a GCE pass.

Languages other than French are in a worse situation because they are learned by so few pupils from the start and their continuation is problematic.

The effect of this failure is to produce a society of complacent monolingual adults, which has serious effects both internally and externally. Externally there are adverse effects on commerce, especially exports (British Overseas Trade Board, Report of Study Group, Foreign Languages for Overseas Trade, 1979), while internally the resultant attitudes of insularity and cultural superiority are socially divisive.

Recent developments in teaching methods and assessment may have slowed the decline, but do not look capable of reversing the trend.

1.2 A context for language learning

The basic argument for Language Awareness courses in schools is that all forms of language learning need to be set in a context, need to be understood by the participants. Without some general appraisal of what sort of phenomenon human language is, language learning can become the meaningless acquisiton of alien codes, either other people's languages or unfamiliar varieties of the native language.

The message which the Working Party passes on from its own experience and investigations is that Language Awareness courses can provide a stimulus to and motivation for language learning which is otherwise often absent. They can clear up muddles, give students a good and positive set towards language learning, and offer alternatives to rigid and narrow attitudes to language and language behaviour.

There are two specific points in favour of Language Awareness courses from the school's point of view.

1.2.1 Basic skills, e.g. education of the ear

Learning to listen is learning what to expect, because language text is substantially predictable. Thinking ahead is important in all language skills, but particularly critical in listening because of the memory constraints; Olsen and Oller have shown that short-term memory constraints can only be overcome by increasing the listener's grasp of pattern. (G. M. Olsen, Developmental Changes in Memory. In: T. E. Moore (ed.), Cognitive Development in the Acquisition of Languages. New York Academic Press, 1973 and J. W. Olsen Jun, CLoze Tests of Second Language Proficiency and What They Measure. Proceedings of AILA Congress, Copenhagen, 1972.)

Learners must know – and may have to be shown – what they are listening for. The Bullock Committee considered the case and, although reluctant to advocate "deliberate strategies", concluded that they might be needed if improvements in listening skills did not develop out of normal activities.

In foreign language teaching the need for education of the ear has become more pressing in the past two decades, which have seen a massive swing from "eye-learning" to "ear-learning", which places emphasis on audio-visual presentation, oral work in class and in examinations, graded tests which require minimal writing skills, etc.

It is not necessary that the ear is educated exclusively with respect to one language only. If it is pursued as a general skill rather than a specific one, it will improve performance in all languages. And if the same principles are applied to the written language ("education of the eye"), particularly training in looking ahead, taught as a general skill, there should be improvement in reading skills. At a most general level, the predictability of text can be offered as a topic for general exploration, and can lead to exciting discussions about the student's available skills.

Such basic and general skills can and should be dealt with against a broader background than that provided by a single language.

1.2.2. Objectives

The objectives of language courses vary along several parameters including:

- the target language, and its status
- whether it is mother tongue, second or foreign language
- the stage in the educational process

If the language is English and it is the mother tongue, then the stage does not matter; the objective of securing mastery over public forms of English is quite clear. Language Awareness work would be useful in elaborating the concept of mastery.

If English is not the mother tongue, then Language Awareness work is important for the student to understand the role of a dominant language and its relationships with other languages used in the community.

If the language is a foreign language not spoken in the community, then a Language Awareness course is necessary to make the objectives clear. Whereas a native speaker of French or German has clear objectives in the learning of English, the English learner of French or German cannot possibly decide in early secondary school which European language, or which skills, will best suit his/her adult needs.

Hence the initial learning of a foreign language shows some of the objectives of a Language Awareness course, and will have different objectives to a language-learning course which is undertaken in the knowledge of adult requirements.

1.3 Co-ordination of language teaching and learning

The above point introduces the need for co-ordination of the language curriculum as a whole. This is first of all a valid and valuable aim in itself, but can also, by bringing teachers together around the centrality of language in learning, constitute a first step towards the Bullock vision of "language across the curriculum".

In other words, we intend that Language Awareness courses will effect two kinds of change. The first will be an improvement in coherence and direction in the language work of the school, bringing in its wake some greater consistency of approach, terminology and methodology. The longer-term changes will be discussed in Section 4 below.

Much of what we are suggesting springs naturally from the Bullock discussion. One of the strongest arguments for our programme may be that it offers the best chance of implementing the best of the Bullock proposals. Our programme differs from Bullock in two main ways: we are suggesting that all teachers of language, with other colleagues (e.g. science, music, home economics) should form a board of studies to plan and teach a specific element in the curriculum, each teacher undertaking that part of the work for which his interests and knowledge are best suited. This is a quite different proposal from the Bullock plan which limited the contribution of teachers other than English teachers to the acceptance of a (vaguely defined) responsibility for or sensitivity to the English demands made by his/her own subject.

We differ from Bullock also in giving a key role to teachers of foreign languages, teachers of ESL, ethnic minority language teachers and teachers of the classics. None of these is even mentioned in Bullock as having any part in "language across the curriculum".

In a large school there may be five kinds of language teaching going on in adjacent classrooms: English m.t./ESL/foreign language/ethnic m.t./Latin. Only the pupils who commute in bewilderment from classroom to classroom know what goes on in the different rooms. The language teachers know only what happens in their own room. They consult infrequently, share no agreed vocabulary in which to discuss language. This problem can be alleviated at school level.

1.4 Language as a curriculum subject

There is plenty of evidence of linguistic parochialism, of failure to appreciate the facts and the opportunities of linguistic diversity in our society. We propose an approach through Language Awareness which sees the students as meeting to explore the phenomenon of language, to which each student brings an individual experience and opinion. We do not expect such courses to work miracles, but they would provide in the regular timetable some opportunity for an important means of social integration.

Such courses can emphasise the linguistic skills already acquired, which the student brings to his/her learning. On the map of human knowledge, such courses introduce a student to an essential aspect of his/her humanity - the subtle articulateness which is often held to be mankind's distinguishing feature.

2.   The Value of Language Awareness work

Most of the previous section concerned the role and value of Language Awareness work in a school setting. It is summarised here from a positive point of view, and then we consider the role and value of Language Awareness work outside the educational institutions.

2.1   In the classroom

Language Awareness work can be a means of social integration through understanding differences and, through understanding, accepting them; or perhaps reformulating personal goals.

2.2   In the curriculum

Language Awareness work is a necessary means of co-ordinating the expertise in language teaching in order to make most efficient deployment of it, and to present to the students a coherent approach to language.

Although nearly all the work noted in this Report is unique to individual schools, the question of co-ordination is also important between schools. One school leads to another, and there are complaints of a breakdown between primary and secondary schools. Also the curriculum as a whole must allow for the increasing mobility of the school population (one in three students finish their schooling in a different LEA from the one they started in).

The next stage in the recognition of Language Awareness work is for regional and national authorities to build in these school-based initiatives and guide their development into local and national policy.

2.3   In the school

This work should gradually raise the awareness of all participants in the educational process of the central and commanding role of language in education.

2.4   For the individual

Language Awareness work will help an individual to acquire an understanding of his/her own linguistic skills and attributes, and how they can be improved. This perception will generate the motivation to learn languages. An individual must formulate goals if he/she is to be motivated or even directional, and this means he/she must know something about a possible destination before he/she actually reaches it.

As well as the educational benefit, the individual will profit by acquiring a greater sensitivity to languge in his/her various social groups.

2.5 In the family

One of the main messages which we would like to put over in this report is the importance of Language Awareness in the family, and the importance of the family in Language Awareness.

On the first point, the cycle of generations produces a microcosm of communication problems which Language Awareness courses must recognise, evaluate and offer solutions to. In particular, the tendency to exclude both older and younger generations from conversational attention is a serious source of problems which awareness can combat. For both extremes of the age-range, interaction is the stuff of identity; social relationships do not stay still or survive periods of neglect of their expression (Berger and Luckman, The Social Construction of Reality. Doubleday, 1966). For the younger generation, from the cradle onwards, the quality of interaction is likely to be the limiting factor on educational attainment, and maybe self-awareness as well.

The matter of offering future parents a language element in 'childcare' courses is one which we adopt directly from Bullock and re-present to the profession. Bullock admirably grasped the importance of this aspect of the preparation for parenthood. The Bullock proposals, far-reaching and radical, have had almost no discussion. They evoked little response from HMI or from those responsible for in-service training or initial training of teachers of English, or Home Economics.

2.6 In the community, and in the workplace

Where a society is in process of fairly rapid change or readjustment, or subject to economic, political or social stress, the importance of understanding social signals is highlighted. Many more events require interpretation than is the case of a relatively stable and isolated society. The most important and complex social signals come in language and so in preparation for a lifetime of interpreting them, students require a reliable basis for their hypotheses. Their ability to support social groups in the community and at work may well depend on their awareness of language. We cannot overestimate the effect of people associating abstract notions and features of language - even surface features like pronunciation, voice quality, loudness, etc. Emotional attitudes, social assumptions, status features and many more can be so linked, provoking a rich variety of prejudice.

2.7 On the national and international scene

This country has a unique ability to criticise itself constantly and complacently about the poor standards of foreign language learning. Despite membership of a multilingual European community, despite a record of weakening industrial competitiveness, despite a continuous display of cultural misunderstandings, there is no surge of effort in the direction of language learning. Instead, we point to another clear trend and put our shirts on the increasing importance of English internationally, as if the world were well on the way to becoming monolingual.

The act of remaining monolingual is an alienating act, telling the world that we will only talk to them on our own terms. The birthright of a native English speaker is to acquire without apparent effort what foreigners will have to work at long and hard. The other side of the coin is the absence of a stimulus to increase our cultural perspectives, or to deepen our understanding of other communities. We see no need, in commerce, to use the language of the customer, and we do not seek the particular delight in international friendships based on an equal footing. Language Awareness courses will increase the likelihood of improved international relations, and better relations between cultural groups within our national group.

3. <u>Problems, snags and pitfalls</u> (see also II. The Term 'Language Awareness' on p 7)

The Working Party is aware that its basic case will not be welcomed immediately by all parties, and so it raises in this section a number of possible difficulties and counter-arguments, and states its own position with respect to them.

3.1 *Language Awareness work is an addition to a crowded curriculum, and it must take time which is at present allocated to something else. In particular, since a lot of Language Awareness enthusiasm starts among the foreign language teachers, time is taken from actually teaching the language. This is a retrograde step, reversing a trend towards full use of class time for learning language skills which has met with the full approval of the profession.*

Our answer to this is first of all to recognise a danger - the danger of the ineffective Language Awareness course, or the moribund one which just wastes time. Language Awareness work will be under constant review, and will only be tolerated if it earns its keep.

Secondly, those who support Language Awareness are also people who support optimising the use of the classroom for direct skill teaching. It is by no means a reaction against that reform, and merely seeks to make the teaching more effective.

The case at this level is that a language will be learned more effectively in a given number of hours if it is presented in a Language Awareness context. It is going to be difficult ever to prove this (see 3.6. below) and at present we rely on the testimony of practitioners, and the distilled experience of our own membership and those we have consulted. If there were no problems for language learners, this Working Party would have had no reason to exist. Nothing in our programme should be seen as replacing the communicative use of the foreign language which is now seen as essential for effective learning. It is now widely accepted that two complementary activities must mutually reinforce each other, for effective learning: insight into pattern must quicken and economise the learning that results from the use of the foreign language in genuine 'speech acts', i.e. language in which the learner expresses his/her own intentions instead of simply acting as a 'post office' transmitting messages which are not his/her concern, from text to teacher or examiner. Almost the whole of the current 16+ examination course consists of such 'non-serious' language (in J. Searle's terms). (J. R. Searle, Speech Acts. An Essay in the Philosophy of Language. CUP, 1969.) Teachers and examiners are challenged to find ways of bringing real communication into the classroom. At the same time the other half of the teaching strategy, developing pupils' insight into pattern, cannot be neglected and it is here that 'awareness of language' has a vital role to play.

3.2 *Language Awareness is little more than a cover for the reintroduction of grammar teaching and all the other discards of recent years. It is linguistics by another name, and an attempt to return to an outdated and discredited methodology.*

This point is particularly sensitive in the mother-tongue English tradition, and it is time to exorcise the Ghost of Grammar Past which still haunts discussions on the subject. It is also time to point out that the effort of getting rid of the old style of grammar teaching required the exclusion of most investigations of pattern in language, and that a lot was therefore lost.

Grammar, and language study as a whole, is barely recognisable compared with the state it was in when it was banished from the English classroom. The Working Party does not wish to engage in detail with the controversy, but does wish to make two crucial points.

(a)   An important feature of current language study is the willingness to work from principles, rather than solely through fully articulated complex and 'given' analytical schemata. From being a subject which appeared to stress knowledge, it has become a subject which emphasises skill.

(b)   There is a growing movement to point up the common ground among students of language, rather than emphasise the differences, and this particularly in a context of language learning.

There is, of course, a danger in this more relaxed professional attitude. It might be difficult on occasions to distinguish between a carefully planned and guided voyage of discovery in language patterning, and a vague, lowbrow wander among trivia that never acquire significance. As in 3.1, there is a requirement of vigilance and self-criticism on the part of those responsible for Language Awareness work.

3.3 *Language Awareness work reinforces the 'nuts and bolts' approach to language teaching, offering students a limited vision of competence. In particular, it does not support or promote the expressive use of language, native or foreign.*

The short answer to this is that if it is true, the Language Awareness course is wrong. We would hope that the limitation is in the understanding of the scope of Language Awareness courses. Although most are brief, they show in toto a remarkable range, and most of them sacrifice any claim to comprehensiveness in order to avoid superficiality.

3.4 *It has been shown that knowledge <u>about</u> language has no effect on one's ability to <u>use</u> language. Hence Language Awareness courses are bound to be ineffective.*

This is a gross oversimplification which we would challenge. On the contrary, some influential recent work (e.g. E.W. Stevick, <u>Memory, Meaning and Method</u>. Newbury House, 1976.) supports the proposition that having a sensitive awareness of language improves learning. Language Awareness courses are a long way from piles of information to be learned.

The Working Party felt strongly that this question had to be aired, and commissioned a paper summarising the psycholinguistic evidence relevant to the question (Paper 7, p 107ff).

3.5 *Language Awareness courses, like so many grassroots innovations, will founder on the problem of teacher expertise. A few enthusiasts with impressive personal knowledge and skill will conceal for a while the fact that hardly any teachers have the requisite qualifications, formal or informal.*

This has been recognised as a serious problem from the outset, and the model courses that we have studied show various attempts to minimise the effects of inadequate training. There is no doubt whatever that the health of the Language Awareness movement will eventually depend on reforms in teacher preparation.

It is not necessary to produce superteachers, polymaths and polyglots. A sound grounding in language study, preferably including some study of languages other than English and supported by reliable and proven materials will suffice. The recurrent theme of those who offer advice in this area (e.g. recently R. Carter (ed.) <u>Linguistics and the Teacher</u> Routledge & Kegan Paul, 1982.) is that all teachers should have a basic understanding of language, since it is their main professional resource; and that language teachers, mother tongue and foreign, should have a good bit more; and that it should hang together better than has been the case in the past.

The coherence and co-ordination that we have recommended for the school policies will have to be reflected, if not created, in properly thought-out language education policies offered in teacher preparation. In this we add our voices to the chorus which has preceded us, and hope that pressure for reform will grow quickly. (See also Paper 6, p 93ff: Some implications of L.A. Work for Teacher Training Courses.)

3.6 *Language Awareness courses are too brief, general and wishy-washy to be assessed with any seriousness. Hence they will never show whether or not the students learn anything, and if so what.*

The assessment of language courses of any kind is problematic, where the ultimate aim is communicative skill. Language Awareness courses do constitute a particular headache, so much so that we have put together a small package to give some guidance (Paper 5, p 68ff). At this stage of development, a full scale evaluation is much preferable to some limited test of student attainment in a short course.

3.7 Conclusion

The Working Party has tried to be aware of the dangers that can be foreseen in Language Awareness work, and to anticipate some of the objections that require to be discussed. We would reiterate, however, that we do not think that any one of these points, nor even all of them together, would be debilitating, and very few would even be daunting. The gains in prospect from Language Awareness courses far outweigh the risks.

4. Longer-term objectives

In section 1 we expressed the need for Language Awareness courses in consideration of the immediate situation and promised to return to the matter of objectives.

Although Language Awareness is not yet fully recognised and its incidence nationally is still patchy, we would like to develop some issues that arise from this discussion, because of their great importance. Even though they may be distant prospects, we hope they may act as an impetus for change.

4.1 Preparation out of school

It was pointed out in 1.1.1 that, in general, the successful language learners are those who bring with them to school the learning
tools which they need. This point ties in with 2.5, where the
importance of adult time in interaction with children was
stressed.

There is evidence from Burstall that reading attainment in the
mother tongue correlates with efficiency in learning a foreign language, so the development of linguistic competence may best be considered very generally, with the school at the centre of a network
of co-operating institutions. At appropriate points in the curriculum Langage Awareness courses should draw attention to this
interdependence of school, home and society.

As a long, slow process measured in generations, we hope that school
leavers will take into their adulthood a better understanding of how
the next generation needs to be prepared for language work. The
Bullock report stressed this need strongly and made recommendations
which appear to have been almost entirely overlooked. The problem is
still with us and will not go away.

4.2 Integration of language teaching in the curriculum

The most part of education is achieved by the exercise of linguistic
skills, spoken and written. The language which is medium of instruction, and any other mother-tongues, are of direct relevance to the
efficiency of the educational process. No doubt many subjects would
claim a central role, but language can make an overt and indisput-
able case for the most careful attention to be paid to it.

The Working Party believes that each unit of the educational system
should begin working towards the integration of language teaching.
We have suggested some obvious and simple overhauls, and drawn
attention to the looming problem of teacher education. But if a
start could be made to the expression of longer-term goals, then
these would be a spur to effort.

4.3 It is likely that language work will assume greater importance
in years to come. Communication is becoming ever more diverse and
complex, and the world has shrunk. Well over a hundred languages are
spoken in substantial communities in this country. Politically and
economically it would seem that interdependence is the order of the
day and the decade. We must be able to get through to people, and
not, as one earlier traveller advocated, by speaking English rather
slowly and loudly.

We may not be able to predict exactly what the next generation will
need, but we can be sure that it will involve language and languages
- hence the suggestion of language courses which are not tied to an
immediate real-world objective.

Any kind of social adjustment or readjustment is going to involve a great deal of discussion at many levels. We seem to be in a period of rapid change, where a high value is placed on articulateness, whatever the language or variety of it. Educational and intellectual standards are changing, so past routine is not a reliable reference point.

A language policy for education at school level would have to be robust and resourceful, paying attention to the requirements of efficient communication within the school itself. Also it would have to consider the specifically linguistic skills that it wished the students to acquire, and how this should be done. Also it would have to consider the outlooks, attitudes and levels of understanding that it should prescribe. And finally it would have to devise a way of presenting and conveying a broad picture of the permanence and importance of linguistic skills, and the way in which citizens should nurture their own and further them in others.

It seems to this Working Party that the concerns which are roughly grouped under the heading of Language Awareness should have a prominent role in any development of the kind envisaged above. At this early stage, we can point to a groundswell of interest, and a number of excellent examples of what can be done. We believe this to be a very important question and one which although still displaying some deficiencies at this fairly early stage of its development should not be overlooked.

V.   RECOMMENDATIONS OF THE LANGUAGE AWARENESS WORKING PARTY TO THE NATIONAL CONGRESS ON LANGUAGES IN EDUCATION

1.   That NCLE create a more permanent body for the maintenance and development of the work as described in the Report. Its obligations should include:

   -   serving as a source of advice and guidance
   -   continued publication of the Newsletter
   -   extension and updating of the annotated bibliography which should be published annually
   -   development of a bank of syllabuses and materials to which there must be professional access
   -   promotion of conferences on Language Awareness topics, encouragement of the writing of papers and maintenance of a list of speakers
   -   encouragement of communication and co-operation between schools, also with other sectors of the education system.

29

2. That NCLE secure funding for further Language Awareness activities, viz:

    - evaluation of the effectiveness of Language Awareness courses
    - production of teacher training modules
    - materials development
    - investigation of factors affecting language learning.

3. That NCLE promote the co-ordination of professional associations and encourage members to use their publication outlets for liaison purposes.

4. That NCLE take further steps in planning the co-ordination of the language curriculum as a whole, whereby all teachers come together around the centrality of language in learning and make progress towards realization of the Bullock vision of 'language across the curriculum.'

5. That NCLE encourage regional and national authorities, in recognition of Language Awareness work, to build on the school-based initiatives and guide their development into local and national policy.

6. That NCLE mount a campaign to ensure that coherent and co-ordinated language education policies are reflected or created in Teacher Preparation programmmes.

7. That NCLE should contact the organisers of all Initial Teacher Training courses and endeavour to ensure the inclusion of a Language Awareness module in all I.T.T. courses for all trainees, with recognition of the key roles of teachers of FLs, ESL, EFL, MCLs and EMT.

8. That NCLE set up a working group to draw up limited and precise proposals for modules for initial and in-service training courses including syllabus, course content and methodology.

9. That NCLE investigate areas of the curriculum lying outside language work, e.g. child care courses, in order to assess the need for Language Awareness work in these areas.

10. That NCLE stress the need for procedures for on-going evaluation as a prominent feature in all courses which are concerned with the design, preparation and organization of Language Awareness courses.

11. That NCLE should encourage a review of the philosophy of language teaching to which Language Awareness initatives are contributing.

Section B

THE PAPERS

LANGUAGE AWARENESS IN SIX EASY LESSONS

J M Sinclair

Language Awareness is very much a "grass roots" movement, taking its lead from the work of pioneering schools, and this has led to a wealth of good ideas and variety of approaches which a more centrally-devised policy could not match. This diversity fits well with the essential vagueness of "Language Awareness", which I have grumbled about on a previous occasion. But a Working Party is bound to exert pressure to tidy things, to define, to abstract, to categorise. It is the natural human seeking of a consensus.

I believe that the creative untidiness of the actual content of Language Awareness courses is in fact unrelated to the fuzziness of the cover-term. They have different origins, and it is a case of a useful concept happily meeting up with a spontaneous school-based perception of a need. This paper hopes to add a little stiffening to a fluid situation, because for many people it is too fluid. Language Awareness courses arise in different schools for different reasons, are devised by different groups and are applied at different stages to different pupils in pursuit of different objectives. There is nothing in the day-to-day teaching that one can perceive as common to all. Also, some of the teachers involved confess that they are at sea when it comes to devising or justifying a syllabus, and teachers who are eager to set up such a course can get little authoritative guidance.

The current pattern of Language Awareness courses highlights a problem that has thwarted many initiatives in language education in the post-war period. There is a gross shortage of time and expertise. Language Awareness courses, in the main, are squeezed into an overfull timetable and are able to secure only a paltry proportion of the attention of a class or school. The priorities of teacher training and the bureaucratic divisions in language education from the DES outward, make it most unlikely that Language Awareness teachers have had adequate preparation, or can feel any security beyond personal conscientiousness.

This unfortunate current situation, when compared with the average run of syllabus proposals, exposes a credibility gap. If one is asked to specify course content in Language, Language Studies, Linguistics, etc. either for pupils or in teacher education, it is difficult to avoid being comprehensive, thorough and detailed. Anything less would seem to be irresponsible. The result is something that will not fit into the time available and/or is beyond the competence of the staff available. I am as guilty of making unrealistic suggestions as anyone else, and hereby repent. I hope that the reception of this paper will not require further repentance.

Hence the title. The great lumbering organisation which educates our children can only cope with modest proposals, and gentle nudges. Instead of thinking of content as coverage, I should like to identify a few important and distinctive features of language which might with profit be offered to pupils in a Language Awareness course. If there are as few as six lessons, something would be accomplished by raising the six points that are outlined below. If there are 12 lessons, so much the better - and so on, for the syllabus is infinitely extendable.

This enterprise has a reputable pedigree, in for example the attempt of R A Hudson to reach consensus.[1] He produced a classified set of 81 statements about language with which most of those working in language teaching would agree; unfortunately, it would probably require at least 81 lessons to put them across. At a more abstract level, the attempt, originated by Hockett, to set out the defining characteristics of language provides a smaller, more manageable menu. As revised and extended by Lyons[2] it offers an interesting set of propositions that could form an exciting Language Awareness course. In essence the claim is that any activity that conforms to all of the criteria is equivalent to a natural human language, and anything that fails on one or more of the criteria is not. It was an interesting defensive response to the revelations in the fifties and sixties that various other mammals - apes and dolphins principally - either seemed to use or could be trained to use a communication system which had a disturbing similarity to language, which had hitherto been regarded as a reliable defining characteristic of humankind.

I commend these criteria as an excellent basis for a Language Awareness course, but fear that the abstract nature of the concepts would take some considerable class time to tease out and exemplify. Also the conceptual steps involved would require very sophisticated management. What is needed is something more direct and concrete, which can be put across in vivid terms in a short time, which does not depend on a heavy input of knowledge, and which can relate directly and spontaneously to the state of language awareness of the average class. There are six propositions which seem to me to express central and crucial features of language. Any pupil who had

---

1. Brookes A, and R Hudson, "Do Linguistics have anything to say to teachers?" in R. Carter (ed.) Linguistics and the Teacher, (RKP 1982).

2. Lyons J, Semantics, vol. 1, p.70, (Cambridge, 1977).

recognised these six would in my view be linguistically aware. Here is a short account of each of them.

1. Productivity

Language is apparently a limited resource for any individual at any point in time. In principle, we could make a list of the words that a person knows and the structural rules that he/she has command of. Yet each individual has the ability to produce an unlimited number of different utterances. The two points should be easy to establish in the classroom with any age of child, and a wide range of devices for extending the set of sentences will be thought out. Perhaps the general mechanism of recursion, or cyclical repetition, will be identified, but perhaps not.

2. Creativity

During exploration of the first point, the question of poetic licence may well arise, and that can be used to examine some features of the literary language. The initial point to be made is that the rules of language are just as interesting and meaningful when you break them as when you follow them. Learners will not need much encouragement to break a variety of rules, and can then be invited to find meaningful contexts for the results. It is likely that this activity will highlight the bizarre side of linguistic creativity as a matter of course by everyone. Because it is so normal, natural and widespread, it is likely that some difficulty will be experienced in latching on to the point, especially since it is suppressed in most language teaching materials. But once grasped, the pervasive creativity of language will provide a powerful tool for exploration. For example, it is natural and everyday to use metaphor to overcome a problem in description.

3. Stability and change

In establishing the second point, it may well be noticed that the rules of a language are not terribly clear-cut or evenly applied. That is a good way into the notion of variation, about which two points are to be made. The first contrasts the relative stability of a language at any point in time with the fact that it is continuously in a state of change. Historical awareness is notoriously difficult to initiate in young children, and language offers one of the easiest ways in, for example through the daily neologisms on the media. Quite important questions can arise from the perception that a society normally includes several generations of speakers.

4. Social variation

The second point about variety will come up in sorting out the historical side - this is the way language varies elaborately with social factors. Again, from the observation that language is an inexact system arises the question of what other meaning is given in side-effects. Of all the issues in this syllabus, this is the most obvious and easy to teach, with stimulus material easy to get. It also provides a good starting point for two further explorations - the variety of languages, and social signalling of a paralinguistic or non-linguistic nature.

5. How to do things with language

Some syllabuses concern themselves exclusively with the fourth point, but this one presses on, picking up the observations in 3 and 4 about individual variation. The fact that no two people are the same is basic to the study of language as interaction; some theories of language are only suitable for clones. The theme of this part of the syllabus is how to get things done, using language, while being aware that it may not be interpreted in exactly the way in which it is intended. Again, it leads to lively, high-activity teaching and good clean fun.

6. The two-layered code

The final point should arise from the preceding by the observation that people in conversations keep checking back on each other. The language of the classroom itself gives examples every few seconds. This is developed into a study of language about language - how we are constantly checking, evaluating, summarising, labelling, scene-setting, etc. Language is seen as a two-layered code rather than as a single stream of speech or writing. The content of an utterance - what message it contains, which in principle could be phrased differently - is seen as taking a particular form because of other important information that must be given in the same structure - how it relates to what has gone before and what is to come, how it may relate to the hearer/reader's position, how it is to be taken, what is the expected evaluation, etc. Because this discoursal information is not as obvious or as well-organised as the conventional content, the learner's attention has to be drawn to it. Some teachers may have difficulty explaining its meaning and force, especially in respect of a foreign language. But since this aspect of language is at the basis of effective use, it is essential to have it even in a minimal syllabus.

A course which brings home these six points will be a lively and effective course. It will certainly give a heightened awareness of language, and will contribute to the linguistic development of learners, whatever their stage. These central features of language would be very difficult to teach by exposition, but easy to teach by discovery. Every speaker of a language actually operates with them, so by delving into their own skills they will readily understand, and become aware of their own language, and that of others.

METHODOLOGY RELATED TO LANGUAGE AWARENESS WORK

A J Tinkel

1.1   Although the concept of Language Awareness in schools now developing is wider than the aims of the authors of <u>Language in Use</u>[1], and in some respects is more ambitious, the basic premises of the two approaches are the same.

1.2   The authors of <u>Language in Use</u> pointed out that "Pupils bring to the class-room a native speaker's knowledge of and intuitions about language and its place in human society. In this sense, the task of the English teacher is not to impart a body of knowledge, but to work upon, develop, refine, and clarify the knowledge and intuitions that his pupils already possess"[2].

The pupils for any Language Awareness course possess a mother tongue plus an intuitive sense of how to use it. Any course designed to exploit that possession must recognise that this is the case. It must not be a lip-service recognition, but one that imbues the syllabus content, guides the choice of materials, moulds the form of any testing procedures involved and dictates the method of presentation. The way the Language Awareness course is presented to the students must inherently reflect in all its aspects the crucial fact they have language already.

1.3   If the premise of 1.2 is accepted, then the objectives of any language awareness course must be to lead the students to a greater awareness of what they intuitively know already. Its objectives must be to explore and thereby to produce a greater familiarity with what is already intuitively known, to get the students to think for themselves about what they can and already do do with their language. Such an exploration of the students' "native speaker knowledge of and intuitions about language and its place in human society" should be, and can easily be combined with the objective of widening and strengthening their awareness of language. Indeed it can be argued that development of the students' awareness is a natural consequence of a proper exploration of their language ability.   When the students bring more than one mother tongue or dialect variation to the group, a Language Awareness course offers the chance to use these different tongues and dialects for comparison. By so doing the course provides a forum to give them proper value and unprejudiced presentation.

---

1. Doughty P, J Pearce and G Thornton. <u>Language in Use</u>. Edward Arnold, 1971.
2. Ibid. p.11.

1.4 The use of the students' own already-possessed linguistic know-ledge in a Language Awareness course means that such a course be-comes an ideal vehicle for student-centred activity. The role of the teacher is to order the material, to shape the presentation, to keep the focus steady so that the students' own knowledge can be explored systematically without their getting lost. In this way Language Awareness becomes a practical subject, with the teacher arranging the guidelines of the course progression and the con-ditions of each exploration. If the teacher talks <u>about</u> language to the students, he/she is far less likely to capture their interest, than if he/she lets them explore it for themselves under conditions carefully prepared and controlled by him/her.

1.5 Within the above concept of a practical, student-centred activity, there will sometimes be a role for the teacher as an imparter of new facts. This will be truer for some kinds of Language Awareness course than for others. For example, when students have a variety of mother tongues which are being used in the course, when facts about first language acquisition are being presented in a parenthood course, when comparisons are being made with foreign lan-guages in a course preparatory to learning those languages, when animal communication or the history of writing and other alphabets are being studied – these and other instances obviously require the teacher to present new items of information to the students that are not part of their already-possessed linguistic knowledge. However, even in such instances, the underlying principle should remain that of examining human language ability through and by reference to that already-possessed language ability.

1.6 If Language Awareness is just an element of a wider course, that element would acquire added immediacy if it is centred on the students' own linguistic ability. This would be true whether there is an imparting of new facts, as, for example, about first language acquisition in a parenthood course, or whether the ability is being explored directly.

If Language Awareness is seen as a course in its own right, its various components need to be held together. Otherwise the course could become a series of disconnected gobbets in the eyes of the students, even more likely when the elements of the course require the teacher to impart factual knowledge, as for example in history of writing, introduction of new languages or animal communications. The particular limited aims of the course, such as preparation for learning a foreign language or introduction to different mother tongues in a multi-ethnic group, may provide such a unifying underpinning, but whether such limited aims are present or not, giving the course the underlying principle of looking at language through the students' own knowledge of it, provides the intuitively most satisfying linkage and underpinning, as well as the guide to the most stimulating method of presentation.

1.7 The unifying nature of the principle of using the students' own language as a 'point de départ' can be taken a step further. It provides a linking concept, not only for the disparate elements to do with language in a particular Language Awareness course. It also provides a vital common denominator for the wide range of Language Awareness courses that have emerged. We could claim that these courses have in common, not just the fact that they all have to do with language in some guise or other, but that they all embody a particular approach to the presentation of language to the student and that this approach predicates the method and even the view of language itself. In this way one of the strengths of the Language Awareness movement (that it is a classroom—led development based on practical solutions for immediate teaching needs) can be protected from the weakness of such a disparate development (that it is so varied as to be amorphous). The idea of exploring the students' already-possessed intuitive language ability can be the defining, as well as unifying principle of Language Awareness courses.

1.8 Greater awareness of how their language — and language in general — functions should bring about greater sensitivity to language on the part of the students. They should become more alert to how they use their mother tongue and — equally important — how it is used by others on them. The authors of __Language in Use__ held this view: "... a basic premise of the volume is that the development of awareness in the pupil will have a positive effect upon his competence ...."[3].

Further, if analysis of the mother tongue is approached on the lines of exploring what the students already know, this should not only produce such an enhanced awareness, but it would be doing so in a manner that makes the methodology of this mother tongue analysis complementary to the approach to mother tongue English teaching that seeks to lead the students to explore and expand their awareness of themselves and their relationship with others through expressing themselves in language.

In both cases the objective is to guide the students through a cultivation of a greater awareness of intuitive knowledge/ability towards development of their possession of that same knowledge/ability. If analysis of the mother tongue can bring about greater awareness of language in the students which benefits their use of it, and if the methodology for achieving that greater awareness is in harmony with the methodology for enhancing the individual by developing a more fruitful use of his/her language, then language awareness can offer a partnership to the 'creative use', 'self-discovery' approach to mother tongue teaching. If this is so,

---

3. Ibid. p.10.

then analysis of language can be incorporated into mother-tongue teaching without jeopardising the developments of recent years and without a return to old-style 'grammar' teaching.

1.9 It has been argued that Language Awareness as applied to analysis of language heralds a return to such old-style 'grammar' teaching. This is viewed with horror by some and with relief by others. The authors of Language in Use point out: "The long argument over the teaching of 'grammar' in schools really concentrated upon the effects of a certain kind of explicit knowledge of the language, such as classification of words and parsing, on pupils' use of language. When teachers discovered that there seemed to be no observable effect of the one upon the other they rejected teaching about language, because they could see no justification for it. It was unfortunate that the study of language came to be identified with a rudimentary and inadequate type of knowledge about language, and that its validity was judged solely upon its power to increase competence[4]."

It is the method of studying language that should have been rejected, not the desirability of studying language itself. The method was counter-intuitive to the students, thereby divorcing what was being taught from the reality of their intuitive language knowledge. The methodology of explicit teaching of one variety of language as right and to be imitated at all times, particularly when based on misconceptions about the nature of language itself, is a more likely reason for the failure of old-style 'grammar' teaching, than the fact that the students were being taught to analyse their mother tongue.

If the methodology is based on working systematically through the language ability of the students, misconceptions about language are more likely to be held in check by the realities of language facts intuitively known by the students. Language analysis centred on the students' own knowledge will offer notions of appropriateness in place of notions of linguistic right and wrong, which will fit the language intuitions of the students.

In this way the horror of those who dread a return to old-style 'grammar' teaching can be avoided, while at the same time relief can be offered to those who want mother-tongue analysis taught.

1.10 From the central idea of the student possessing language and the teacher's role being to guide his analysis of it, we are led to prefer a particular method of teaching. This student-centred method ensures that the native speaker's intuitions are in harmony with the

---

4. Ibid. p.10.

teacher's presentation, which in turn offers some insurance against counter-intuitive concepts being advanced by the teacher, since the the student is offered the initiative to protest by being raised to the status of partner already possessing language knowledge. He/she merely has a less developed awareness of that knowledge.

2.1 The teacher's role in language analysis elements of a Language Awareness course, as foreseen in 1, is that of a planner of a guided journey of exploration of the student's own knowledge of his/her mother tongue and his/her intuitions about language. It is inherently interesting for the student to be made aware of facts about language that he/she knows but does not realise he/she knows. Once alerted the student can work alone and prefers on balance to do so. Materials should therefore be geared to this fact. They should be explorations of language facts that he/she can think about for him/herself. He/she will in fact want to explore for him/herself once the interest is alerted and that interest is therefore likely to wane, if he/she is subjected to too much talk about language. The term "talk about language" here covers not only talk by the teacher: it also refers to general discussion in class and to the writing of essays discussing language. Essays of research on a particular language topic would qualify as handling language under this distinction between handling language in order to explore it and talking about it; essays discussing ideas about language would qualify as talking about it. General class discussion about language ideas would qualify as talking about language; the volunteering and discussion of particular examples of language would be handling language facts themselves and, it is proposed, would be inherently more interesting to the student. It is only when the student develops a penchant for language study as an academic discipline that the 'talking about' – the theoretical discussion – should be allowed into prominence.

This emphasis on the student being guided to explore for him/herself holds good for all ages and ability levels. The nature of the exploration will, of course, have to be adjusted to suit the level being taught, but not the principle itself of working through the students' own language knowledge.

2.2 One important contribution the teacher must make in any kind of Language Awareness course is to make sure that the progression of topics handled in the syllabus is sequenced in the most effective way. The handling of some topics can be more effective if they are preceded by others. The notions of variety of language and register are clearer in their presentation to the students, if they have already been introduced to differences between written and spoken language, for example.

Equally important, once the order of presentation of topics is decided, is that there is a focussing on one topic at a time. It is probably easier to go off at tangents when handling language than in almost any other area. Such tangents blur the focus on the particular point and hence jeopardise the build-up of the explicit aspect of language awareness defined by the aims of the syllabus.

2.3 The premise of working through the students' language ability to bring them awareness of it can also be of help in the matter of terminology.

If the teacher aims to concentrate on exemplification first to illustrate the concept and on naming second to label it, the focus is once again placed on what the student intuitively knows in line with the basic premise advanced in this paper. The importance of the teacher at this point lies in his/her being able to 'tee up' the examples effectively to lead the student towards the concept.

The progression in presenting a topic should therefore be along the pattern of:
    i) a brief introduction, informally expressed, of the area of language to be studied;
    ii) a handling of material to illustrate the concept through exemplification;
    iii) (if i. and ii. achieve their objective) a production by the students of their own examples, their own objections to and refinements of the concept. If the third stage is reached there should be no trouble about attaching a name to the concept.

For example, the concept of the morpheme can be presented in terms of there being units of meaning smaller than a word; accompanying examples should be plentiful, both invented and - as much as possible - actual, such as Sam Goldwyn's "In two words - im-possible". Then the students explore problems for themselves revolving around the concept of minimal units. The students will then be volunteering comments on the problems and variations involved in trying to define the concept, which can now be labelled 'morpheme'.

2.4 The premise of working through the students' language ability to teach the language analysis aspect of language awareness, the allied premise of it being more effective for the student to handle carefully prepared language problems rather than talk about language - these premises entail dealing with language analysis at a pre-theoretical level. The students are looking at the language facts that linguistic theories seek to classify and describe - whether the theory is the inadequate description that inspired old-style 'grammar' teaching or a description of the order of systemic or transformational generative grammar.

2.5 In 2.3 we looked at the notion that the focussing on a linguistic concept should be with emphasis on the exploration of examples, in preference to emphasising the name first. The question of how to introduce terminology and what terminology to use is complicated by the fact firstly that some linguistic terminology – noun, verb, sentence – is in the everyday language, secondly that there are a number of terms – prefix, suffix, relative pronoun – firmly established from traditional language analysis usage, and thirdly that more recent terminology can have varying interpretations or go out of favour.

This variety in terminological usage is an added reason for concentrating on exploration of examples to reach the concept. In addition the amount of terminology should be kept to the essential, even for older students, and that essential can be supplied for the most part from the familiar or the traditional. For example, one may need the more technical term of 'morpheme' (if one needs a term at all) to cover the overall notion of a minimal unit of meaning, but the traditional terms of prefix and suffix are available for particular types of morpheme. In such cases the familiar and the traditional should be preferred.

It may be argued that linguistic terms of familiar or traditional use may be too loose in definition, but this is no different a situation to that facing a Physics teacher when required to present students with a more rigid definition of the term 'work' than the one they attach to it in everyday usage. It is, in fact, the purpose of Language Awareness courses dealing with analyses requiring such terminology, that they should seek to define more precisely in the students' mind concepts of language to which that terminology applies, whether the terms are already to some degree familiar or not.

2.6 It may be argued that the Physics teacher presents the student with a formula definition of the narrow sense of 'work' required in Physics, namely that it equals force times distance moved, and that this firm equation provides something for the student to grasp while acquiring the concept. No similar security of formula is available to help the student grasp the concepts behind linguistic terminology. The inadequacy of any attempt to define terms such as 'noun', 'phoneme' is notorious. They are either semantically-based and the vocabulary does not fit the grammatical function, or they are defined by other terms in a meaningless circularity.

The solution to this dilemma is found yet again in the underlying premise that the students already possess intuitive knowledge of language. If that is accepted, then it must also be accepted that, unlike in Physics, they are secure in their possession of the experimental data. They do not have to acquire it. Therein lies their security in handling the aspect of language awareness that considers analyses of the mother tongue. This is a further reason for arguing the approach to linguistic concepts through emphasis on language facts rather than through emphasis on terminology.

If this latter point is accepted, then confusion through complexity of language – as opposed to confusion caused by complicatedness of presenting how it should be analysed – is not a danger, since the students' language intuition tells them that they have the security of the native speaker's knowledge.

This security of control of the data means that the terminology can vary, the main considerations being those of consistency and familiarity of the terms. It also means that a rigid theoretical statement is less vital as a framework to hold on to. All that is needed is a guideline of clear syllabus progression and clear presentation of each topic to help the students make and order their insights into their intuitive knowledge, which is a pedagogic matter of course planning and preparation.

A further implication of this security of control of the data is that the language-analysis aspect of language awareness could provide for older students a good context for teaching the nature and importance of theory construction.

REQUIREMENTS OF A LANGUAGE AWARENESS PROGRAMME FOR THE PRIMARY TO MIDDLE YEARS

Florence Davies

It is clear from the papers published elsewhere in this book that a number of distinct models of Language Awareness courses for the middle-secondary level of education have been developed and are in the process of being tested. To date no model of the kind of Language Awareness programme which might provide a foundation for those courses at the primary-middle level has been developed.

It is not my intention here to attempt the task of presenting such a model. Rather, I shall seek to identify certain basic conditions which I believe will need to be met if the development of language awareness in our primary and middle schools is to become a practical reality. I will then consider the extent to which these conditions have been met and go on to explore what might further be required for the development of Language Awareness programmes.

I suggest that there are four basic conditions required for the development of a Language Awareness programme:

i)   a willingness on the part of the teachers to devote time and resources to the study of language in the classroom;

ii)   the availability of a coherent policy and guidelines for selecting appropriate contexts and methods for studying language in the primary classroom;

iii) the availability of a policy and guidelines for selecting content, that is, the units and features of language to be studied; and

iv)   an awareness and acceptance on the part of teachers of the practical potential of the policies and guidelines outlined above.

I suggest further that the evidence indicates that the first three conditions are already established, that is, that the majority of teachers in primary schools are committed to involving their pupils in a study of language, and that a coherent policy and guidelines for selecting appropriate methods and content has been available since the publication in 1975 of the Report of the Bullock Committee, A LANGUAGE FOR LIFE. The condition which has not been met, the evidence suggests, is a recognition by teachers of the practical potential of the guidelines available.

The evidence on which these observations are based is drawn from two basic sources: first, DES reports and surveys such as the Bullock

Report, the HMI survey, "Primary Education in England" (1978), and the APU survey "Language Performance in Schools" (1981), and secondly, samples of the language books and materials traditionally, and still widely, used in the great majority of primary classrooms.

It is in both Bullock and the Primary Survey that evidence about teacher commitment to language study is documented.

Thus, drawing on the results of questionnaires summarised in Tables 56 and 57 of the Report, the authors conclude not only that there are no grounds for the belief that language study is neglected in primary schools, but that more time is spent on language study in primary schools than in secondary.

The conclusion is based upon data relating only to the formal study of language, i.e. exercises in comprehension, vocabulary, grammar and punctuation, where the primary aim is to focus attention on the way language works, rather than to practise skills or to develop sensitivity and appreciation. Nonetheless it cannot be doubted that the exploration of how language works is not restricted to such contexts. In the primary classroom a study of how language works is an integral part of reading instruction and of the preparation for, and follow-up to writing; time spent on spelling, too, must be counted as a language study activity. When time spent on these activities is included as part of language study time, as shown in Tables 1 and 2 of the Appendix to this paper, it seems reasonable to estimate that a minimum of at least three hours a week is devoted to the study of language in most primary classrooms.

Furthermore it appears that the Reading Practice which is a vehicle for language study for six-year olds (and in which a study of language use and spelling patterns may in fact be obligatory) is increasingly replaced by the more formal study of Language Use and Spelling at the nine-year old level. That this trend continues up to the eleven-year old class is indicated by the Primary Survey. Textbooks containing comprehension, grammar and language exercises intended to provide children with knowledge of "language techniques and writing conventions including spelling and syntax ... featured in the work of almost every nine and eleven year old class ..." Language course kits fulfilling a similar function were used in about half of nine and eleven year old classrooms, along with other kinds of assignment cards

"... providing exercises in grammar or spelling ..." (5.45 p.51).

Furthermore

"in nine-tenths of all the classes teachers ensured that children's vocabulary was steadily extended." (5.24 p.46)

With respect to the provision of resources for language study, HMIs observe too, that

> "... in the vast majority of classes reading schemes and courses were used to provide children with material at the right level of difficulty and were used regularly." (5.46 p.51)

Stimuli for language study such as television programmes

> "were introduced in more than four-fifths of classes, and radio in about three-fifths." (5.43 p.50)

> "Libraries and book collections were available almost universally ... In three-quarters of the classes the books had been selected with care and represented a range of reading material containing, for example, interesting plots, good characterisation, clarity of illustration, factual accuracy and an index where appropriate and suited to the age and reading activities of pupils." (5.44 p.51)

In sum, the evidence indicates a widespread willingness and commitment on the part of the teachers to provide time and resources for the study of language, a commitment which is highlighted when provision for language study is compared with that, for instance, for science:

> "Although some science was attempted in a majority of classes, the work was developed seriously in only just over one class in ten ..." (5.69 p.58)

Nonetheless, what the evidence also indicates is that the guidelines which were formulated in Bullock have made little impact on schools. Indeed, the observation of the HMIs undertaking the Primary Survey suggest not only that teachers have not recognised or accepted the practical potential of the guidelines, but also that the implicit model of language study which governs classroom practice is one which is at variance in most important ways with that presented in Bullock. The mismatch between classroom practice and Bullock policy is clearly reflected in HMI observations about the way in which the awareness of language function is developed, the context in which it might be developed, and the range and authenticity of written material to which children are exposed.

With respect to Oral Language, HMIs observe that

> "... in only about three-fifths of these [11-year old] classes were children learning to follow a sustained discussion and contribute appropriately, and in fewer

47

still were children taught to follow the line of
argument." (5.21 p.46)

"... in only about a fifth of the classes were
children encouraged to formulate and pose pertinent
questions or helped to find alternative ways of
expressing themselves clearly and accurately." (5.24,
p.47)

With respect to the written material to which pupils were exposed,

"it was evident that teachers devoted considerable
attention to ensuring that children mastered the basic
techniques of reading but there was a tendency at all
ages for children to receive insufficient encouragement
to extend the range of their reading." (5.27 p.47)

For the abler readers there was little evidence that the more
advanced skills were being taught. The work which the ablest readers
were given to do was too easy in about two-fifths of the classes,
while the teaching of the more advanced reading skills did not occur
in three quarters of 11 year old classes.

The range of functions explored in written work was also restricted:

"It was rare to find children presented with a writing
task which involved presenting a coherent argument,
exploring alternative possibilities, or drawing conclusions
and making judgments." (5.36 p.49)

Furthermore, the potential of children's own writing as a basis for
language study was not exploited:

"Surprisingly in only about a third of classes were samples
of children's written work regularly used to monitor their
progress. In fewer than half of the classes was children's
written work used as a basis for teaching spelling, syntax,
sentence structure, or style." (5.38, p.50)

With respect to the deliberate study of language as a system, the
widespread reliance of teachers on textbooks gave cause for concern:

"Reliance on isolated exercises presented in textbooks
does not necessarily provide children with the right
kind of asistance in improving their capacity to use written
language fluently and to some purpose. (5.45, p.51)

HMI disquiet about the use of exercises for the study of language
echoes that expressed throughout Bullock (see for instance paragraphs 11.18 - 11.20, 8.14 - 8.15). It serves to highlight further

the gap between Bullock policy and guidelines, and classroom practice. Not only does the 'isolated exercise' persist, but the potential of practical alternatives of the kind recommended in Bullock, such as "group attention to text" (albeit, for Bullock, in the context of a study of literature) does not appear to have been recognized. HMI authors of Bullock Revisited (1982) observe that:

"... though many teachers read to their classes...
group attention to text is rarely observed."

In sum, the evidence suggests that Bullock guidelines about the ways in which awareness of language might be developed have either not been accessible to teachers or have not been accepted by them.

Data from the APU Survey of the Language Performance of primary children indicates too, a gap between Bullock guidelines about content, the features of language which might be the focus of attention, and those which are selected for attention in primary classes (albeit through the hidden curriculum of correction of written work). Thus for most eleven-year olds in the sample, an editing task was interpreted as an invitation to correct spelling while other features such as grammaticality and coherence were ignored. This fact may be interpreted on the one hand as a reflection of the features of language which children have been 'taught' to focus on, or, on the other, as a reflection of the much greater complexity of editing at a level above spelling. HMI authors of Bullock Revisited accept the interpretation of the writers of the report:

"This finding may be an indication of what eleven-year olds take to be the main requirement of making corrections to a text" (2.2)

Support for this interpretation would seem to come, too, from the evidence given in the Secondary Survey (1979) that

"weak writing by fifteen year olds was more likely to be found inadequate in terms of content and style than in relation to grammatical or orthographic conventions."

Thus it is with respect to what is taught, as well as to how it it taught, that the differences between Bullock policy and classroom practice are revealed. The formulation in Bullock of a policy and guidelines for the study of language and for the development of language awareness was not, of course the only, nor the primary objective of the Committee. Nonetheless, the guidelines which are presented, not only within the section entitled Language Study, but throughout the Report, are sufficiently comprehensive for them to represent an explicit model for the development of language awareness: a model which may be compared with the implicit model of the primary classroom.

I suggest that a recognition of the distinctions between the two models, and an understanding of their relative accessibility to teachers is a pre-requisite for the acceptance of, and practical realisation of, the Bullock model in the classroom.

The two models may be contrasted with respect to the selection of contexts and of methods for the study of language and the development of awareness, and with respect to the selection of units and features of language to be studied.

The context for the development of language awareness in Bullock is a functional one - the objective is to develop in children an awareness of the function of different varieties of language in use.

> "What is needed is to create the contexts and conditions in which the ability can develop." (5.9, p.54)

Amongst the language uses which are to be explored in the early years of schooling are reporting, collaborating, projecting, perceiving relationships, explaining, expressing and recognising tentativeness, problem-solving, creating imaginative experience, justifying and reflecting. (5.30, p.67)

The development of awareness of function is expected to involve attention to both spoken and written language. As children gain increasing control over the written language they are to be encouraged to become aware, not only of the variety of purposes for which they might read, but also to become aware of the different strategies they can consciously deploy in their reading. Development of this kind of awareness is seen to be progressive throughout the primary, middle and secondary years:

> "The development of reading skills is a progressive one and there are no staging points to which one can attach any particular ages,... We believe that the primary teacher needs an understanding of the reading demands of the later years so that the line of development is clearly recognized." (8.1 p.115)

> "It will often be helpful for teachers to encourage their pupils to identify their purposes before they undertake a particular piece of reading." (8.12. p.119)

> "We have suggested that pupils should learn how to read for specific purposes, how to organize their material, and how to apply appropriate techniques." (8.19 p.122)

In organizing their own writing, too, pupils are to be encouraged to develop a conscious awareness of their own intentions, and of potential audiences and when writing for audiences outside the classroom, pupils should be

> "faced with the need to analyse the specific task, to choose the language appropriate to it, and to establish criteria by which to judge what they have achieved." (11.9 p.100)

With respect to the use of written language for learning, a strong case for an explicit awareness on the part of teachers and pupils of the way in which study skills may be developed is presented:

> "... a reader has considerable control over the learning situation and he needs particular skills to take advantage of the possibilities this opens up to him. We can sum these up by saying that reading for learning will be most effective when the reader becomes an active interrogator of the text rather than a passive receiver of words. A second principle is that these skills should be developed in close association with other aspects of language use and in particular with the oral activity recommended in Chapter 10." (8.10, p.118)

For Bullock, as for linguists like Crystal (1976) and Sinclair (1983), a necessary corollary of the study of language function and variety is that the language studied is authentic – the language used in the classroom and playground, in play, and drama, and in the wider world – the spoken language of the children themselves and of the society which meets their interests and needs, and the written language which serves these functions. A central objective is that pupils develop an awareness of the purposes and functions which govern their own language use. Implicit in this view is a recognition of the linguistic competence children bring to schools.

> "Children bring to school a spoken language far more complex than anything they encounter in [these] early readers. They use and can appreciate a wide range of sentence structures. Reading schemes which present highly contrived or artificial sentence structures therefore lack predictability. They prevent children from developing the capacity to detect the sequential probability in linguistic structure." (7.18, p.105)

The need for the written language of the classroom to be authentic is stressed throughout the report. An important feature of authentic texts is that they can serve as a vehicle for a wide range of values and attitudes:

> "We do not suggest that reading schemes should be

passed through a kind of ideological or ethical
scanner. But we do believe that children's experience
should not be confined to a narrow range of attitudes."
(7.17, p.105)

Not only is it important for children to be exposed to authentic
language, they should also be given the opportunity to produce it:

"If, as Chomsky argues, the normal use of language is
innovative, it becomes a vital principle that the
teacher should create opportunities most likely to
produce innovation and generate natural language."
(10.36, p.159)

One means of developing awareness of a variety of natural language
forms is through drama:

"An increasing number of teachers of drama, ... do in
fact see their work as productive of such [natural]
language. They would add that it helps to establish
confidence in social intercourse, as well as
familiarity with a variety of speech forms. ... Drama
thus has the capacity for sensitizing the ear for
appropriate registers and responses. It encourages
linguistic adaptability, often accustoming children to
unfamiliar modes of language." (10.36, p.159)

The functions of language to which pupils are expected to become
sensitised range from the basically instrumental, to the persuasive
and heuristic functions of language in small group discussion, to
the imaginative, evaluative and discerning functions, which are
evoked in response to literature. The opportunity for pupils to work
in small groups and to discuss what they are doing is seen to be
fundamental to learning.

"Most nursery and infant teachers recognize that when
young children are involved in some activity the talk
that accompanies it becomes an important instrument
for learning." (5.22, p.62)

"Reading is an instrument for individual learning but
it is also a collective activity, and we believe that
group discussion based on co-operative reading is a
valuable means of learning." (8.10, p.118)

In Bullock one of the most effective ways of encouraging discussion
is seen to be through group attention to text:

"In recommending an expansion of supported individual
reading in schools we see it as a complementary process
to group attention to a text. Some of the best and most

lasting effects of English teaching have come about through
the simultaneous encounter of teacher, pupil and text,"
(9.21, p.134).

Even in the early years:

> "A good deal of incentive can be provided by well
> organized small group work where the interaction draws
> upon shared experiences in reading. The children can
> be encouraged to discuss what they are reading, to ask
> questions and offer answers, and to compare their
> ideas of what the book said." (7.31, p.112-113)

The ultimate objective is the development of conscious discernment:

> "Most teachers of English would include among their
> most important aims growth of discernment in their
> pupils." (9.12, p.130)

The means by which discernment is to be developed is through the
extension of voluntary reading for pleasure;

> "As we see it the main emphasis should be on extending
> the range of a pupil's reading. True discernment can come
> only from a breadth of experience. Learning how to
> appreciate with enthusiasm is more important than learning
> how to reject." (9.15, p.132)

The role of enjoyment in developing extensive reading and discernment is seen to be critical.

> "We can sum up by saying that whatever else a pupil
> takes away from his experience of literature in school
> he should have learned to see it as a source of
> pleasure." (9.28, p.137)

The written language to which pupils are introduced is not only to
be authentic but also representative of the extensive range of
varieties: from those deployed in pupils' own written work, to the
language of textbooks, the media and literature.

> "There has not been enough thought given to the
> different varieties of English and to the stages of
> language development at which children can begin to
> cope with them." (11.6, p.164)

Pupils

> "should be given the opportunity to explore many
> different kinds of media and learn how to obtain what
> they need." (6.43, p.95)

Awareness of language varieties is seen to be developed through writing as well as reading. Differentiation of function in writing should be developed throughout the school years:

> "We believe that progress in writing throughout the
> school years should be marked by an increasing
> differentiation in the kinds of writing a pupil can
> successfully tackle. ... Their reading interests will
> be an influential factor, particularly in the early
> stages. To develop they must take in written forms of
> the language and articulate these with their own
> general language resources built up by years of
> listening and speaking." (11.8, p.166)

Awareness of language varieties is seen to be developed through the reading of texts in the subject areas and literature:

> "Subject teachers need to be aware of the processes
> involved, able to provide the variety of reading
> material that is appropriate, and willing to see it as
> their responsibility to help their pupils meet the
> reading demands of their subject. The variety of
> written forms a child meets in his reading will be an
> influence upon the development of his writing abilities.
> To restrict the first can result in limiting the
> second." (12.7, p.191)

Literature is seen to offer pupils experience of an even wider range of forms:

> "Literature brings the child into an encounter with
> language in its most complex and varied forms. Through
> these complexities are presented the thoughts,
> experiences and feelings of people who exist outside
> and beyond the reader's daily awareness. This process
> of bringing them within that circle of consciousness
> is where the greatest value of literature lies." (9.2.
> p.125)

The aim is not to prescribe invariant rules about language and language use, but to develop sensitivity to language and to initiate a search for pattern, the outcome of which might be the formulation of tentative rules or hypotheses which we all make use of in speaking, listening, writing and reading.

A related objective is to illustrate the dependence of such patterns and rules on social and linguistic context:

> "We have already placed special emphasis on the
> importance of pupil's intentions as a writer and have

suggested that this will arise out of the context of
work in the class or the broader one of his out of
school-life, as shared with his teacher and class-
mates. It is upon these contexts that the teacher
works with a view to rousing specific individual
intentions,...." (11.7 p.165)

The role of experimentation in the development of language is also
seen to be crucial:

"If a pupil is progressively to develop in his
handling of the language he needs opportunity to
experiment with new forms and to do so with security.
(11.10 p.167)

The study of language in context is contrasted with a prescriptive,
exercise-based approach. With reference to reading workshops and
laboratories it is observed that

"any real gain in reading development must come
through the generation of a strong motivation and this
means reading to satisfy a purpose. This is more
likely to arise from the wide-ranging opportunities of
the curriculum than from the arbitrary stimulus of
'laboratory' materials. (8.8 p.117)

The disadvantages of a prescriptive approach to language are seen to
relate both to content and to modes of learning:

(11.18).. "We do not conclude [from this] that a child
should not be taught how to improve his use of
language; quite the contrary....what is questionable
is the practice of setting exercises for the whole class
.. what is also open to question is the nature of
some of these exercises... Most give the child no
useful insight into language and many.. mislead"
(11.19 p.171)

In sum:

"Explicit instruction out of context, is in our view
of little value" (11.21 p.172)

With respect to linguistic context, the necessity for pupils to be
able to utilize context and anticipation, is stressed as is the role
of hypothesis testing:

"Our analysis of the problem has led us to the view
that it is better for children to learn phoneme-
grapheme relations in the context of whole-word
recognition, at least in the early stages of schooling

... children will be developing their own hypotheses about
phoneme-grapheme correspondences and this process
should certainly be encouraged as opportunities arise."
(6.26 p.89)

The integral relationship between use of context and prediction of
language patterns is recognised:

"All the points already made about letter sequence and
probability apply equally to phoneme sequences. Thus a
listener not only has to recognize phonemes as they are
uttered but to anticipate very efficiently those that
are likely to follow... what we emphasise here is the
fundamental importance of prediction in attacking
unfamiliar words (6.31 p.90/91)

Anticipation and prediction of likely sequences in context is seen
to operate at every level from phonemic to syntactic sequences:

"Word recognition is also made easier by the ability
to anticipate syntactic sequences. This means that
for the young child certain kinds of reading material,
must present a problem" (6.34 p.92)

This role of context and prediction is seen to be equally important
at the level of meaning.

"The anticipation of sequences is also called into
play at the level of meaning... The ambiguity of
letters considered in isolation is almost trivial when
compared to the ambiguity of isolated words. Only by
using the surrounding sequences can the reader identify
which of the many possible meanings an author intends
in a given passage. The most effective teaching of
reading, therefore, is that which gives the pupil the
various skills he needs to make fullest possible use
of context cues in searching for meaning." (6.35 p.92)

Indeed the notion of context is central to the Bullock model. It
determines not only the situation in which language is studied, but
also what is studied.
The situation in which it is studied is one of enquiry, involving
teacher and pupils collaborating in an exploration, in the analysis
of data and in hypothesis formulation and testing. Awareness and
control of language is seen to be developed through involving pupils
in a wide range of situations and in conscious analysis of language
in these situations:

We have advocated throughout this section that
children should progressively gain control of

language by using it in response to a variety of
demands. They can be helped to do this by studying
how it works in various situations, not in any sense
of choosing models or opting between stereotypes but
by insight into its richness and infinite
possibilities." (11.29 p.176)

"What we are suggesting then, is that children should
learn about language by experiencing it and
experimenting with its use." (11.25 p.173)

Furthermore the units or features of language which receive
attention are of all sizes - from the macro-units of the complete
story or exchange, or report, at one level, to sentences, phrases
and collocations of words at another, to the micro units at the
level of the word and its constituents. Increasingly pupils are
expected to be able to perceive 'themes' and structures as they
read, and to determine

"... what is essential supporting detail and what is
peripheral." (8.15 p.120)

Close study of text is seen to further these objectives:

"Even when skimming at speed [the reader] must be able
to pick out certain features and identify general
structures and relationships. It may help pupils to
acquire this ability if on occasion they make a close
analysis of a passage to identify the significant
words in sentences, and significant sentences in
paragraphs, working out in group discussion the
relationship between position and function. ... By
recognizing the function of various sentences in the
structure of the paragraph the pupils are helped to a
grasp of the theme." (8.15 p.121)

Attention to lower-level features of language such as morphology,
parts of speech, punctuation and collocation is also seen to be
necessary:

"Though in every instance the need should create the
opportunity, the teacher ought to ensure that in a
given period of time the pupils cover certain features
of language and for this purpose might find a check-
list useful. We believe these features should
certainly include punctuation, some aspects of usage,
the way words are built and the company they keep, and
a knowledge of the modest collection of technical
terms useful for discussion of language." (11.21
p.172)

57

> ..."it is perfectly reasonable that by the end of the
> middle years children should know about the parts of
> speech, but they should encounter them in the course
> of looking at language in a living context." (11.23
> p.173)

Nonetheless it is up to the teacher to construct a syllabus

> ".. it is reasonable to set clear targets which
> children recognize to be achievable. With this in
> view the teacher should determine appropriate language
> objectives, devise his own ways of fulfilling them,
> and assess the extent to which they have been
> achieved." (11.22 p.173)

In sum, it is only with respect to possible syllabuses that the
Bullock guidelines are less than comprehensive.

In other respects the Bullock model is both comprehensive and
explicit. It involves a functional context, exposure to authentic
language varieties, a conscious and deliberate search for pattern at
all levels of the system and the opportunity for pupils to generate
and test hypotheses and to discuss language phenomena. By contrast
the evidence examined earlier suggests that the language study (as
opposed to use) undertaken in most primary classrooms, is not
undertaken in a functional context, nor is it concerned except
incidentally with language variety and the authentic use of
language. The model on which it is based is one which not only
involves a reliance on textbooks but itself owes a substantial debt
to the implicit model of the traditional question-and-answer
exercise of the text book. It is this exercise-bound model of
language study which may be contrasted with the Bullock model.

When we examine the traditional language study of the primary
classroom we can see that it is the textbook exercise itself which
determines the extent to which function and variety may be explored.
The provision in textbooks of exercises, by definition, de-limits
both the context and function of the language being studied. The
exemplars of language used in exercises, whether they are texts,
sentences, or smaller units, have been pre-selected out of context.
Thus while they might incidentally represent different (written)
varieties of language, their connection with the real world of the
classroom, the ongoing curriculum, and society is inevitably remote.

Furthermore, because the exemplars are used as the basis for written
exercises, their original function must necessarily be obscured. It
is difficult to explore the function and variety of a unit of
language, a story, a description, a report, without a consideration
of its real life and linguistic context, its function in that
context, and the patterns and forms which distinguish it from

another instance of language. Such an exploration demands richer resources than can be made available in a textbook; it requires an awareness and an acceptance on the part of the teacher and pupils of the objective of the study; it requires tentativeness, time and the opportunity for discussion. In short, it requires active problem-solving on the part of pupils, and interaction between pupil and pupil, and pupil and teacher. As I have argued elsewhere (Davies, 1983b), the textbook has advantages over the teacher as a source of information; as an initiator and monitor of active learning, however, it is severely constrained. Thus even when the objective of an exercise is a consideration of function, the obligatory means of doing this through the setting of simple questions like:

"The writer wrote this story to:

a) give information
b) give an opinion
c) amuse the reader"
restricts such a consideration to a superficial level.

The particular linguistic form of the question and answer, or multiple-choice exchange which constitutes an exercise determines a prescriptive view of language, and the selection for study of only those units and features of language which can be handled in a prescriptive way. Thus it is that the language study promoted by the exercise presents a model of language in which spelling patterns, morphological and inflection rules, simple definitions of word meanings and parts of speech predominate. That such features of language are worthy of study for certain purposes and in certain contexts is not at issue; what is in question is the validity of the model as a representation of the language system. It is what is excluded which gives cause for concern.

What cannot be handled by the model is a study of the patterns and forms which distinguish one variety of text from another; and one exchange from another, there is no place in the traditional exercise for the study of the collocations of words and phrases which characterise a distinct unit of language, or of the cohesion of lines and signals which link one part of a text with another, and which open and close exchanges, or of the structures which underly distinct registers and genre.

Furthermore the exercise which requires of pupils only a written answer to a simple question, prevents them from utilizing their own resources and competencies for the study of language. There is no space here for pupils to formulate tentative hypotheses and test them, to draw upon and make explicit their own intuitive knowledge of language, to discuss language phenomena, or to collaborate in pushing their understanding forward.

In sum, a study of language which is promoted through the exercise, based as it is on a deficit model of language and of learning, is inherently designed in practice to restrict and distort awareness of language rather than develop it.

The question is, what is it about the exercise-based model which accounts for its apparent appeal to teachers in comparison with the Bullock model, and what is to be learned from asking this question?

It would be tempting to suggest that a programme of exercises makes life easy for the teacher; it obviates the need to collect resources and to prepare lessons, it keeps pupils busy. Such an explanation, I suggest, is too facile and does a disservice to the commitment, creativity and rationality of primary teachers. It also fails to recognise the actual demands made on teachers by pupils working on exercises. Classroom observations show that exercises which are designed in principle to elicit simple right and wrong answers, in practice, are frequently ambiguous - trying to help pupils interpret questions is for most teachers a full-time task, and one which is harder to manage successfully than almost any other.

I propose that there are other features of the exercise-based model which suggest an explanation of why it might recommend itself to teachers. Specifically, the programme or textbook offers teachers exemplifications of a model in the form of pupil **activities**, it offers a **syllabus**, and it is **accessible**.

The exercise, by definition, is a concrete exemplification of the implicit model of the text book or programme - it is a realisation of the model in the form of activities which can be undertaken in the classroom. A comparable realisation of a programme derived from Bullock has not to date been available to teachers, nor, as I have tried to show elsewhere, is the textbook format ideal for the realization of such a policy. In this respect is it worth observing that the published programme which comes closest to representing Bullock policy, 'Web of Language', not only provides activities which are alternatives to the exercise, but is also dependent for its successful use on the extra resources such as tapes which support it.

It seems then, that for teachers, a policy is neither recognisable nor acceptable unless it is represented through exemplars of pupil activities of one form or another. Where the only exemplars available are traditional exercises, it can be predicted that these will be preferred, by all but a few highly experienced teachers, to general guidelines.

Closely linked to the need for concrete exemplification of a model, too, is the need for a selection of the content which is to be studied. Again it is the text book or programme, rather than a policy, which makes this selection, and in effect provides a syllabus. For the teacher without specialist training in language to draw upon, the provision of such a selection by an authority must be welcome. So too, must be the apparent authority and reliability of the linguistic rules which are exemplified in the exercises. For teachers who are sharply aware of the limitations of their own knowledge of language, the textbook in effect functions as an apparently reliable source of reference about the language system, and about what pupils need to learn about the system. What is more, in practice, it is the only reference accessible to most teachers. It is the reference and implicit guide, which, as the Primary Survey showed, is actually to be found in the classroom; alternative sources of reference, whether drawn from in-service courses or from school-based initiatives, are rarely available in schools and hence are much less accessible to teachers. It is striking too, that even the standard sources of reference, which underpin the teaching of English as a Foreign Language, are virtually unknown in schools.

In sum, if the Bullock report provides rational and explicit guidelines for the study of language, what the textbook or programme does is to provide implicit guidelines, and more critically, actual exemplification of what children might do with language, and of what a syllabus might be.

It is, I suggest, these features of the exercised-based programme, especially the actual exemplification of what pupils might do, that accounts for the continued reliance of teachers on the textbook; a reliance which has inevitably been established in the absence of alternatives. In the classroom, the most rigorous test of linguistic theory and methodology is what it tells us about what children might do. If teachers are to become aware of and to accept guidelines for the development of language awareness, then it seems that a further requirement must be provision of exemplars of children doing things with language and the provision of sources of reference, which can be used to describe and explain these things.

The question is, what sources other than the textbook might provide exemplars, with supportive references, of what children can do with language? The answer, I propose, is sources which historically have been utilised only to provide occasional insights into aspects of language development, rather than for the construction of an integrated picture of the way in which language awareness might be developed. The sources I have in mind are established research investigations which provide evidence of children's naturally developing awareness of language and classroom-based observations and studies which provide exemplars of the way in which this natural awareness can be further extended in the classroom. That there is a wealth of such sources could be demonstrated through an exhaustive listing; more useful at this stage, I believe, will be the provision of illustrations of the kind of sources envisaged.

Illustrative, for instance, of research studies which provide exemplars of the development of awareness of language at the macro-level, as manifest in spontaneous speech is Halliday's analysis of dialogue showing the gradual acquisition of these basic functions: Instrumental, Regulatory, Interactional, Personal, Heuristic, Imaginative and Informative, in: Halliday M.A.K. 'Learning How to Mean: Explorations in the Development of Language', Edward Arnold, 1975.

Illustrative of children's sensitivity to function in writing in the classroom are exemplars collected by the author while supervising students in primary classrooms in Cambridgeshire, and while working in South Yorkshire classrooms.

A source which provides a discussion of the educational implications of such material is provided in:

HALLIDAY, M.A.K. 'Relevant models of language' in Wilkinson, A. (ed) The State of Language. Vol. 22, No. 1 November 1969 issue of Educational Review.

Likewise documentation of children's awareness and use of the Interactive, Heuristic and Informative functions in small group discussion is provided by:

BARNES, D and F Todd (1977.) Communication and Learning in Small Groups, Routledge and Kegan Paul and by ROSEN, C and H Rosen (1973) The Language of Primary School Children, Penguin

While an analysis of children's use of hypothesis testing strategies is available in:

DAVIES, F and T Green 'Directed Activities Related to Text: Test Analysis and Text Reconstruction' in ERIC Clearinghouse on Communication Skills and Reading Abstract in Resources in Education, March 1982

Evidence of children's knowledge of story structure is equally well documented in:

MANDLER, J M and N S Johnson 'Remembrance of things parsed: story structure and recall', in:Cognitive psychology Vol. 9, 1977 p. 111-151

and in:

APPLEBEE, A N (1978) The Child's Concept of Story: Ages two to seventeen, University of Chicago Press

while the role of story structure in young children's reading is illustrated by:

STEBBING, J and B Raban (1982) 'Reading for Meaning: an investigation of the effect of narrative in two reading books for seven year olds', Reading 16.3, pp.153-162.

Evidence that pupils can also learn to utilize text structures other than story-structure and a description of the classroom activities which can be used for this purpose are provided by:

DAVIES, F and T Green Reading for Learning in the Sciences, Oliver and Boyd (1983) and by LUNZER, E A and K Gardner Learning from the Written Word, Oliver and Boyd, 1983.

Equally informative of children's awareness of language at the micro-level are research studies of children's sensitivity to parts of speech in reading such as those by:

CLAY, M M 'A syntactic analysis of reading errors', Journal of Verbal Learning and Verbal Behaviour, vol 7 1968 pp 434-438 and WEBER, J M 'First-graders use of grammatical context in reading' in LEVIN, H and J P Williams (eds) Basic Studies in Reading, Basic Books Inc., 1970.

Evidence that this sensitivity is found in the daily intercourse of the classroom can, of course, be provided by the many thousands of teachers who have undertaken miscue analysis.

More critical perhaps for teachers is the availability of a comprehensive set of classroom activities designed to develop awareness of language at all levels of the system. This too is available in the materials produced by Helen Arnold and colleagues in Suffolk, namely Suffolk County Council Education Committee: Language Guidelines, and in materials currently being developed and exemplars being collected by Anne Darnton at Bromford Junior School, Birmingham.

It is the use of exemplars drawn from sources like those above, which would, I suggest, meet a number of critical conditions:

they would serve to focus attention on the linguistic and heuristic resources which children bring to the classroom, and on what children are trying to do with language, instead of on performance limitations which are determined by artificial tasks;

as such, the exemplars would provide a solid foundation for a range of different but practical syllabuses;

because they would demonstrate what children can do, they would be accessible to teachers and would hence provide models for the development of classroom activities;

they would also provide direction for the use by teachers of standard references on language and learning and would serve, too, to initiate further classroom observation and data collection.

Taken together I believe the exemplars would provide a solid foundation for the development of language awareness programmes consistent with Bullock policy. What is envisaged through the provision of such exemplars, is not in itself, then, a programme, but a resource for teacher groups in which each exemplar, with details of the context in which it was produced, would serve to illustrate the way in which a particular feature of language may be explored with children. It is a resource of this kind which, supported by the basic classroom references listed in the bibliography, would meet the final requirement for the development of a language awareness programme: a recognition by teachers of the practical potential of the guidelines available.

Finally, and perhaps most importantly it would also go a long way towards meeting Halliday's minimum requirement for an educationally relevant approach to language, i.e. "that it takes account of the child's own linguistic experience defining this experince in terms of its richest potential and noting where there may be gaps which could be educationally or developmentally harmful".

Basic Classroom References:

QUIRK, R et al (1973) A University Grammar of English. Longman

LEECH, G and J A Svartik (1975) Communicative Grammar of English. Longman

DOUGHTY, P, J Pearce and G Thornton (1971) Language in Use. Edward Arnold

TRUDGILL, P (1975) Accent, Dialect and the School. Edward Arnold.

HMSO (1981) Language Performance in Schools: Primary Survey, Report No 1 (1975).

HMSO (1978) Primary Education in England: a survey by H. M. Inspectors of Schools.

HMSO (1982) Language Performance in Schools: Secondary Survey, Report No 1

HMSO (1982) Bullock Revisited.

SINCLAIR, J, (1983) Linguistics and the Teacher in Linguistics and the Teacher, pp.16-30. Routledge, Kegan and Paul.

PENMAN, T and Al Wolft (1981) Web of Language. Oxford University Press .

CRYSTAL, D (1976) Linguistics and the Teacher. 'Child Language, Learning & Linguistics.' Edward Arnold.

LANGUAGE AWARENESS IN A CHILD DEVELOPMENT COURSE - A CASE STUDY

P J Downes

Introduction

Teachers of Child Development courses, which mainly appear on the timetable as 4th/5th Year options, have an excellent opportunity to develop language awareness with specific reference to first language acquisition. Most teachers of this course come from a background of Home Economics training so it is not surprising that the traditional emphasis in such courses has been on the physical development of babies, their dietary needs, their clothing, their play and toys. Many of the text-books used as a basis for these courses give only a passing reference to language development but it is pleasing to note that some more recent examination papers have included specific questions on aspects of child language, with special reference to social context.

Many Home Economics trained teachers of Child Development are anxious on two counts: a. they are afraid that teaching about language development as such may divorce it, in the pupils' minds, from the overall family context; b. they are uneasy about the abstract nature of the ideas and the complicated vocabulary used by specialists in linguistics. It is, however, possible to devise a short course which focuses specifically on language development and which could be incorporated in a two-year course as, say, a 12 week module, preferably early in the two-year cycle, with the possibility of a little follow-up work later.

In such a course, the main aim would not be to pass on theoretical knowledge of the nature of child language even though some transmission of factual information may be necessary from time to time. The primary aim would be to sharpen pupils' awareness of language development in the young children they meet in their everyday lives and in particular in relation to the specific individuals they are studying as part of their course. The teacher would seek to draw out the main strands of linguistic theory from the observations made and would then encourage pupils to try out language strategies in their contact with young children, whether in playgroups, at infant schools, as big sister/brother or as baby-sitter.

The Course

The following is an outline of a course tried out by Paul Baker (Banbury Teachers' Centre) and Peter Downes when the latter was Head of Linguistic Studies at Banbury School. With modifications, the same course has been tried out subsequently with pupils at Henry Box School, Witney and at Hinchingbrooke School, Huntingdon. The academic level has varied from non-exam pupils to O level candidates and the length of the 'module' from 6 weeks to a term.

The main 'headings' for the work are:

a. The miracle of language. The aim here is to create a sense of wonder and amazement at the baby's achievement in learning to talk and communicate in such a relatively short time. Comparisons and constrasts are made with how the young of other species develop communication without speech and the uniqueness of the human being is brought out.

b. Ages and stages. The main developmental stages in language are explained, principally by reference to tapes and videos, as well as by direct observation of children known to members of the class. Care is taken to ensure that variations from the 'norm' are not allowed to be cause for anxiety but hints can already be made about the effect of the parental and adult context in which the baby is reared.

c. Talk in everyday situations. The point is made that babies are learning every day and all day (contrast learning of foreign language) and that all routine experiences of everyday life form the structure in which they learn to communicate. By means of observation and role play, it is possible to sow the seed of the idea that the way parents 'use' everyday events as language material can have an effect on the way children learn to talk.

d. Language and play. Much of the baby/toddler's day is spent 'playing' so the effect of the different kinds of play is looked at: imaginative play, dressing-up, playing with toys, using everyday objects, adventure games, construction toys, jig-saws etc. By watching how parents talk to children as they play with them, the class can begin to see what aspects of language are being developed by the various activities undertaken. Pupils working with playgroups set out to try out specific strategies with their charges.

e. The language of control. By looking at transcripts of recordings made in shops and in the street, and by adding their own observations, the class looks at the way language is used to bring about acceptable social behaviour. The 'conditioning process' not only produces a behavioural response but also creates a way of looking at the world.

f. Rhymes, songs and stories. By recalling their own childhood songs and rhymes and by listening to others commonly used, the pupils try to come to an understanding of the contribution made by rhythm and intonation in the developing speech of the young child. It is possible for them to discover that words are in themselves a source

66

of pleasure and entertainment and this leads on to discussion of what we mean by a sense of humour and its close links with linguistic mastery. Pupils prepare for themselves stories to be told to young children and then report back on their success.

g. Reading and books. By bringing in to school a wide selection of books used by pre-school children, it is possible to study the strengths and weaknesses of various approaches to pre-reading for young children. The point is made that if children associate enjoyment with books from a very early age, long before they can actually read, they are more likely to be well-disposed towards reading and book-based learning in future.

h. Television and young children. This has become an increasingly important part of the course over recent years as the impact of television and television-based entertainment has intensified. The positive and negative aspects are looked at and pupils try the experiment of watching a programme with a toddler and then trying to 'exploit' the content in play.

i. The wider implications. Depending on the maturity of the group and the relationship between the teacher and the pupils, it is sometimes possible to draw out some or all of the wider implications of the studies undertaken: that all children other than the severely handicapped do learn to understand and talk but the speed and effectiveness of the learning process is directly affected by the adults surrounding the child; that the time that parents have to give to their young, with its social and financial implications, is a crucial element; that family size and paternal role are more important than commonly assumed; that later attitudes and progress in school are dependent on what has happened before the child comes officially within the education net of 5 - 16; and so on.

Teaching method

Most of the above topics can be dealt with actively and practically and this is much more effective than a more didactic, information-giving approach, even when the watching of television programmes on child development is included. The use by the pupils of tape-recorders with subsequent transcription of baby utterances was found to be far too difficult and ultimately counter-productive. A great deal of guidance was needed to train pupils in listening for specific aspects of language e.g. on visits to playgroups.

Problems

1. Sex-stereotyping. In all the schools in which this course has been tried out, the membership of the teaching group was entirely female. There is a danger that this reinforces the view that the job of bringing up children is solely that of the mother,

whereas, in a number of aspects of the course outlined above the distinctive and important role of the father is emphasised.

It can be argued that the rearing of children is too important to be sex-stereotyped in this way and an alternative approach is to include language awareness in a social studies course taught to both sexes or in a parentcraft course, taught as part of a number of core courses to 4/5th Year pupils.

2. Teacher-pupil relationships. On a number of issues, the relationship between teacher and pupil touches on sensitive areas. There could, for example, be an implication that a low-achieving pupil, possibly one taking mainly non-exam subjects, is in this situation because of a linguistic deficiency which can be attributed to parental neglect or ignorance. Some of the points referred to in (i) above could be the source of ill-feeling and resentment if handled insensitively.

3. Social class implications. A common misunderstanding in the early lessons of this course has been that 'teachers want to make us all talk posh'. This serves to remind anybody thinking of trying out such a course that the material must start from what the pupils observe of the world around and not imply the imposition of a superior model of language.

4. Teaching personnel. In the courses referred to, the teaching has been led by a teacher who was not a member of the Home Economics department, i.e. either an English specialist or a modern linguist with a special interest in linguistics. In discussion at conferences for Home Economics teachers where this course has been presented, there has been frequent reference by Home Economics teachers to their self-confessed inadequacy to teach this aspect of a Child Development course. Reassurance that there is a relatively low level of specialist knowledge required has not been easily accepted and it would appear that, if this course were to develop more widely, there would be a need for in-service training for Home Economics teachers, supported by specially produced materials and teaching notes. Where a specialist teacher can be imported from another department, assuming timetable logistics make it possible, there can be an uneasiness of relationship and, more dangerously, an implication that language can somehow be divorced from the rest of child development.

Conclusion.

In spite of the difficulties referred to, I remain convinced that there is an important role for language awareness to play in the later years of secondary schooling, quite apart from the other examples shown in other case-studies in this report. Ideally, I would like to see it as part of a wider policy for increased public awareness of the essential role of parents in the early years of their children's lives. Such a policy would need support from the health authorities, from social services and from the education service at all levels; it will not come about as long as these different departments of care and provision remain in isolation from each other and particularly as long as the Local Education Authority, coming under increasing financial pressure, restricts its oversight to the so-called compulsory period of schooling from 5 - 16. Those who have had much experience in dealing with slow-learning and demotivated children are often heard to say that what has happened to the child in his social and linguistic environment before he enters the official period of schooling is the most decisive factor of all in his education and, arguably, in his whole life.

Select bibliography

There is now a vast list of books on linguistics and various aspects of language development. Those mentioned below are just a few of those which have been found to be specifically useful for teachers working on the course outlined above.

FRAILBERG, Selma H The Magic Years. University Paperbacks, Methuen.

HOSTLER, P The Child's World. Penguin.

LURIA AND YUDOVICH, Speech and the development of the mental processes in the child. Penguin.

WILKINSON, A The Foundations of Language. Oxford University Press.

BARTRAM, Gwenda E Not Yet Five. Creative Learning Ltd.

OWEN, R. ed. State of Play. BBC Publications.

BRITTON, J Language and Learning. Pelican.

BECK, M Susan Baby Talk. Plume.

LEWIS, D The secret language of your child. Pan.

LEE, V ed. Language development. Open University Press.

LEWIN, R ed. Child Alive. Temple Smith.

Journal of Child Language published twice yearly by Cambridge University Press

APLIN et al. _Introduction to Language_. Hodder and Stoughton.

BULLOCK, Alan _A Language for Life_. HMSO.

PICTON, M _Understanding Parenthood and Child_. Blackie.

Child's Talk. ILEA and Heinemann.

EDE, J and J Williamson _Talking, Listening and Learning_. Longman.

BALDWIN, D _All about children_. Oxford.

EVALUATION AND ASSESSMENT

B G Donmall, J M Sinclair & A J Tinkel

SECTION ONE - INTRODUCTION

This is a package of short papers which members of the Working Party
have assembled as a first response to the need for monitoring of
Language Awareness courses. The wide variety of individual
initiatives in the subject area makes it very difficult to
generalise, and we are anxious not to suggest an orthodoxy so early
in the development of Language Awareness. However, it became clear
that the Working Party would be dodging its responsibilities if it
remained silent on the issue of assessment, so we set about
preparing some guidelines. The package is made up as follows:

SECTION ONE:	INTRODUCTION: John Sinclair	
SECTION TWO:	PROGRAMME EVALUATION: Gillian Donmall & John Sinclair	
SECTION THREE:	FORMAL EXAMINATIONS: Tony Tinkel	
SECTION FOUR:	IN-SCHOOL ASSESSMENT OF INTRODUCTORY COURSES: Gillian Donmall	

The first point is to separate evaluation and assessment. By
evaluation is meant a critical report on a course as a whole -
materials, teachers, students, timetable, working conditions, place
in curriculum, and anything else that is deemed to be relevant. We
believe that Language Awareness courses should strive to be
self-evaluating, so that any external evaluation will be straightforward, and, hopefully, positive. That is the professional
priority. Language Awareness courses have to justify themselves,
and because of their general character they will not be likely to
justify themselves on student performance in terminal assessment.
Wherever this is possible, of course, we advocate terminal
assessment, and Section Three gives useful guidelines for this. But
most Language Awareness courses share features which make assessment
less than straightforward. They are often of short duration and
intended to serve as a basis for further language learning; although
dedicated to improvement in student performance, the improvement is
of a kind which is very difficult to measure. They are designed to
awaken interest, to contextualise language learning, to examine
attitudes, to stimulate motivation, and to heighten perception of,
responses to and manipulation of language in a wide range of
operational situations. Conventional assessment has little to offer
in the measurement of factors such as these.

We understand by assessment the measured results of student
performance in carefully constructed test conditions. The concern

71

is with how the student has coped with a given course of instruction. Despite our worries, expressed above, concerning the relevance of this information to Language Awareness courses, we are conscious that the conventions of the educational system pressure teachers to vindicate their courses by some such assessment. Section Four offers suggestions and comments related to this.

The main problem is that retrieval of content may take precedence over the more subtle objectives that motivate the course. A course can be trivialised if its initial objectives are lost sight of, and short Language Awareness courses are particularly vulnerable. A few scraps of information may seem paltry as the only retrievable evidence of what could be major reorientation.

Where it is necessary in a course that some straightforward assessment will be conducted, we urge that this is designed and carried out as a part of the more general self-evaluation of the course as a whole. Then it will be clear to all what part the assessment plays in the overall programme. Section Two offers some principles for setting up a programme evaluation.

John Sinclair

SECTION TWO - PROGRAMME EVALUATION

Introduction

In this paper we shall concentrate on the evaluation of a course
while it is in progress - whether it is in the initial stages, under
development, or fully up and running. We shall draw mainly from
experience with language skills courses; often ESL (English as
Second Language) and LA (Language Awareness) but also EFL (English
as Foreign Language), EMT (English Mother Tongue) and FLT (Foreign
Languages in EMT context).

A thorough evaluation of a course would be ongoing and would slice
through and examine the total process at regular intervals. The
'ongoing' cannot be fully separated from the 'before' and the
'after', so we should like to place our remarks first of all with
reference to those other points of evaluation, pre- and post-course
evaluation.

In general, we think that retrospective evaluation of a course
should be designed separately from the course itself. The external
evaluator needs to be free from even the most basic assumptions of a
course, and the assessment of student performance should also be
done in isolation from the course, both to avoid self-fulfilling
results, and to avoid the backwash effects of assessment. This
separateness will protect the integrity of the course but at the
expense of increasing its vulnerability.

So it is to the vulnerability of a course that we turn, and that
feature leads back to the very beginning. A course whose design
recognises the need for continuous evaluation will be much less
vulnerable than one which does not. We find it useless to consider
ongoing evaluation without reference to the original design of the
course. This kind of evaluation does not need to be external, nor
do we need the slightly absurd notion of internal evaluators who are
distinct from participants. It becomes a part of the progress of
the work, in which everyone participates.

We shall concentrate on two important design features of a course,
and show how they lead to reliable self-evaluation. These are:

A. Explicitness of documentation
B. Two - tier management structure, one tier playing a monitor
   role.

We all get involved in courses, sometimes helping to design or
implement them, sometimes to revise and develop, and sometimes just
to serve as a team member when a course is well-established. If
these two features are present in the design, and properly
articulated in the course itself, then the course is fairly safe,

73

and will stand up to external evaluation at any time. If they are not present, the course is vulnerable, and the people working on it may be subject to unfair criticism.

A. EXPLICITNESS OF DOCUMENTATION

In this section, we must again distinguish between what happens before and after, this time taking a course stage by stage.

1. Forward-looking documentation

In general, the implementation of a course from design to reality requires that we take a series of steps in realisation. The characteristic progress is from abstract to concrete. Each step taken produces a sub-plan which can be checked against requirements in the more abstract plan which stimulated it. So a Language Awareness course might decide on a syllabus item "variety" and then decide what aspect of language variation would be appropriate, and then how available resources could be used to plan a series of lessons, and then what would actually happen in the classroom.

The question here is fidelity of realisation. Each step requires a number of decisions, and the exercise of creative imagination, in how a concept can be brought to life in the classroom. At this point the direction of the course could shift, priorities could subtly change, a misunderstanding could be given licence. Unless the more abstract statement is explicitly made before the step in realisation is taken, the check cannot be made, and the control is lost.

There are additional advantages to an explicit step-by-step design, for example simplifying late stages of implementation like materials-writing. With reference to evaluation, it ensures that the elements of the design are maintained right through the complex process of putting it into practice.

Here is an example. In most language courses of all types, learner motivation is a problem. Despite progressive developments in teaching, it is often difficult to stimulate a class with the prospect of fairly distant goals in order to get them to tackle what is undeniably hard work. There may be few external factors to show them the value of language skills. Hence motivation should be a major design element. If the course is to be successful, each lesson should be interesting or compelling enough in itself. This is a grave design constraint; many teachers may feel that it should figure in every educational course.

If the requirement to provide lesson-by-lesson motivation is to be carried right through, then the specification for each activity must include a statement of the reason why a learner should bother doing it. When the activity is fully articulated, it can be checked

74

against the motivation statement; when the activity is piloted, it will be discovered if the prediction was correct.

The process of specifying everything step by step in advance is laborious, and can appear unnecessary to experienced teachers in a course team. There is a human tendency to skip the red tape and try something out - a confidence in improvisation which, in its proper place, is essential for teachers who have to survive bad courses. But to avoid bad courses, the discipline of explicit documentation is necessary, and turns out to be highly educational for the participants.

2. Backward-looking documentation

The type and quality of decisions taken in a course should be a matter of record. All sorts of decisions are taken and memory cannot be relied upon. In a course of any size, some individuals may be implementing decisions in ignorance of how and why they were taken.

We shall first of all pick out a few of the ways in which decisions can vary, giving examples from experience.

(a) Decisions can range between principled and arbitrary. Arbitrary decisions are often necessary, and there is nothing wrong with them so long as everyone knows that they are arbitrary and can be varied if good reason arises. For example, in one course, the pilot materials were arranged in four sections of equal size, and the syllabus prescribed one lesson from each section in rotation. Each section became a book which approached the target skills in a different way.

After piloting, this organisation was queried on the balance of the sections (were they equally important?), on the daily switching from one to another (was it unsettling?), and on the distinctiveness of each approach (were they actually separate in practice?). The initial decision to make four sections was a purely operational one, in that there were four senior members of the team, and the most efficient organisation of effort was to divide the job into four parts, each part focusing on a particular priority. The course improved noticeably when three of the four sections were integrated in revision, the placement of lessons next to each other became non-arbitrary, and the balance between sections gave way to a better deployment of the various approaches.

In another project, however, there were and still are four sections because that division was the result of decisions in principle, unrelated to the team structure. Research had shown that the target learners were weak in listening comprehension, vocabulary richness, and interactive skills, and that remedial attention to syntax was needed for some. These four areas therefore retained their separate identity.

(b) Decisions may be internal or external: external ones are not decisions taken by the course participants, but are delivered from outside. It is very important to record these because they often conflict with internal opinion. For example, it used to be necessary (and sometimes still is) to devise hour-long sessions in the language laboratory, because the booking systems allowed nothing less, and classes which did not use the time fully were placed low in priority.

(c) Decisions may range from theoretical to practical – in the sense of arising from practice. Course designs are all the better for a strong theoretical orientation, but as the implementation proceeds the need for attention to practice becomes stronger, and needs to be accommodated. For example, there once was a course based on formal grammar which introduced words and structures according to the grammar's estimate of their difficulty. The teachers had problems because question forms were regarded as difficult and didn't appear for some time, and information questions were held to be very difficult indeed.

(d) Decisions may range from considered to spontaneous, as contingencies arise. The spontaneous ones must be identified as such so that they can be retrieved for a more searching appraisal at a later stage. Many valuable and innovative features of courses have had their origins in chance or coincidence.

The importance of recording the type and quality of decisions becomes clear when a course is to be revised, adapted or updated, because people develop a fierce loyalty to their creations, and tend to resist the necessary upheavals that keep a course healthy. They may identify with superficial features of the course which can be shown to have little solid support in the design.

Since in an explicit design any feature of the course can be referred to the decisions which originated it, it becomes possible to assess the seriousness of a problem. If changes are proposed, their effect on other parts of the course can be discerned, and disturbance can be kept to the minimum. For example, a good course will try to achieve a balance between theoretical and practical concerns. But once the course is at the piloting stage, and from then on, the feedback is almost entirely from practice, and the influence of theory could disappear altogether. Only if the decision chains are traceable back to source can a theoretical point which is called into question be dealt with at the appropriate level.

In this way a course can remain flexible, and yet consistent with its origins. Flexibility is essential because there are many variables which lie outside the control of the course team. Even fundamental constraints presented as external decisions can turn out to be negotiable, and basic "given" facts can turn out to be wrong. Rigidity is the enemy of good courses, because the problem is changing all the time. One's own course is unlikely to be the only one affecting the total educational pattern. Hence, for example, the expected competence of learners may vary against time, either upward or downward, or change in character. Or the course itself may reveal that an assumption made about the learners is unfounded. A good course will respond to these upsets very economically.

It is worth noting here, with regard to flexibility, that modern technology is making possible the production of materials of high presentation quality, but without the fossilisation of conventional publication. At last, materials can be granted their proper status as by-products of educational courses, and not as the ultimate course goals. With equipment such as word-processors, changes can be made locally in materials to implement revisions, without necessitating extensive overhauls. The advantages to be gained by explicit documentation are thus well worth the labour involved. The course becomes potentially self- evaluating. We turn now to a feature of the management structure which will bring out that potential.

B. TWO-TIER MANAGEMENT STRUCTURE

The suggestion is that each course will set up for itself a monitoring system, which will ensure its relevance from the outset, and give early warning of problems. The first step is to ask who is going to be affected by the course. The full answer will no doubt differ from course to course but typically the list will include

(a)   learners
(b)   teachers and other staff
(c)   institutions, authorities and sponsors
(d)   the profession at large.

For each group, we ask the questions - What does the course offer them? What is their method of evaluation? How does the course take account of this?

Within the group, there may be two sets of answers to the questions, one from those who are directly involved in the course and one from those who are only indirectly affected. We must also expect the course to affect groups in ways to which their own evaluation is not sensitive. For example, the question of coverage of a syllabus may not be raised by learner evaluation.

From the concern of interest groups, a report structure and a committee structure can be devised which will further help the course to be self-evaluating. This monitoring tier should be as fully developed as resources allow, and should be seen to be as important as the teaching. It should not be seen as a necessary chore or a waste of resources or a hindrance to innovation.

Here are some brief examples of the point of view of those affected directly by a course. One avant-garde scheme overseas attempted to teach purely communicatively, but the learners tended to stick to their traditional learning patterns. The learners secretly worked out an underground methodology; for example, there was no rote-learning of vocabulary, so they maintained their own lists.

In some parts of the world teachers do not allocate a lot of time to preparing a lesson based on a text. They expect to be provided with a bank of selected texts, each with a set of conventional exercises following, and they have an efficient, generalised method for getting through the text. They tend to be initially hostile to a course which requires a lot of personal preparation, different for each text. Educational institutions prefer courses to be as standardised as possible, and will examine new proposals to see if they fit into the existing pattern. If there are likely to be discrepancies - for example, a Language Awareness course involving several departments can look anomalous and cause timetable pressure if it takes place in one term only - the course designers can save a lot of trouble by anticipating such a viewpoint, and designing the course so that it fits in.

Information bulletins, etc. are usually welcomed by others in the profession. Not all course organisers are coy about this, but too many are. The slow and patchy spread of information about Language Awareness courses is a case in point.

Let us say a little more about some of these interest groups.

(a) The learners

Learners require a perception of relevance and personal progress to gain confidence in a course. The criterion of relevance can be subdivided - for example, in the area of subject matter. To many staff, the choice of subject matter is regarded as fairly cosmetic, especially when they are working from general principles. To the learner it may be critical, catching a fashion or an interest at just the right time to motivate.

Learners will also be very conscious of the level and tempo of their courses, and time spent in studying their needs will bring dividends. The style of teaching, too, should be carefully matched to expectations. This does not mean that there can be no innovation, but rather that the monitor system constantly checks that the features of the course are correctly interpreted to learners.

We are led once again, and not for the last time, to a plea for explicitness. Whoever the learners are, we feel an imperative to make sure that they understand the aims and methods of the courses they are taking. Otherwise the opportunity for genuine co-operation in the teaching/learning process may be lost.

This is a unilateral responsibility on the staff side. Many learner groups respond with indifference to initial statements of aims, etc. and retain little understanding of the rationale of the course. There may be many reasons for this, ranging from inability to believe that this level of co-operation and involvement is seriously being sought, to a lack of appreciation of the opportunities offered. When there are difficulties in the way of communication, the effort should be increased.

We have stated this point as forcibly as possible in a short space; obviously it is a design factor like any other, and has to be fitted into the course as a whole. No matter how strongly we feel certain principles, they will be ineffective if they are not integrated into a design which is acceptable to all parties.

Learners must have confidence in their teachers, because through the teachers they will gain confidence in the course as a whole. This is a serious issue in Language Awareness courses, because teachers may be tempted beyond their competence both in their understanding of the principles of language structure, and their control over data, say, from exotic languages.

The learners' perception of progress is another essential feature of a course. Particularly with innovative teaching, we can observe a situation where the students are actually learning well, but do not realise it. This can blunt motivation and lead to confusion about objectives. The course should provide throughout for frequent and regular feedback of an encouraging kind, showing the learners that they are gaining command over language skills which they did not have before, and understanding more about language. This is a particular problem in the area of Language Awareness, which resists simple assessment techniques.

A course is institution-based, but frequently is required to select only some of the learners. A particular group or subject may be picked out, or learners with a particular profile on early assessment. Pilot stages of a course may have to keep the numbers down. It is important to consider the course in the context of the total membership of the institution, and to deal with the interest of both those within and those outside the course. Quite often an excluded group can attack a course because of its very effective-ness, on the reasonable ground that it is only available to some; equally an included group can perceive a course as adding substantially to their burdens, and attempt to opt out.

(b) The teachers

Very similar considerations apply to teachers on a course, and their colleagues outside. They must have an explicit understanding of the course, and confidence in the management team – confidence in the design, the recruitment of colleagues, and the infrastructure. They must have a clear perception of role. Throughout a course it is desirable that all the teachers are participants in the development of materials, methods and organisation, and the course itself is seen as a valuable training exercise.

For this to be effectively achieved, an important load is again carried by documentation. Initial briefing of new teachers, and orientation in the early stages, will be carefully planned, and at the centre of it will be an up-to-date presentation of the course, at an appropriate professional level. This is a major requirement when the turnover of teachers is anticipated, but is good practice in any course to minimise confusion and to support the day-to-day traffic in information. In a modest course it may be no more ambitious than a file or two, and as well·as the big courses we must not forget the individual initiative of a teacher, where design and monitoring matters are no less important, and where discussion with others on planning may enlist their sympathetic support, even though they are not involved in the actual teaching.

Guidance on an organised basis should be continuously available from experienced colleagues. It may seem on the verge of insult to make a point of this, but in large courses, in an ongoing stage, experience is that it is rather rare. New teachers are frequently ushered into the classroom with no support beyond a set of interim materials. Once the first flush of enthusiasm and creativity is over, there is less chance of attention and resources being given to a course, and unless provision is made from the start, then decline sets in. New teachers fail to appreciate the good qualities of the work, and react against it; lack of maintenance leads to ad hoc patching or simple neglect, and in a short time the course becomes an embarrassment. Sadly, we have to record that institutions do not show a strong desire to protect their investments, and each course must set out to be self-perpetuating. This can best be achieved by creating a full range of feedback mechanisms, particularly involving the teachers.

We have mentioned the importance of any course as a training exercise, but we want to make a further plea for opportunities for teachers on an innovative course to have formal professional training. It is a difficult organisational point, particularly in the early years, and teachers can become shackled by their own value to a course. Not only does this increase the isolation of a course and threaten its up-to-dateness, but it can cause loyal teachers to feel that colleagues who have gone for further training have improved their relative positions in the institution. Teachers must be guaranteed that their participation in a course, with the extra effort that is so often asked of them, will enhance their professional standing. We believe that this point carries implications for those who provide advanced professional qualifications, but the issue cannot be pursued here. Let us instead give a couple of examples to support the general argument that the course should make specific provision for the teachers, and listen to them throughout.

Many courses in recent years have concentrated on the production of materials for the learner, and the word "teacher-proof" has frequently been used. New methodologies, especially with technological innovations, have appeared to reduce the role and importance of the teacher. Coupled with inadequate orientation and guidance, teachers have often become alienated from a course unable to adapt their skills and experience.

A new development is just appearing, where materials are constructed for the teacher, and not immediately for the learner. If this becomes fully accepted, the teacher will re-assume a central role, incapable of being bypassed, and the state of his/her professional awareness and skill will dominate the planning and maintenance of the course. We can only hope that this development will be supported by all parties.

To take a more specific case, it is not uncommon for groups of teachers to be recruited into a course which was not designed to exploit their skills. A clear and recurrent instance of this is the recruitment of native-speaking teachers to a course whose materials are designed for non-native-speaking teachers. We shall not elaborate on the serious problems that arise, but only point out that however much the native speakers are seen as having special attributes, their special needs are just as vital, and should be anticipated, analysed, provided for and supported strongly.

We mentioned the perception of progress when talking about the learners; it is equally important that the teachers have a clear understanding of the way their learners are progressing, and it is a factor which can affect their confidence and morale. It may be the case, although evidence is lacking, that individual progress in the interactive, communicative kind of teaching is as difficult for the teacher to perceive as it is for the learner. The fact that learners are not all learning the same things at the same time, that we easily forget a previous state of incompetence, that solo performance is hardly relevant - these all obscure the subtly growing command of a language, and make it almost impossible to apply simple measures so that the teachers can check their intuitions.

(c) Institutions and authorities

The course is part of the work of an institution, and must relate to
it both internally and externally.   There are so many variables
here, and so many stories to tell, that we shall confine ourselves
to broad generalities and a few examples.

First of all, external liaison between the course and those with
authority over it must rest on a clear understanding of objectives.
Most courses in our experience, are misunderstood by significant
segments of the authority structure.   Yet understanding is crucial
when the course is under way and external priorities change, as they
always do.   The negotiations that take place to accommodate such
changes depend on goodwill, good communications, but above all on
detailed, explicit, agreed and understood objectives.

For example, it is almost inevitable that the authority's perception
of the role of a course will change as experience grows.   Some of
the resources allocated may seem attractive for purposes that were
not envisaged at the outset; or the course may be under pressure to
accept learner groups whose needs are subtly different from those
for whom the course was devised.   Motives ranging from over-
enthusiasm to cynicism may lead to these diversions.   The course
organisers require an explicit starting point for negotiations, or
they may be accused of the most irritating failure of all - failure
to do what they did not set out to do.

It is also a fact of life that assumptions made at early stages in a
course need to be revised.   Some of them are just wrong and since
one of the early tasks of a course is to examine all assumptions,
their inaccuracy emerges perhaps even in an embarrassing way.   Some
initial positions are modified by the early experience of the course
itself, and some are changed by external factors.   Examples:
assumptions made about the competence of learners may be proved
wrong by the course assessments; assumptions made about the likely
rate of progress may be optimistic or pessimistic; assumptions made
about learner numbers may be changed by educational policy.
Assumptions made about the learners' acquiescence may be challenged
by the learners, or may be sabotaged by political changes.

Institutions tend to value stability over experiment, and tolerate
innovation only reluctantly and in the short term.   Courses are
expected to cause a brief flurry and then to settle down,
consolidate and work to routine.   This is difficult to align with
the volatile state of language teaching methodology; changing
patterns in the schools invite frequent adaption by the teachers.
Such broadly antipathetic positions can become polarised and
entrenched, and cause crippling difficulties.   One of the recurrent
problems is the unwillingness of institutions to allow a continuing
element for Research and Development beyond the first stages of a

course. The balancing problem is the opposition of the more creative members of a course team to any sort of compromise or plateau stage in, say, material production.

These considerations point to a course organisation which tries to be explicit about the interface with the institution, authority or sponsor involved, and which tries to allow evaluations in both directions.

Let us turn now to the internal responsibilities of the course with respect to institutions, etc. Factual documentation again takes pride of place; the diary of work, the functions of sections and individuals, the newsy items are all valuable components of what should be very active communication lines. The process of internal documentation and reporting, which we dealt with earlier, can and should lead to the right sort of external documentation.

But it is very rarely found. Usually the two processes are separate, and the external documentation is full of meaningless data, supposedly impressive tabulation, with all the burning issues damped down. Very few internal documents could simply be transmitted outwards, and the course organisers can become information losers, suppressors, distorters and manipulators. This is one of the most intractable problems in the profession, and it seems to arise from faulty perceptions of role, and often also from inadequate resources for proper documentation. Real or anticipated reactions from authority can sometimes be held responsible, but we would also include bad course design, and often a narrowness of outlook of participants. We don't want to appear idealist here, naively believing that truth will always triumph, or that information is neutral; but rather that since these difficulties can confidently be anticipated, and can be seriously debilitating, they should be reckoned as shaping factors in the course from the outset.

(d) The profession at large

It may not seem at first sight that there should be any pressure on the designers or organisers of a course to provide for continuous contact with the profession at large. The individual teachers, of course, will be interested in self-advancement and the more energetic of them will be anxious to attend conferences, write papers, and help in the publication of course materials. Many courses are sympathetic to requests of this nature. Some go farther, and plan stages of presentation to the outside world, using the conference circuit and the journals as vehicles for attracting professional attention.

We believe that one of the biggest dangers facing a language-teaching course anywhere in the world is isolation. Once begun, it has a tendency to be inward-looking, as the problems strike, as the complexity increases, as the brainchild becomes the obsession of the doting parents. Perhaps because of an imperfect understanding of the course, participants can become very defensive, resisting criticism and losing any analytic detachment. The unique or innovative features of the course are thought of as a professional lifeline.

The enthusiasm and productiveness which this attitude engenders is invaluable, and few if any courses would get far without devotion well beyond the call of duty. Our point is that if contact with colleagues in a wider context is built into a course design it should not inhibit motivation or inspiration but will remove the need for secrecy and defensiveness. Any good course should be spurred on by regular positive feedback and constructive criticism. There should be a dialogue from the start with other groups and individuals, seeking views and suggestions. It has to be efficiently organised because of the turnround time of comments, but it allows the course team to identify at any time the professional importance of their work, encourages them and others to draw out the likely lessons for other courses, and reduces the depressing delay that we usually have to suffer before good work becomes available. Properly planned, it is a major feature of ongoing course evaluation.

Some courses devise a halfway house for professional contact in the shape of an Advisory Group or the like. That is better than nothing, but not very satisfactory. For one thing, the members of such a group tend to become as inward-looking as the team itself, and for another, they rapidly become sophisticates and therefore unrepresentative. One of the very first courses of a communicative nature, back in the sixties, had really magnificent support from its representative advisers, but was still too innovative when it appeared on the market. The hardbitten heads and their staff were just not ready for it, and the advisers had apparently acted as a buffer from reality rather than a route through to it.

In conclusion, we should like to summarise the central theme. Evaluation is always a sensitive issue, and it can be faced without fear only if courses are properly designed and fully documented. The documentation, while laborious, has a wide range of uses beyond course control. A feature of the design of any course should be a monitoring system so that all groups affected by the course will be conducting an efficient two-way dialogue with the course team. When a course is safeguarded in this way, then external evaluation is no problem, and if possible external evaluations should be based on different principles from those which have guided the course.

Gillian Donmall and John Sinclair

SECTION THREE - FORMAL EXAMINATIONS

1.   This section of the paper on Evaluation and Assessment is
concerned with terminal assessment of a Language Awareness course by
means of an externally administered formal examination. The
questions that need to be considered when setting up such an
examination are defined through describing the experience gained at
The Oratory School in setting up the GCE A/O Level Principles of
Language examination. This experience is, of course, based only on
groups of able A level students who had elected to follow the
course. There are, however, certain fundamental questions that
should be faced by anyone setting up any formal assessment at any
level.

2.   Why is formal external assessment desired?   In the case of The
Oratory the answer was fourfold.

i)   to show that is was possible and feasible to set up an
examination in Language Awareness through a mainstream   examination
system. (see Section 5)

ii)   to enhance the validity of the course in the minds of the
students.   The success of the Graded Objectives and Tests movement
has shown that motivation is increased if the course can be seen by
the students to culminate in demonstrable and tangible achievement.

iii)   to provide a stimulus and a guide for the better internal
functioning of the course, as, for example, in the case of the
extended essay element of the examination.   The preparation of this
2500 word essay on a subject of their choice made the students think
more deeply in an aspect of the course than would otherwise have
been the case.

iv)   to help define and confirm the nature of the course in the
minds of teacher, students and onlookers.   The content of any
examination paper and the way in which the questions are framed have
a powerful influence on people's view of the syllabus and how it
should be taught.

3.   What is the nature of the course being assessed?

i) Before starting to plan the form that an external examination is
to take, it must be decided what the course is meant to achieve in
those who follow it.   In the case of The Oratory the course aims
were:-

a)   to make the students more sensitive to their own and people's
     use of language, and in the process
b)   to provide a pre-theoretical introduction to the basic
     principles of linguistic study.

ii) It must also be decided what means are to be used to realise the aims of the course. The syllabus content of the course at The Oratory is detailed in the next section of this publication, <u>Reports and Initiatives in Core Schools</u>. Briefly it covers:-

a)   definition of human language and communication
b)   analysis of English
c)   examination of change and variety in usage.

iii) It must be considered carefully whether the objectives of the course will lead to the aims being realised. Will the syllabus have the intended effect on the students? In the case of The Oratory this question becomes:- Would coverage of the syllabus in 3.ii develop the students' awareness of what language is and how it functions? Would that increased awareness of language produce increased sensitivity to how it is used? Unless the probable answer to such questions is positive, the course is not linked to its stated aims.

iv) The way in which the course content is presented to the students is also important. Does the teaching of the syllabus suit the content of the syllabus? Do the manner of exposition and the format of the materials lead the students effectively towards achieving the aims of the course? The methodology of the course at The Oratory is based on the fact of the students' native speaker knowledge of English. It is felt that the best way of making the students more aware of language is by guiding them to explore what they intuitively know and use already. The students are guided towards an awareness of linguistic concepts primarily through the analysis of examples of that concept. If the process is successful, then it should lead on to their producing further examples of their own. (Further discussion of this methodology can be found in the paper <u>Methodology Related to Language Awareness Work</u>.)

4.   What form should the examination take?

i) If the form of the examination does not correspond to the nature of the course, then the nature of the course will change to fit the form of the examination. Conversely, the aims, objectives and methodology of the course are reinforced, if the form of the examination coincides with them. If an examination terminates the course, the teaching will inevitably be directed towards the form and content of the examination.

ii) The content of a course may be primarily concerned with increasing students' knowledge, or alternatively with increasing their skill and performance. The course at The Oratory is of the latter type, since it aims at increased sensitivity to language use through developed awareness of its nature and function. The questions in the examination had, therefore, to reflect the fact that it was performance in being aware of language that was to be tested, not knowledge of how to talk about language.

iii) More specifically the questions in the A/O Principles of Language examination had to fulfil a twofold function:-

a) to ascertain whether there was an improvement in the awareness of the student about language. Such improvement was deemed to have been shown by the satisfactory completion of the linguistic tasks in the questions;

b) to state the linguistic tasks in such a way that individual insight on language could be shown, either in the form of an unexpected slant on the task in hand or of seeing wider implications.

iv) The format of the questions had to replicate the methodology of the course at The Oratory. The emphasis in the course presentation was on guided exploration through examples, on the students' approaching analysis and definition through handling examples of language for themselves. The examination questions were framed to fit this pattern, thereby reinforcing it. (For examples of the questions see Report of Work at the Oratory School, Section 7.)

v) If the Principles of Language examination was restricted to a question paper composed of language examples presented to the candidate for handling (as outlined in Section 4. iv), then they would have little opportunity for continuous writing in the context of the examination. This objection was rectified by introducing an extended essay into the examination. The students were required to write about 2,500 words on a topic of their own choosing related to the syllabus. This essay would be researched and written over a period before the question paper was sat. It gave the students the stimulus to investigate more closely an aspect of the course that interested them, thereby reinforcing the objectives and aims of the course by another means. (Topics chosen by candidates for their extended essays are listed in Report of Work at the Oratory School, Section 8).

vi) When the form of the terminal examination has been decided, the results of the first sittings must be monitored to see whether the examination is doing what it is intended to do. For example:-

a) Do the results coincide sufficiently well with the pre-examination predictions of the teachers? Is there a good spread of results? Have the better candidates been given the opportunity to shine?

b) Do questions produce the kind of answers expected? Do questions have equal value or is it easier to gain credit by anwering some questions in preference to others? If it is not already the case, should some questions be made obligatory and should the paper be sectionalised? Is the time limit too generous, too short or about right? Is the lay-out of the paper a help or a hindrance to the candidates? Are the overall examination instructions clear? Is there any question rubric which is misleading? Could the candidates have been expected to know the terminology used? If not, was such terminology explained?

c) If any component of the examination has been completed before the written examination, such as the extended essay referred to in Section 4.v, has the opportunity to work in greater depth been taken up by the candidates? If not, is this the fault of the terms of reference of this part of the examination?

d) If the candidates have been taught by one teacher or a small group of teachers in the same school, what problems would be involved in opening up the examination to a wider public? How far do the teaching on which the examination is based and hence the preparation for that examination depend on particular teachers in particular circumstances? Can the syllabus, method and materials be taken up by other teachers in other schools and used in their individual contexts, allowing for the fact that they can still make personal contact with the original source in case of difficulty? Can they be taken up more widely when the only feasible contact between participating schools is that of a formal statement of syllabus content and formal instructions on examination procedure?

e) What adjustments would have to be made to the arrangements for setting, marking, moderating and administrating the examination, if it was offered to a wider public?

5. i) It is always possible to approach the ruling body of an examination system with proposals for a formal examination under its aegis. In the case of the Oratory's Principles of Language examination the initial proposal to the Oxford and Cambridge Schools Examination Board contained a statement of aims and objectives, an outline of the course syllabus, an indication of the intended age and ability level of the candidates and an outline of the proposed examination. When the Board decided to investigate the proposal, it asked for further information in the form of a specimen examination paper, detailed guidelines on how it would be marked and a marking scheme. Detailed consultations produced a format that the Board felt was sufficiently consistent with the aims and objectives of the original submission, as well as with their own examining standards, for the proposal to be given a three-year trial period restricted to candidates from the place of submission. In this way the proposal could be tested in practice, free from the problems that would occur in sharing an experimental course and examination between schools.

ii) In obtaining approval from an examining body for a formal examination, attention must be given to the financing and marking of the proposed examination. How will the costs of the examination be covered? Who will set, check and produce the question papers? Who will mark and moderate its various components? How far will the teachers of the course be involved in the setting and marking of the question papers? An examination body will offer guidance and opinion on these questions which will vary according to the nature of the board, depending in particular on how teacher-based it is. Such mundane questions are crucial, since their answers will decide the smoothness of the routine administration of the new examination and thereby facilitate its being offered to a wider spread of candidates, if and when the initial pilot testing is successfully completed.

iii) A formal examination must respond to expectations of what a formal examination is like. If the reality falls short of such expectations, the formal assessment will not be seen as a serious examination and will not be treated as such by students on the course, other teachers or members of the public. If the underlying aims and objectives are thoroughly thought out, if the examination itself is properly planned and prepared in the context of those aims and objectives, if the presentation is that of a serious public examination, then it will evoke a serious response.

A.J. Tinkel

SECTION FOUR: IN-SCHOOL ASSESSMENT OF INTRODUCTORY COURSES

(It is appreciated that some of the following will not be new to
many teachers, that some of the points made are applicable to all
testing situations. However, they are offered as a composite source
for reference with the particular circumstances of Language
Awareness initiatives in mind).

A number of the points made in Section Three of this paper with
regard to the setting up of a formal assessment scheme with an
outside examining body are as important to any internal assessment
scheme. Few teachers can be unaware of the problems of setting
tests which successfully do what is required of them; testing is no
easy matter even for experts. Few teachers are given thorough
training in the setting of tests/examinations and yet the results of
internal assessment procedures are often crucial determinants of the
shape of a pupil's further learning. For example, as a result of an
internal examination a pupil may be excluded from any further
learning of the subject or allocated to a specific learning level.
Alternatively, poor performance in a test may have a strongly
negatively reinforcing effect on his/her learning of that subject if
inadequacy rather than achievement has been underlined.

It should be said again, as was first pointed out in Section I, that
we do not favour formal assessment procedures for Language Awareness
work, that on-going evaluation should be a much more effective
monitor of a course, its teachers and its learners. Since most
Language Awareness courses in existence at present are of relatively
short duration, not destined for qualification as O- or A-level
subjects, since they are designed to further competence in learning
in all curricular areas, since emphasis is on skill and performance,
not factual knowledge, and that is per se more difficult to assess
with a measure of objectivity, assessment as a means of determining
a pupil's progress (and thereby the value of the course as a whole)
is not especially to be recommended.

Foreign language teachers are only too well aware of examination
techniques which in order to attempt a measure of objectivity and
allow for standardization incorporate conventions of examining far
removed from the language use in most schools' teaching syllabuses.
Furthermore, they are well aware of the "backwash effect" of
examining techniques on teaching methods.

Where assessment is still required, however, we should wish to
emphasise that it should form only a part of a whole evaluation
process within which all work produced plays an important part in
the profile of a pupil's learning and development, thus ensuring
that conclusions are not drawn from an assessment undertaking which
it cannot logically be expected to provide.

Why ?

For whom or for what purpose is a formal assessment process to be carried out?

If it is sought by the head, for other staff, for parents, as a means of justification of the course in terms of improved pupil conscious awareness and performance, so be it, but its place in the overall evaluation process should be underlined. It should not stand alone as the sole determinant of the value of the course defined in these terms.

If the response is "for the pupils", the teacher might question that necessity. It should be a built-in on-going feature of a Language Awareness course that learners perceive and give evidence of their own progress.

If the answer is : to use as a means of discriminating between pupils in order to determine placement, for example, into ability sets, this would run counter to the philosophy underlying all Language Awareness work. The intention with such a test, is to arrive at a spread of marks, whereby a substantial number of pupils are labelled as "less competent". However, in Language Awareness work the basis is pupils' already high performance skills in language; its purpose is to make conscious and develop those skills to higher levels. We should intend any assessment of pupils in Language Awareness to record levels of <u>achievement</u> not inadequacy.

When ?

Assessment is usually sought at the end of a teaching programme and we should not wish to recommend any greater frequency. Diagnosing and putting right pupils' problems and ensuring continued progress will form part of the teaching programme of a Language Awareness course which is subject to continuous monitoring.

What ?

a) The essential setting-off point is : the aims and objectives of the course, the objectives of each teaching module within the course and of each small section within the module, firstly in order for goal-orientated teaching to take place and secondly for proper assessment of it to be tackled.

e.g.

Aim:
Appreciation of the variety and range of expression present in the United Kingdom and the circumstances and appropriacy of their use.

91

Objective:
Knowing to which part of the country different expressions belong through familiarity with their use in speech.

Assessment:
Listen to recordings of speech and indicate on the map provided in which part of the country they are widely used.

b) All Language Awareness courses have an affective as well as a cognitive aspect (see The Report, section: The Term Language Awareness). This aspect in itself defies <u>assessment</u> but it would be wrong to overlook it when seeking a view of the value of a course as a whole. This is an important part of the <u>evaluation</u>.

c) As the core school descriptions show, most, if not all, Language Awareness courses have some input of knowledge content. This can be a relatively simple kind of area to assess if extension of knowlege in certain defined fields is a complete course objective in itself. Pupils may, for example, be required to reproduce that knowledge on the stimulus of a request for the same.
e.g.

In which countries is German/Greek/Spanish spoken?

However, it is important to remember that knowledge content in Language Awareness courses is usually subservient either to the affective sphere or as a preliminary to and ultimately part of the conscious awareness, skill/performance sector. In these circumstances the knowledge aspect should not be assessed separately but as part of the whole activity which reflects the course objective.
e.g.

Knowledge of intonation patterns allied to awareness of how they affect meaning, may allow a pupil, for example, a. to say a sentence with at least 4 different stress patterns to indicate 4 different meanings ("we'll paint the garage red and white as well") and b. to state what the different meanings conveyed are.

d) In Language Awareness work two important concerns are appropriacy and effectiveness of language use. A pupil might be asked to indicate the most appropriate response in given circumstances.
e.g.

Situation : pupil late for athletics training because he/she had been chatting to his/her friend.

Possible comments to the teacher: (a) I'm very sorry, (b) I'm stricken with mortification, (c) I do apologise profusely, and to give reasons for his/her choice.

Or again, a pupil might be asked to express him/herself as effectively as possible, e.g. persuade a customer to buy fruit from your stall in a market.

Objectives related to an appreciation of styles and registers ᴦof language may invite an assessment item of the following kind:

Situation: man returns home after work to find that his house has been burgled.   Many valuable items have been taken and also his guard dog!

Task : quote briefly his description of what has happened to the following people : (a) his wife when she comes home from work, (2) the policeman who comes to investigate (3) the postman who delivers the mail early next morning (4) his friends in the pub. It will be appreciated that assessment of these, especially the latter, types is not easy but the assessment must respond to the objectives, the objectives must not be lost in the interests of standardization or objectivity.

How ?

a) Syllabus:

The teaching syllabus and methodology allied to aims and objectives must be detailed as an essential factor in the design and implementation of a Language Awareness course.   Any assessment procedure must relate, as best as it can, to these.   It is not acceptable for limitations or conventions of assessment to condition either course content or teaching methodology.

b) Validity:

Not only must an assessment process reflect the content and teaching methodology of the course but every item must actually achieve the intention assigned to it in order for it to be valid.   For example, if pupils have been learning to discriminate between regional speech patterns based on listening to examples on tape, it is not valid to assess their competence by giving them examples on paper!

c) Reliability:

The larger the number of items, the more likely the test is to be reliable, i.e. the same statistical pattern would again be produced. In any case it would be unsatisfactory to use the single instance to make a statement about the generality of a pupil's progress.

d) Balance:

It is important that the balance of skills to be assessed reflects the balance determined for them in the course design. It is only too easy, for example, to include a number of items which are easy to assess, such as those related to extension of knowledge, and then to weight them in accordance with that, although the course design and purpose gives only small value weighting to this area per se.

e) Instructions:

Not only should these be absolutely clear but should be familiar to the pupils from classroom teaching use.

f) Time allocation:

The intention is to assist pupils to give the best account of themselves in circumstances most conducive to that. We should not wish to advocate that speed of writing, for example, should also be assessed. For this reason adequate time should be allowed for the tasks set, or if the constraint of time has to be the first priority, the tasks must be limited to suit those constraints.

Marking

a) All Language Awareness work is based on achievement. Pupils already have high performance skills and the intention is to advance these together with their conscious perception of language in use. Tests therefore should show what the pupils have achieved, not what they have not. The test will be set in such a way as to reflect this and thereby give stimulus to pupils' further learning. The philosophy underlying the Graded Proficiency test scheme is important to the Language Awareness field.

b) Appropriate marking must reflect the defined objectives of both teaching and testing, e.g. if correct spelling is not a defined objective, it should not be marked. The determining of parameters is always difficult but examiners must discipline themselves to mark only what it was intended to assess or otherwise run the risk of invalidation. (Consideration may be given to additional marks for especially good work in defined areas).

Evaluation

In the case of evident success, few problems arise. In the case of lack of success this may be due as much to, for example, teaching methodology, materials, course design, assessment design as to pupils' incompetence or laziness or the impossibility of achieving positive results in Language Awareness work. A proper evaluating and self-amending programme should ensure avoidance of most, if not all, of these but it is important to realise that an assessment process itself should also be subject to evaluative scrutiny. The following sample questions may give guidance for this:-

- do the results coincide with predictions and evidence given in class work?

- have all ability levels had the opportunity to show what they can do?

- was it possible to "play the system", i.e. by choice of some questions in preference to others?

- were the kind of responses intended actually supplied?

- was time allocation reasonable?

- was it a positive undertaking?

- did the marking scheme reflect the balance of objectives?

- what was the customers' response? i.e. what were their views of the assessment procedure?

In conclusion, the limitations of assessment processes and the problems with which they are beset underline how important it is that results obtained from them should not be used as the sole determinants either of pupils' achievement or of the value of a Language Awareness course. Section IV is offered to assist teachers to assess as effectively as possible when this is necessary but we hope that it serves also to emphasise the need for an on-going evaluation programme of which any assessment undertaken would simply form a part.

Gillian Donmall

SOME IMPLICATIONS OF LANGUAGE AWARENESS WORK
FOR TEACHER TRAINING (PRE-SERVICE AND IN-SERVICE)

B G Donmall

This paper concerns the training of all teachers, both as
contributors to the teaching of Language Awareness courses and as
teachers of language within their own subject areas.

Developments in the sphere of Language Awareness have their roots in
the Bullock Report of 1975, A Language for Life. The title itself is
a pertinent reminder of the significance and scope of the field. A
number of perceived truths, half-known truths and intuitions
concerning inadequacies in school pupils' operational skills in the
sphere of language, both as mother tongue per se and as an
instrument in the learning/teaching of all curricular subjects were
articulated (although regrettably, foreign languages were ignored).
Despite the breadth of coverage in the report and an appreciative
response among educators, however, lack of clear direction and
guidance as to how to tackle the issues raised meant that a number
of initiatives taken failed to stand the test of time. Attempts to
marry the insights of applied linguistics experts to the field of
practice have suffered sufficient setbacks for a further call on the
area of linguistics for support and guidance to seem for the time
being unlikely to be fruitful.

Some initiatives have survived profitably, however, and at this
grassroots level, eventually in combination with specialists in
language, it is developing a coherence and direction under the term
Language Awareness.

AWARENESS OF LANGUAGE (IN USE)

What is our topic? If we have to handle "it" we must know what "it"
is.

The term Language Awareness has at times been challenged as
indefinite, woolly, unclear. The writer suggests, however, that
these criticisms arise from educators' familiarity with a curriculum
heavily weighted with courses of factual knowledge content which is
readily retrievable for regurgitation in test conditions, and
assessed according to criteria of the ilk of 'right or wrong', 'good
or bad'. Those of us who are conditioned to gear all our teaching to
examination requirements rightly anticipate that assessment of
"awareness" and associated competencies would be difficult. While
the nature of some courses may be susceptible td formal assessment
(see the work of A.J. Tinkel at The Oratory School) others may serve

purposes for which formal assessment is inappropriate if not impossible (see paper on Evaluation and Assessment). First, let us consider the language element:-

a) Language

Language is the prime means of human communication. It facilitates - or inhibits - our progress through life. It is at once the focus of learning and the means of learning other things. It is also the means by which we are taught. Competence in language - perceptive reading of messages as well as the effective conveying of them, the ability to use language as a tool for one's own learning purposes and in development as an individual in a complex social environment - is the first basic factor which affects a pupil's progress in all sectors of the curriculum and in all extra-curricular areas. 'Language in use' is necessarily in an environmental context. The context affects the language use and may also be affected consciously by the language user.

b) Awareness of language (in use)

'Awareness of Language (in use)' is a person's sensitivity to and conscious perception of the nature and functioning of language in both his/her immediate and wider environments. We use the expression 'Language in Use' to underline the fact that it is the purposeful functioning of language in operational contexts which is the focus of our attention.

c) Language Awareness activities

Language Awareness activities and methodological procedures are described in detail in other papers (The Report, Methodology Related to Language Awareness Work, descriptions of core school activities and the paper by A.J. Tinkel). The following may serve as a useful reminder of some points which are particularly pertinent in the context of this paper.

Broadly speaking, work in the field of Language Awareness is directed towards the development of that conscious perception of and sensitivity to language allied in explicit terms to skill and performance. The latter may both precede as well as succeed the former. The pupil already has high performance skills in and intuitions about language. These are the springboard for pupil-based investigations during which the unconscious and intuitive becomes conscious and explicit.

However, if at this stage of discussing 'language in use' categories are established and terms applied to denote them, it is important to remember that it is not the categories themselves nor the terms of demarcation but the criteria governing their identification which must be the focus of attention and remain so in any application to language activities. We must underline that this is no reversion to "purposeless parsing pastimes". Our purpose is not description but interpretation.

The following may serve to give an indication of our intentions. Insights gained into 'language in use' permit attention to be directed, for example, to appropriacy of language in use not to value judgements about it. (Not "that's not proper English" but "when might you be more likely to say that?"). We may hope that, in addition, appreciation of appropriacy of language use may lead to tolerance of difference rather than condemnation through ignorance. Heightened perception may also allow us to concentrate on effectiveness of giving and reading messages rather than commenting on accuracy of language use. ("I think he's got the message over that he wants his son to wash his car but I think he'll have to make it a bit clearer that the son can borrow the car afterwards before he'll actually get round to doing it".)

To sum up: we have established the ·importance of language for human inter-action in life and its significance for the pupil in all operational areas of the school curriculum. We have seen that it is our responsibility to develop our pupils' sensitivity to and conscious perception of language in use. We have indicated what we mean by the term Language Awareness and have given an indication of the essential nature of Language Awareness activity. We have ascertained that the resource base is to be the pupil himself/herself and it is his/her development as an individual in society which must be fostered. What does this mean in the school context?

LANGUAGE AWARENESS IN THE SCHOOL CONTEXT

a) Courses in Language Awareness

There is considerable variation in the objectives, content and design of these courses in schools which as a result may be taught at any point in the pupil's school career, but their special nature is the focus on language itself. Broadly speaking, we may say that they share the following intentions: to arouse interest and stimulate motivation, to examine attitudes, affect positively the conveying of messages and to heighten perception of responses, to improve manipulation of operational situations and to contextualise learning. Given that this is the case, it would not be unreasonable to suggest that courses of this kind will also serve to foster pupils' progress via language in other curricular areas. However, these must also be addressed in their own right.

It should be stressed that teachers of these language-specific courses may well not only be linguists by training. For example, the musician has an important role to play in the training of the ear, the biologist in the handling of the processes of the physical activities involved in production and reception of language and the historian on the topic of language development and change conditioned by prevailing circumstances.

b) The subject-specific classroom

For all teachers of all subjects there is subject-specific matter expressed in subject-specific language to be conveyed to pupils. That language, be it vocabulary items, phrases, expressions, or language conventions (e.g., use of the impersonal statement in preference to the first person singular form) must be taught and must be learnt. They may first be encountered in the teacher's speech, in the text book or other materials. The teacher must be ready:

a. not to assume either the pupil's knowledge or the pupil's 'natural acquisition' competence;

b. to anticipate the language and respond accordingly, both in his/her own controlled use and teaching of same and in the materials in use in the classroom;

c. having ensured understanding by all pupils, to check retention of understanding, for example, in the next lesson but also subsequently and by all pupils, to ensure the pupils' capacity to respond to and/or use actively the language appropriately;

d. to ensure pupil participation in the teaching/learning process.

We see then that there are three clear areas requiring attention: the teacher's own use of language, the language contained in materials and the pupil's own reproduction of language. Clearly the teacher must be in a position to control all three.

In addition to subject-specific language and conventions of language use, however, there are other exchanges, e.g., instructions or evaluative comments made by the teacher which may incorporate new vocabulary items and phrases and novelty of expression or complexity of structure which require mastery.

The pupils for their part must learn to express themselves in the classroom context, for example, in asking questions, expressing difficulty, seeking help or clarification.

c) <u>Study skills</u>

There has been a burgeoning of courses in study skills with a greater or lesser explicit emphasis on language aspects in the post-Bullock period. These may include:

a.   how to take notes
b.   the use of a dictionary
c.   the use of a library
d.   how and where to seek information in and out of school
e.   how to learn for specific purposes.

Again, one thing is abundantly clear, viz that at the very heart of all the above lies language as the means of access.

d) <u>The spectrum of language learning</u>

In the Language Awareness class all language interests meet. It is no coincidence that this Working Party was set up after ground work had been carried out by previous working parties for example, into areas of convergence of interest and operation between teachers of mother tongue English and foreign languages and into considerations associated with minority community languages. History, variety, range, register, common and disparate elements of language(s), for example, which are common to most Language Awareness courses are of direct relevance to EMT, ESL, EFL to MCLs and FLs[1] in all their forms and with their many varied intentions. It should serve to foster their interests, both collectively and individually. (It is no <u>replacement</u> for them).

In language-based classes pupils who already speak at least one language in addition to English are an especially rich resource.

THE TEACHERS' NEEDS

It must now be clear that all teachers, be they teachers of language or languages or teachers of other subjects have need of instruction and guidance in language on their initial training courses. Ideally

---

1   EMT-English as Mother Tongue, ESL-English as second Language, EFL-English as Foreign Language, MCLs-Minority Community Languages, FLs-Foreign Languages.

this work should feature fully at the initial stage, and indeed on a number of courses very useful work is carried out despite difficulties, most notable of which is perhaps the limited time available. Since language use is fundamental to every area of teaching and learning, however, the suggestion that it can be tackled "briefly" or "superficially" on initial teacher training courses, to be developed more fully at some later stage during service is simply unhelpful. However, it will be necessary for some time to come, no doubt, to extend into the in-service area what in some cases has been inadequately tackled on initial training courses. Nor may we forget the masses of teachers already well launched on their careers whose needs must be met during service. Given the considerable disparity between individual initial training courses it would not be helpful to try here to indicate demarcation points between pre- and post training but to pin-point needs and to suggest responses and to emphasise again the importance that the responses be made early.

a) Language in use/Linguistics

Clearly, in order to programme and sequence their pupils' development in the field of Language Awareness, the teachers too must have a conscious and specific awareness themselves. They must acquire a knowledge of the structures and functions of language(s) and master the techniques of purposeful language analysis. As Ronald Carter expressed it: "The rules governing 'language' must be a vital part of the teacher's knowledge; otherwise pupils' engagement with language whether it be in spelling or in poetry or in the lived experience of the individual, can never really be progressive, systematically developed, or properly evaluated and assessed".[2]

The teacher must have control of the language he/she uses, of that contained in the teaching materials and of that received and used by the pupils, and in the subject-specific classroom, in Language Awareness classes and in interaction for the pupils' personal development. He/she needs to be able not only to foster progress but also to perceive problems and to analyse them in order to make appropriate corrective responses. In learning these skills he/she must acquire the tools for analysis and the language of description of language structures, functions and the features of discourse appropriate to his/her own learning.

This systematic study of Language in use must indeed be,

---

2 Ed R Carter. <u>Linguistics and the Teacher</u>. Routledge and Kegan Paul. 1982, p.8.

according to widely accepted definitions of the term, an area of linguistics; nor should we shy away from use of the term, as long as we are clear about the criteria for its use. We are not concerned here with 'categorisation for its own sake', nor with unintelligible jargon, nor again with long-winded investigations at the end of which little useful about practice can be stated. In Language Awareness work in the school context theory and practice coincide to their mutual benefit and in order that this development may continue, the association of Linguistics with Language in Use in Given Contexts, must not only be maintained but strengthened.

b) <u>Teaching techniques</u>

In spite of the controversies which still abound concerning pupils' acquisition of new language, indeed, what constitutes "learning language", there are none-the-less some statements which may be agreed by practitioners as well as theorists of most schools of thought on procedures which are either necessary or helpful in the controlled development of language skills. These may incude, e.g.:

- explicit training in the listening skill;

- frequency of hearing of new language items;

- frequency of use;

- pupil participation and involvement in the learning process;

- contextualised language learning;

- checking the various acquisitional stages;

- building in and responding to feedback.

These techniques may be new to non-language teachers or overlooked, for example, by foreign language teachers when involved in interaction via the mother tongue.

c) <u>Teaching roles in Language Awareness courses</u>

It has been emphasised in other papers[3] that essential to the methodology of teaching in Language Awareness courses is the pupil as the base point, as the springboard and as resource.

---

3 See especially A J Tinkel, <u>Methodology related to language at work</u>.

Pupil involvement in the whole process is paramount. The nature of the work is investigation and discovery by the pupil. It is the role of the teacher to define the objectives and draw up the syllabus, to select materials and programme the course.

He/she is to impose the start and end of each section, to sequence them to best effect, to supply the unifying thread(s) to the investigations, to guide pupils' analyses, to lead from the intuitive to the consciously perceived. In addition to all this he/she does also have a role as imparter of knowledge, since some Language Awareness courses may include, for example, aspects of unknown languages, how hearing and speech organs function etc. The skills appropriate to these kinds of methodological approach must feature, too, in teacher training.

(d) <u>Observation strategies</u>

With the focus on classroom language activities, teachers in training must be equipped with strategies for observation. Even experience and success in teaching do not necessarily bear with them the capacity to observe the teaching and learning of others and to comment with discernment and discrimination on interactive processes. Nor do teachers necessarily possess the language of comment or categorisation. In the former instance we might well say that the teachers' intuitions and insights need to be brought to the point of explicit and conscious awareness, and then, with acquisition of language of the second instance, to analyse and discuss systematically and purposefully.

Most importantly perhaps, the teacher must acquire the capacity for observation of his/her own classroom and the language activities operational in it.

(e) <u>Teacher involvement</u>

Whenever possible it is important that the teacher him/herself should be a full participator in the production and functioning of any course he/she teaches. Where the course is new, all who may teach it should be involved in establishing the aims and objectives, in the overall design as well as the selection (and production) of material, determining methodology (methodologies) and in the making of decisions affecting the development of the course. Especially he/she must be a part of the continuing monitoring process - preferably not the only source of evaluatory response - but most certainly not excluded from it!

In many, if not the majority of instances teachers in school are presented with courses "to be taught", material "to be covered", language structures or functions "to be learnt" by the pupils and materials " to be used". This is determined often, for lower classes by the head of department and by examination requirements higher up the school. The dreadful negative effects on teaching to examination syllabuses which do not reflect agreed teaching syllabuses are well known. Less frequently emphasised but none-the-less real are the dreadful negative effects on the teachers themselves. However, it has been seen that whilst Language Awareness courses may lead to qualifications based on assessment (see work at the Oratory School), many serve interests which defy formal or even informal assessment. Thus, the focus may be placed and remain firmly on the objectives of the programme and on the agreed teaching of the same. The positive benefits to the teacher and, it should follow, to the teaching/learning process should be considerable.

Teacher training courses should therefore usefully take account of the necessity to train participants in the skills of course design, structure, programming and monitoring as well as the methodology of teaching.

Additionally, just as it is true for pupils that they are their own best resource in developing their skills in Language Awareness, so also are the teachers, who must necessarily acquire their own Language Awareness, a valuable basis for their own investigations at teacher training level. Involvement and participation is as important for the learners/trainees at this level as for the pupils they will eventually teach.

TEACHER TRAINING COURSES

The focus of work of this Working Party has been Language Awareness courses and these, as can be seen from descriptions of core school activities as well as from initiatives taken elsewhere which have been brought to our attention, may take any one of a variety of forms in order to cater for a wide range of objectives. They are being taught in primary classes, in sixth forms and at stages in between. It is clearly not possible, therefore, to be too tightly prescriptive about the training of teachers of courses whose purposes are of such diversity. Similarly, each subject has its own language items and conventions of language use which require specialised attention and will require specialised training. However, drawing together strings from the points already made in the paper, the following stages are offered for consideration by those setting out to train teachers to teach Language Awareness courses as well as other individual curricular subjects.

a)   Common to all teachers

    1.   Development of the teacher's own language awareness

        a. in general use
        b. specifically related to the school context.

2. Acquisition of the language of description and analysis
    (for defined purposes).

3. Understanding of the development of the person through and
    in tandem with language including relevant aspects of
    socio and psycho-linguistics.

4. Finding out how pupils learn and how the teacher can
    foster pupils' learning both of language per se and of
    other matters via language.

5. Observation skills.

6. Inter-action and language development in all classes,
    including problem-analysis and response.

b) <u>Divergence according to specific circumstances</u>

(e.g. Language Awareness in the Physics class, learning to use
the Library etc.). At this point we address ourselves solely
to:

<u>Language Awareness Courses</u>

1. Understanding the topic.
2. Defining objectives.
3. Designing, structuring, programming a course.
4. Establishing methodology.
5. Decision-making and monitoring.
6. Evaluation (and assessment).
7. Materials production.

For further suggestions the writer would recommend reference to
the Bullock report and to the detailed as well as the summary
sections.

Language Awareness work is still in its infancy. Developments
in schools will influence training programmes and vice versa.
This is to be encouraged. We are not at a stage where we would
wish to make decisive statements about training course contents
and design. The writer feels able to speak on behalf of the
Working Party in expressing the hope that this work will be
developed further. We should wish to support NCLE involvement
in the teacher training sector, to include Language Awareness,
if this should be proposed as an area needful of further work,
for the next cycle of NCLE activity.

References

1. BULLOCK, A (1975) A language for life. HMSO.

2. CARTER, R, (Ed) (1982) Linguistics and the teacher. Routledge & Kegan Paul.

3. DOUGHTY, P, J Pearce and G Thornton (1971) Language in use. Edward Arnold.

4. DOUGHTY, P and G Thornton (1973) Language study, the teacher and the learner. Edward Arnold.

5. HAWKINS, E W (1981) Modern languages in the curriculum. Cambridge University Press.

6. TINKEL, A J (1981) 'The relationship between the study of language and the teaching of languages'. In: Issues in language education. NCLE Papers and Reports 3. CILT.

TRANSFER, KNOWLEDGE AND SKILL IN SECOND LANGUAGE DEVELOPMENT

S H McDonough

This paper is intended to contribute to the language awareness debate by exploring what can be extrapolated from the general theory of transfer of knowledge and skill in learning second and foreign languages, in the belief that how people learn and how people apply what they have learned to new areas is an important factor in any discussion of teaching languages and about language. Naturally, it is written from an exploratory point of view and is not committed to any particular position, for example that language awareness training is either a necessary prerequisite for foreign language learning, or a necessary consequence of that, or an activity that cannot stand in its own right as an important component of a school curriculum. Such considerations are more properly the subject of other contributions to the Working Party.

There are several relevant questions in which a psychology of transfer of knowledge and skill might be useful. Probably the most important for present concerns is the likelihood that some kind of training in the general nature of language might beneficially influence the acquisition of foreign languages. A secondary question arising from that concerns the nature of the training, whether it be in general principles, in direct experience of learning foreign languages, or in sensitivity to the mother tongue. Another question (which this paper can hardly address) would concern the likelihood that explicit training in language per se would benefit the mother tongue and other subjects to be learned at school. However, at present the general understanding of the process of transfer of training is so limited as to make these wider questions unanswerable. This short paper must be restricted to statements that can be made relevant to the first question. Broadly the paper will fall into three sections. Firstly, some classical notions of transfer and generalisation will be looked at. Secondly, some more recent work on cognitive principles will be reviewed in the light of the main question above. Thirdly, some current second language development theories will be examined to see what predictions concerning transfer can be made from them.

The notion of transfer of training in classical learning theory was encompassed in two general areas of experimentation and theorising: generalisation of responses (or stimuli) and interference between different learning tasks. 'Generalisation' refers to the chances of a learner transferring a response which has been learned in connection with one stimulus to a new stimulus, or learning that two responses are appropriate to the same stimulus. Both of these found their way into language teaching via general educational psychology but also more particularly through the assumptions of the audio-lingual approach. Briefly, a typical generalisation experiment would involve training an animal to go to the white side of a T maze rather than the black side. Put into a differently painted T maze with light grey and dark grey arms it would highly probably go to the light grey side, rather than run about at random. A graph of the "gradient of generalisation" could be plotted if the probability of choosing that arm were drawn against the degree of difference between the original white arm and the new more or less grey arms. The obvious assumption is that the likelihood of the animal making any particular choice is directly related to the degree of similarity that exists between the original stimulus it was trained to and the new stimulus that animal is exposed to. What the behavioural scientists were unable to specify was how the notion of similarity was represented: that is to say, why the animals were able to class and rank environmental stimuli in some kind of order of similarity without training, while at the same time claiming that all intelligent behaviour was learned by a process of training by reinforcement. The well known experiments on "interleaved" learning tasks involved learning a task, perhaps a set of nonsense syllables or a list of independent words, or a particular manipulation of some equipment, then learning a second one. If, when tested again on the first task, there was an influence on time or errors from the second, 'retroactive interference' was said to have taken place. If, when tested again on the second task, there was an influence from the first, 'proactive interference' had taken place. Both of these examples of transfer of training could in principle be beneficial (positive) or interruptive (negative) when compared to learning the tasks in isolation. The general principle which both kinds of experiment seemed to support was that transfer of training takes place in proportion to the number of elements which are identical in each task, or the proportion of each task which is covered by the same principle of organisation. Thus transfer was seen in terms of physical similarity of the tasks (The law of Identical Elements) or the organisational similarity (the transfer of principles). While these have been very influential ideas, they have not gone unchallenged. As well as the theoretical vacuum that surrounds the notion of 'similarity', it has been shown by Tulving (1966) that in verbal learning, it is by no means the case that transfer occurs in proportion to the number of identical elements. In fact if a list of nine words are learned, and then a list of eighteen including those nine are learned, memory for the eighteen is worse than if a list of eighteen quite different words had been learned. With half the second list being identical with the first, learning should have been facilitated. The explanation must be that learning the nine old plus nine new words was made more difficult because of the subjective organisation the nine old words were already embedded in, which had to be 'unlearned' or at least considerably modified to accommodate nine new words. For these reasons we cannot continue to base teaching on assumptions about transfer of training derived from classical behaviour theory.

The more recent literature on skill acquisition and information processing in cognition has produced some interesting indicators, but it remains true that little of this literature has been devoted to the question of transfer of training. The skill acquisition literature has usually concentrated on particular skilled activities, very often in applied contexts such as training aircraft pilots or plant supervisors (eg studies of motor co-ordination and vigilance under stressful conditions) and has therefore not been extended often into areas of possibly related degrees of complexity like learning linguistic rules. Walford's (1968) book remains a classic introduction to the field, and his comment that skill acquisition studies have tended to look at ancient questions such as 'massed' learning of large chunks or 'distributed' learning with rests, the order of learning simple and complex tasks, the learning of anticipation, timing, and integration of the component parts of a skill is still true. If language learning is related, at least by analogy, to motor skills, then the finding that in learning two tasks of different difficulty, doing the more difficult first (p.311) shortens the total learning time for both compared with doing the easier one first, is an instructive one both for syllabus design and for the relationship between learning about language and learning languages. However, these perhaps unexpected results may well one day be directly usable in language teaching; their relevance to that long process has not yet been adequately tested.

In the area of cognitive processing much interesting work has arisen out of the re-adoption in psychology of the notion of a 'schema' (Bartlett, 1932). This comparatively old idea received a new lease of life when it was found to be a useful explanatory concept for results which showed that in learning information expressed in language – comprehension experiments with sentences and connected prose texts – people typically used some form of cognitive organisation at a more abstract and general level than linguistic structure. The use of a such a level – usually called a schema (script and frame are alternatives) – enables people to relate information from different sources (in the experiments, different sentences) to some common organisation and therefore both to make inferences about information not present to them and to make prediction about relationships and facts that are strictly beyond the information given. Therefore this schema approach potentially offers a great deal to the understanding of transfer of knowledge, since knowledge is seen as a structured level of representation of particular areas of experience. One example of this kind of work we owe to Thorndyke and Hayes-Roth (1979), who investigated the use of schemata in the acquisition and transfer of knowledge. Their experiment concerned the degree of transfer of knowledge, measured by accuracy of recall, from training texts to test texts. Where the test text was of the same form but one component was changed, accuracy of recall was high, indicating use of the underlying form of the information in the training texts as a schema for assimilating the test text; when training and test texts were formally unrelated, overall accuracy was low. It is important to note, however, that these authors were using only very simple texts ("This constellation was first recorded at Mount Palomar observatory") in one of the experiments and only slightly less simple stories in their second, in the interests of being quite explicit about the knowledge structures constructed; it would be dangerous to extrapolate from these experiments to the much larger knowledge structures and much longer time spans involved in school language learning programmes.

A development in educational psychology which interestingly parallels the use of schemata as a theoretical tool in cognitive studies or psycho-linguistics is provided by the work of G Pask (1976, and see N Entwistle, 1978). In what Pask calls 'Conversational Techniques' - in computer aided instruction - is the operation of a rather rigid schema which he calls an 'entailment structure', which is an analysis of the topic to be learned reconstructed as an arrangement of sub-topics with logical relations between them which provides a 'map' for the student to guide his understanding of the subject matter. It can be tailored to particular student differences like preferences for large chunks or small steps. Entwistle comments that it seems more adaptable for science learners than for arts learning. However, in the present context Pask's work seems worth examining not specifically for its possible use as a teaching method but for the obvious underlying assumption that learning - which for him subsumes understanding - proceeds by way of logical steps derived from the internal structure of what is to be learned (and not, as in a Skinnerian learning programme, from a rather arbitrary and empirical breakdown into the smallest learnable steps). It would be very interesting to test if language(s) learning might benefit from a similar concern with the 'entailment structures' of the general theory of language. However, there is one finding in the transfer of learning literature that casts doubt on the universality of transfer, even if a Pask-like teaching system could be set up. Sullivan and Skanes (1971) showed that transfer of training was much greater in 'bright' 9 - 12 year olds than in 'dull' ones, where intelligence was measured on one of the Otis tests and the tasks were simple letter series problems. It is of course not particularly surprising that bright children should see connections and perceive parallels between otherwise dissimilar tasks or facts better than dull children, but it is a warning about individual differences in children that cannot be forgotten. It is also not an isolated finding. Gagne and Pardise (1961) had found a similar result.

It is possible to derive predictions about transfer from several recent and current approaches to second language development; the weight to be given them depends on the strength of the evidence supporting the theory in general.

The proponents of habit-formation theory drew out of stimulus/ response theory the concept of positive and negative transfer, and generalisation and discrimination learning. It is possible to view the standard language teaching syllabus as training sequences of generalisation and discrimination learning as each new grammatical item is introduced, developed, and then given limits of applicability by contrast with another item. Generalisation however was strictly in terms of analogy: little attempt was made to get the student to induce general principles from the language data, and indeed it became a precept to "teach the language, not about the language". There was also no suggestion that one might teach about language either in the process of or as a means to teaching proficiency in a language. Jakobovits (1970) explored the extant literature on transfer between languages and the 'extrapolation of knowledge' (Chap. iv) and came to the pessimistic conclusion that transfer effects were highly complex and not at all as simple as the audio-lingualists' espousal of constrastive analysis would lead one to suspect. However he comments interestingly at the end of his section on teaching generalisations:

"I would like nevertheless to suggest that in language learning we can maximise transfer effects by concentrating in the early stages on the acquisition of general principles and only later should we worry about automatisation of phonological habits, fluency, and correct pronunciation. (Note that this is the reverse of audiolingual practice.)" (1970, p.216)

Predictions that are perhaps more in accord with Jakobovits' suggestion can be derived from hypothesis testing theory, sometimes known as 'cognitive code' learning theory. Incidentally, Jakobovits himself suggested that this kind of theory was more appropriate to second language learning than to first language acquisition. In most forms of 'cognitive' theory, languages are thought to be learned by a process of creation and elimination, by negative feedback, of alternative hypotheses about the structure underlying a set of examples of the language. J Dakin (1973) presents a well worked out scheme for guiding this hypothesis testing activity. In general educational psychology such hypothesis testing guidance systems have been labelled 'discovery methods'. The role of transfer of general principles of language or of general experience with languages, in such a theoretical approach, is clear: it is in the students' initial creation of hypotheses about the structure and conventions of the new language. The richer the hypothesis formation process can be, the greater the case with which new structural devices can be understood and 'internalised'. It is this kind of theoretical approach that supported the great amount of work in Error Analysis performed in recent years. However, not all theorists are agreed that negative feedback on formulated hypotheses is the main driving force in language learning: people do not only progress from example to rule to proficiency but sometimes from example to proficiency (by feel) to statable rule.

From a less 'cognitive' point of view, Stern suggested (1974) that good language learners might be distinguishable from unsuccessful ones in terms of a set of strategies for learning which they seem to adopt unbidden. One of these was the use of "technical know-how about how to tackle a language". The obvious suggestion is that that kind of knowledge can be taught, both with reference to the first language, and with reference to other languages. In the empirical project at O.I.S.E. which arose out of this approach (Naiman Frohlich, and Stern, 1975) that particular strategy was 're-distributed' in a new formulation, but the central idea was still there, and was found to be supported by the interview data which they collected. In this connection it is probably signficiant that in the various tests of language aptitude that are available, the most robust predictors are those which are most obviously "language-knowledge" tests, like the test of grammatical sensitivity in the MLAT (Carroll and Sapon, 1959) and the exotic language learning task and the mother tongue vocabulary task in the LAB (Pimsleur, 1968).

The idea that second language learning was more closely related to first language acquisition than suggested by, for example, Jakobovits or Dakin, became a popular one as evidence was compiled which seemed to show either that learners' sequences of mastery of grammatical items were the same as native childrens' or that while different from native childrens' they were still apparently independent of teaching syllabus and thus were 'natural hierarchies' or 'natural orders' of difficulty. Dulay and Burt (1974) suggested, to explain their results on the consistency of the order of acquisition of grammatical morphemes, that there was a 'creative construction' process which essentially is the re-activation of the innate mechanisms which construct grammars for children acquiring the native language. It therefore allows the real possibility that innate knowledge of universal principles of languages, for example, the subject-predicate distinction, are brought to bear directly on the development of second language proficiency. However, its proponents have not attempted to assess the effectiveness of training in awareness of such principles.

The general nature of language acquisition would argue for there being no conscious component in the use of universal principles of language, and therefore no role for explicit training in awareness of them; however no test has been performed of this attractive possibility.

Perhaps the most controversial current theory is that of Krashen (1981) in which strong assertions are made about the relationship, in second language learning, between first language-type processes ("acquisition") and conscious rule-learning in constrained teaching environments ("learning"). In his theory, knowledge of language per se would affect proficiency in two ways; unconsciously through "acquisition" and consciously through the formation and evaluation of rule systems and language features as in "learning". However, it seems impossible for Krashen's model to allow language awareness training to affect acquisition because he states that this is unconscious. One criticism levelled at his "Monitor" theory is that it does not allow "seepage" from consciously learned knowledge to unconscious sensitivity; if this possibility is allowed for (as argued by Stevick (1980) Chap. 21), then "acquisition" can benefit both from first language development processes and other experience of the general nature of language. Krashen himself, however, would strongly resist this idea, because it diffuses the sharp distinction he wishes to draw between acquisition and learning. In fact he further subdivides learning into learning 'rules of thumb', which are the contents of the 'monitor' which checks on the output of the model, and thus the accuracy of the learner's productions, and learning about the structure of the language, which he sees as an optional, interesting 'extra', a kind of language appreciation class, which has no role to play in the actual process of developing proficiency. As an afterthought, he adds (1981, p.118, note 3) that teaching structural rules may give confidence to students who have developed proficiency but do not have confidence in their 'acquired' ability.

In conclusion, it is evident that the work briefly reviewed above cannot be used to support or refute any particular about transfer of knowledge of general principles of language to or from experience of particular languages. It is possible to draw out predictions from schema theory and from various current second language learning theories; they are as yet untested and in any case subject to the fate of the base theories in the testing ground of empirical research. Those theories that emphasize the role of universals and the first language acquisition process in second language development are silent on the role of explicit or school-like teaching of awareness of those universals. The hypothesis testing and stimulus-response theories are silent (largely) on whether transfer could occur only from previous experience of language learning or from general principles of language. The 'cognitive' approach of Pask implies strongly that general principles are involved at all stages of learning, in different forms according to the subject matter and the student characteristics.

However, this interesting area is ripe for a concerted empirical attack and the nature of transfer in these circumstances will remain a matter for vigorous debate in the discussion of second and foreign language learning and teaching. It should be evident from this brief review that several important questions remain open. For example, it should not be supposed that enhanced ease of learning foreign languages cannot result from transfer of principles from language awareness courses. Indeed the current activity in such courses may well provide positive evidence for this possibility. Equally, the conditions under which transfer has been shown to operate are relatively restricted. However, the possibility of transfer to practical proficiency cannot weaken the claim that Language Awareness courses are justifiable in their own right as part of the curriculum.

References

BARTLETT, F C (1932) _Remembering_. Cambridge: Cambridge University Press

CARROLL, J B, and S Sapon (1959) _Modern language aptitude test_. New York: Psychological Corporation

DAKIN, J (1973) _The language laboratory and language learning_. London: Longman

DULAY, H, and M Burt (1974) 'A new perspective on the creative construction process in child second language learning'. In _Language Learning_, vol 24, No 2, pp 254-77

ENTWISTLE, N (1978) 'Knowledge structures and styles of learning: a summary of Pask's recent work'. In _British Journal of Educational Psychology_, Vol 48, pp 255-65

CAGNE, R, and H Paradise (1961) 'Ability and learning sets in knowledge acquistion'. In _Psychological Monographs 75_ (14 Whole No 519)

JAKOBOVITS, L (1970) _Foreign language learning_. Rowley, Mass: Newbury House

KRASHEN, S (1981) _Second language acquisition and second language learning_. Oxford: Pergamon

NAIMAN, N A Frohlich, and H Stern (1975) _The good language learner_. Modern Language Center, Dept of Curriculum, OISE

PASK, G (1976) 'Conversational techniques in the study and practice of education'. In _British Journal of Education Psychology_, Vol 46, pp 12-25

PIMSLEUR, P (1968) _Language aptitude battery_. New York: Harcourt, Brace and World

STERN, H H (1974) 'What can we learn from the good language learner?' In Canadian Modern Language Review, vol 31, pp 304-18

STEVICK, E (1980) Teaching languages: a way and ways. Rowley, Mass: Newbury House

SULLIVAN, A M, and G R Skanes (1971) 'Differential transfer of training in bright and dull subjects of the same mental age'. In British Journal of Educational Psychology, Vol 41, pt 3, pp 287-93

THORNDYKE, P, and B Hayes-Roth (1979) 'The use of schemata in the acquisition and transfer of knowledge'. In Cognitive Psychology, Vol 11, 82-106

TULVING, E (1966) 'Subjective organisation and effects of repetition in multi-trial free-recall learning'. In Journal of Verbal Learning and Verbal Behaviour, Vol 5, pp 193-7

WELFORD, A T (1968) Fundamentals of human skill. London: Methuen

THE RELATIONSHIP BETWEEN GRADED OBJECTIVES AND TESTING IN FOREIGN LANGUAGE TEACHING AND LANGUAGE AWARENESS WORK

Michael Byram

1. Introduction

This paper is to discuss from the standpoint of the foreign language teacher the relationship between two developments which affect foreign language teaching. One of them, Language Awareness, has its origins in a wider context than foreign language teaching alone; the other, Graded Objectives and Tests, is largely an initiative peculiar to foreign language teaching, although there are parallels in the underlying principles elsewhere (Harrison, 1982). For some foreign language teachers, the two developments may appear at first glance to be contradictory. To put it baldly, the ethos of Language Awareness is likely to appear to some advocates of Graded Objectives and Tests a retrograde step, a return to the kind of language teaching from which Graded Objectives and Tests have liberated them. I shall argue that this apparent mutual contradiction is superficial and misleading. In order to appreciate the unease aroused by Language Awareness, it is necessary to consider the model of language teaching which teachers enthusiastic about Graded Objectives and Tests are - rightly - attempting to cast off permanently.

Foreign Language teaching in schools has, from its beginnings in the nineteenth century, been in search of a methodology. Initially, as the label Modern Languages indicates, it took its methodology from its predecessor and higher status companion, Classical Language Teaching. It also took its purposes from the same source: to enable pupils to read and write in the foreign language. Although the late nineteenth and early twentieth centuries brought an appreciation of the importance of being able to speak and converse in foreign language, the higher status of the written language - which is a common perception, not peculiar to teachers - has dominated the language teaching and examining process until well into the fourth quarter of the twentieth century. One of the significant differences between spoken and written language is that the latter is fixed in time, whereas the former flows irretrievably past. (The advent of sound recording alters this but little in so far as the intention of most speakers is not to say something which will be listened to later and heard over and over again). It is possible therefore - and perhaps particularly necessary with the high literacy texts which pupils were being prepared to read - to study the relationship between the form and meaning of written text, and to do this an understanding of the grammatical structure of the language in question is a sine qua non. In the course of acquiring such an understanding, pupils' attention was drawn to their own language and indeed translation was used both as a teaching and as a testing method. Thus pupils learnt about the language as a step to using the language; "language" meant however only written language. The comparative emphasis of the so-called grammar-translation method also had the corollary that pupils began to understand something of the nature of human language, although this was limited to insights into grammar. In view of the purposes, the method was reasonable and successful. There has however been a gradual change of purposes - to the teaching of language for oral communication. The change began many decades ago but was given a surge of strength in post-war years, particularly with the influx of a new clientele of learners from comprehensivisation. The change was however not a revolutionary one; the new purposes did not replace the old ones but were added to them. There was not an immediately corresponding change in methodology, although the introduction of audio-lingual/audio-visual courses and language laboratories helped to provide for the teaching of spoken language. Yet the traditions of the grammar-translation method were strong and there was confusion about which purposes should dominate and which methods were most appropriate. Furthermore the audio-lingual/ audio-visual methods did not produce the success expected of them. In the 1960s and 1970s the situation was, in broad terms, confusion about purposes for pupils of widely differing abilities and, in an atmosphere of insecurity due to failure of new methods, a tendency to continue the traditions of the grammar-translation method which had at least proved its worth for its original purposes. The H.M.I. survey of 1977 summarised the situation, but the summary held no surprise for language teachers themselves:

> In all but a few of the (83) schools the learning of modern foreign languages was characterised by some or all of the following features: under performance in all four language skills by the abler pupils; the setting of impossible or pointless tasks for average (and in particular less able) pupils and their abandonment of modern language learning at the first opportunity; excessive use of English and an inability to produce other than inadequate or largely unusable statements in the modern language; inefficient reading skills; and writing limited mainly to mechanical reproduction which was often extremely inaccurate. (D.E.S., 1977:8)

2.   The nature and origins of Graded Objectives and Tests

2.1 Origins

A year after the H.M.I. report, there appeared a booklet written by the Oxfordshire Modern Languages Advisory Committee entitled New Objectives in Modern Language Teaching. It is perhaps significant that the word 'objectives' is used, implying that the aims or purposes remain unchanged and uncontroversial. The introduction refers extensively and approvingly to the H.M.I. report and the latter describes the aims which "must be central to (the) teaching" in terms of the ability to speak to a foreigner in his own language and to understand the gist of both the spoken and the written word

(D.E.S., 1977:3). Within five or six years, the Oxfordshire group - and another important group in Yorkshire - had been imitated in their initiative by more than sixty other groups throughout the country. They had said in their introduction that there are widely differing opinions concerning the reasons for the present state of affairs but agreement that there is failure due to setting 'inappropriate targets and objectives' - again avoiding the word 'aims'. It is also very difficult to document those opinions but some of them will be expounded here in order to describe the climate in which the Graded Objectives and Tests movement flourished.

There were three broad areas of dissatisfaction: with the definition of the 'object', of what is to be taught; with the success rate; and with the motivation of pupils towards learning a foreign language.

2.1.1 In the strictest sense, there was no definition of what was to be taught. Examination papers and text books formed the basis for a consensus on what was 'expected' of pupils after five years of learning the foreign language in a secondary school, but this 'definition' was - and often still is - at best imprecise and at worst misleading as a basis for decision on what was to be taught. The Oxfordshire group therefore produced defined syllabuses, for the earlier stages of learning, and tests which tested only what was in the syllabus.

In broader terms the object on which a consensus was reached was unsatisfactory in nature. The language taught was that required for assertions about the world and for putting a number of assertions together to form a narrative. Pupils learnt to make statements in response to questions - more rarely to ask questions - and to tell stories. Their knowledge of the limited range of language required for this was tested by having them translate narrative texts and write their own stories within narrow guidelines. Yet the telling of stories is only one use of language and not the most frequent one. Pupils did not learn how to use language to discover a person's point of view or persuade them of their own, to greet people or take leave, to congratulate and so on. They learnt only the written language - with its formal style - not the vocabulary and different structures of spoken language, whether formal or informal. This was an unsatisfactory state of affairs if the purposes of language learning were to include learning to converse with a native speaker. Furthermore the skills involved in the use of written language - for production of narrative or understanding of narrative text - are of a different kind to those in use in conversation. There is time and opportunity in the written language to formulate precisely and accurately both in meaning and grammatical form. The skill involved is based in part on knowledge of the grammar of the language and an ability to carry out grammatical and semantic analysis. In conversation the grammatical and semantic analysis is supplemented by the ability to work together with the conversation partner(s) to establish common understanding. That working together requires other linguistic, as well as social, skills: the ability to seize the drift or gist of the meaning by anticipation of what is going to be said, through knowledge of the discourse structures appropriate to the context of the conversation. Essentially, then, the 'object' was not sufficiently defined and was too restricted in nature.

2.1.2 It was already evident in the 1970s that the success rate – measured in terms of examination passes or of the number of pupils abandoning language learning as soon as possible – was low. The Secretaries of State for Education have emphasised this in a recent paper (D.E.S., n.d.). The failure rate was attributed by some to the limited relevance of the kind of object being taught. The ability to do linguistic analysis and to write simple narrative is not one which makes immediate appeal to pupils. Those who completed a five-year course were driven by other needs – especially to obtain qualifications – rather than linguistic ones. Those who saw little hope of obtaining qualifications, or little use for them, were not attracted by the 'object' itself. It was also thought that the very distance of the target set was problematic, in two ways. First, the examinations providing the qualifications were too distant in time: a five year course was too long for many pupils to apprehend. This is a factor common to many subjects and which has led mathematicians for example to consider intermediate testing. Unique to language teaching, however, was the sense in which little of what was learnt during the course could be used realistically before the whole course was completed. Already the ability to tell stories is of limited use on its own, but pupils could not even tell stories adequately until they had been exposed to all the necessary grammatical knowledge. And the grammatical, and semantic, knowledge was fed to them little by little over the whole course in such a way that items vital for narrative, and even more so for conversation, were withheld because, though common in conversation, they were considered to be too complex for the learner who had to have his knowledge of the grammar built up from simple to complex structures. (The basis for deciding what is complex or simple was unclear but not challenged).

2.1.3 The nature of the 'object', the distance of the target and the opportunity for pupils to opt out of language learning usually after three years combined to reduce their motivation. Motivation was particularly low in the year previous to opting out, and the lack of pupil motivation infected teachers too who, like their pupils, saw the task as impossible. Thus pupils dropped out of a course before it was complete and with no sense of having learnt anything which was usable or whole. They had no complete skill or knowledge, no matter how limited in nature. They had nothing to show for their efforts in another sense, too, because they obtained no qualification. Thus teachers were dissatisfied with the motivation of pupils towards the language and the people and culture it symbolised.

2.1.4 The climate of opinion and belief sketched above is one facet of the origins of Graded Objectives and Tests. The origins in the more positive sense of the contribution of ideas and the initiation of work could be the object of a fascinating piece of research on curriculum innovation. Harrison (1982) traces some of the relationships with other forms of graded testing, especially in music. The purpose here, however, is to describe the nature of the movement and its purposes in order to relate them to Language Awareness and because Language Awareness may be perceived as a retrograde step it is necessary to have clarified the state of affairs 'before' the onset of Graded Objectives and Tests. It is necessary now to clarify the nature of Graded Objectives and Tests as a response to the dissatisfactions described above.

2.2 The nature of Graded Objectives and Tests.

A Schools Council evaluation of the undoubted success of Graded Objectives and Tests documented above all a change in attitude to language learning:

> There is, then, an impressive amount of evidence to support the hypothesis that pupils working with graded syllabuses and tests in French have very much better attitudes towards learning French than do other pupils.....As far as the pupils are concerned, the introduction of graded syllabuses and tests seems to bring considerable gains and no losses. (Schools Council, 1981:31)

Attitude and motivation are, however, dependent on other factors and it is important to consider what changes have been made to meet the factors causing the dissatisfactions outlined above. There are two facets of the innovation: the notion of grading — and the attendant certification procedures — and the notion of defining and re-defining the content, the 'object' to be taught. These two facets have developed together and contributed to the success in attitude change. It is not possible therefore to say which facet has contributed how much to that success. Yet the two facets are logically separable and need not co-exist. It is possible to consider each in turn.

2.2.1 As Harrison points out (1982), the notion of grading is commonplace. In language teaching there has been a grading of language content and presentation of 'simple' grammar before 'complex' grammar through textbooks and examinations. By consensus and tradition, for example, the French subjunctive is excluded from GCE O level, but the German subjunctive is included, thus implying that the French is more difficult than the German, or less necessary in some way or maybe some other basis for grading. The innovation in the Graded Objectives and Tests movement is to introduce more grades, more steps towards the target, steps which can be fully apprehended by pupils. To help them see the steps more clearly,

certificates are introduced for each step. Precisely the same
procedure could be applied to the 'object' taught until the advent
of the movement: for example, pupils could be rewarded with
certification for learning the French Imperfect Tense and then move
on to some other section of grammar. In fact, however, the grades
are described in terms which refer to the use to which the acquired
language may be put rather than to the terminology used in
'traditional' linguistic analysis. More precisely, the certificate
refers to the activities which pupils can carry out with the help of
the foreign language, that is to their behaviour. This owes much to
the method of determining learning objectives in the form of
behavioural skills. This is helpful to the pupil because more
readily understandable and to the teacher because it is possible to
use a meta-language which the pupil understands and appreciates.
Furthermore, should pupils give up study after any given grade, they
would nonetheless have learnt usable language with potential
applications. The close definition of the behavioural skills, of
the ways in which individuals make language work for them in contact
with others, has origins in sociolinguistic analysis. Through
terminological confusion however, the definition may be identified
with the behaviourist tradition in language teaching. Thus the
meta-language in current use may seduce both pupil and teacher into
a view that language is learnt through habit formation, a theory
which is much disputed (cf McDonough's paper Transfer knowledge and
skill in Second Language development).

2.2.2   The description of grades in terms of use is facilitated by
the second facet of the innovation: the re-definition of the
'object'. The language taught is no longer only or indeed primarily
the language of assertion and narrative in the written mode. The
differences between spoken and written language are recognised and
uses other than narration are introduced: for example, the language
for expressing preference or requesting help. At the same time there
tends to be less emphasis on analytic skill and knowledge of the
grammar of the language and more on the ability to perform, to
produce appropriate language in defined contexts. This is a question
of degree but can lead to training in performance without any knowledge about grammar. Doubts have then been expressed whether the
performance is language or 'language-like behaviour', a problem of
which those leading the graded tests movement are aware.

The change to a description of the language to be learnt in terms of
use and context is accompanied by an explicit and detailed
definition. Thus teachers now have lists of vocabulary items and of
grammatical structures which they know will be the basis of the
corresponding test. Pupils can also feel more secure and see an
'amount' of language which they will be able to learn in the fore-
seeable future. Furthermore the description in terms of use helps
pupils to see the potential relevance of the language, which clearly
helps maintain their motivation.

2.2.3 There are then several factors which coincide to encourage teachers to reduce and sometimes entirely abandon the teaching of knowledge about language. The new meta-language they have in common with pupils refers to use and to context as the criteria for choice of the language to be learnt. Previously the meta-language referred to the structure of the foreign language and if this was to be used with pupils they had to have some knowledge of the structure and the terminology. Second, the syllabuses and tests are described in terms of what pupils can do with the language rather than their knowledge about it. The tests are also devised in such a way that 'success' is defined in terms of the ability to use the language together with other inter-personal skills, and not in such a way that a knowledge of comparative grammar will be directly tested: translation is shunned. Any teaching about the language is only valuable if it contributes to skill in performance in the language.

3. The nature and origins of work on Language Awareness

Language Awareness work differs in two essential respects from the Graded Objectives and Tests movement. First it has its origins in other kinds of teaching as well as in language teaching. Second it involves a change from the aims of language teaching as identified by the H.M.I. report and implicitly accepted by the Graded Objectives and Tests movement, that 'communication' shoud be central. It involves putting equal emphasis on 'communication' and on "an awareness of the nature of language and language learning", as a recent document expressed it (GCE and CSE Boards, n.d.)

3.1. Origins

There is also a third difference: that the work which can be labelled Language Awareness work is far more heterogeneous. Again it is not the intention here to trace the literal origins of the diverse kinds of work, nor to speculate on the reasons for apparently simultaneous and independent innovations which have underlying common interests. Detailed descriptions are available elsewhere in this report. The purpose here is to list some of the purposes and thinking which lie behind the work involved.

3.1.1 Some foreign language teachers consider that their pupils will be more proficient learners if they are given the tools and techniques for learning. (cf. McDonough's discussion of 'technical know-how'.). They usually consider that these techniques - which may be acquired in the course of language learning - ought to be made explicit <u>before</u> the process begins. Therefore they teach about languages, including the mother tongue, in a course which precedes the beginning of the foreign language course.

3.1.2 A second impetus is the desire to raise pupils' interest in language for its own sake. Behind this lies the belief that education should extend pupils' knowledge about themselves and the world around them and that language here plays a central role. Thus pupils will be more sensitive to their own and other people's use of language.

3.1.3   Other work goes a step further along the same road by providing pupils with the tools for the study of language once their interest and wonder has been aroused. Such courses treat language as an object of academic study.

3.1.4   Some work springs from the desire to enable pupils who are almost certainly future parents to appreciate the importance of a rich linguistic environment in the development of their children and to show them how to provide such an environment. Such courses have been linked with Child Care courses.

3.1.5   Elsewhere, teachers of language from a number of backgrounds – English as a Second Language, languages of ethnic minorities, foreign languages – have joined together to establish common interests and attempt to make sense, for the learner, of the different styles of language teaching. In particular, the teaching of ethnic minority languages within the normal curriculum is seen as a way of raising the status of the languages and hence increasing the self-esteem of the pupils who speak them.

3.1.6   Foreign language teachers who are concerned that the justification of languages in the curriculum should rest on more than the provision of skill in languages have developed that part of their teaching which makes pupils aware of the nature of language.

3.1.7   Teachers of English as the mother tongue have in their discipline a strand of work on the nature of language, on an understanding of "Language in Use". Some teachers who have wished to give particular emphasis to this have joined with teachers of foreign languages; others have developed the notion within their own discipline, sometimes linking it with the techniques of drama teaching.

3.1.8   The seven areas of interest and the brief indications of how groups of teachers are working together do not exhaust the field. Furthermore there are many cases where the reasons for work in Language Awareness are combinations of the seven mentioned and others. In view of the variety, the following characterisation will attempt to deal with the common ground rather than the particular versions which have developed.

3.2 Nature of Language Awareness work

The common ground shared by the different groups is essentially a belief that language and languages are a worthwhile object of study in themselves; a belief that pupils' education will be all the richer if they are aware of language. Pupils tend to 'see through' language and be ignorant of the role it plays in their lives, until occasionally it causes them a problem. They are not then in a position to understand their problem because they are not sensitive to language. Thus in a sense language and languages become an object of study in a way which superficially looks, to the foreign language teacher in particular, like a return to the 'grammar-translation' method which they have rejected. It is the danger that Language Awareness work may be rejected out of hand for this apparent identity, which this paper is concerned to remove. The similarity is misleading both with respect to the nature of the 'object' taught and to the methodology. It is more obvious that the aims of Language Awareness work differ from the aims of grammar-translation teaching of foreign languages.

3.2.1 The 'object' studied is different because the conception of what language and languages are is much more differentiated and developed. Whereas the 'traditional' language teachers were concerned only with grammar - especially with syntax and morphology - the definition of what is to be studied in Language Awareness includes sociological, psychological and anthropological aspects of language. It includes, for example, the study of varieties of a language and social attitudes to them, the study of child language and language acquisition, and the study of the relationship of human language to the systems of communication of other species.

3.2.2 The methodology of 'grammar-translation' was concerned with teaching the generative rules of syntax and morphology which would enable a pupil to produce correct and meaningful sentences, and at a later stage text, and to analyse and understand the meaning of sentence and text in the language. If the pupil acquired an interest in the generative nature of language, this was a valuable but essentially incidental corollary. The methodologies of work in Language Awareness stress both the learning of skills and the acquisition of some propositional knowledge about the phenomenon under study.

The skills may be behavioural: emphasis on the skills of language learning arising from an increased understanding of the nature of what is to be learnt and the processes involved. The skills emphasised may on the other hand be those of rational analysis: pupils may be taught how to analyse language - and not just textual meaning - on scientific principles, although the emphasis in method is likely to be on the doing of analysis rather than on the principles themselves.

The acquisition of knowledge about language and languages plays a significant role in Language Awareness work, although the role may be large or small depending on the kind of work. For example, pupils know that there are relationships between languages, that there are differences between spoken and written varieties, that infants learn a mother tongue in particular ways. It is assumed that knowledge of this kind is an integral part of the learning process out of which a greater sensitivity towards language will arise. In most cases, it is not part of the ultimate aims that such knowledge should necessarily be retained and recallable. It is however assumed that the aim of sensitizing pupils to language is best done - and possibly only done - through a process which includes some knowledge about language. Such knowledge is more wide-ranging than that concerned only with syntax and morphology.

4.   Points of contact and divergence

In my description so far, the emphasis has been on the removal of misunderstanding. By analysing the origins and nature of the two concepts, I wanted to clarify their historical position within foreign language teaching and in particular to anticipate the possibility that Language Awareness might be assimilated to a conception of language teaching which has rightly been rejected. This final section will be founded on the assumption that Graded Objectives and Tests and Language Awareness both have a role to play within foreign language teaching. It will therefore examine how the roles relate to each other. It will view the relationship from two angles: the process of learning one or more foreign languages, and the justification for language teaching in the secondary school curriculum.

4.1   Learning foreign languages.

4.1.2   The aims of Graded Objectives and Tests are usually formulated with exclusive stress on the use of the foreign language for communication:

> The most worthwhile objectives would seem to be the ability to use the language for realistic purposes rather than, for example, the ability to describe the language or use it for purposes which the actual user would rarely need to employ. (Harding et al, 1980:4)

It remains unclear what contribution knowledge about language and languages can make to the ability to use a language. This issue is addressed by McDonough elsewhere in this publication. Krashen's Monitor Theory offers an attempt to clarify the relationship. (Krashen 1981). In so far as such knowledge is helpful however, Language Awareness work which emphasises lessons to be learnt about approaches to language learning (cf. 3.1.1) is also clearly supportive. In practice teachers in Sussex and at Archbishop Michael Ramsey School in London have written courses which include both Language Awareness and Graded Objectives elements. Such courses reflect an intuitive theory, by which many language teachers work, that knowledge about the language is necessary to proficient language learning.

4.1.3 Although, as stated above, the origins of the notion of defining language behaviour for the purposes of graded tests are in sociolinguistic analysis, the determination of behavioural objectives for language examinations antedates the developments in Graded Tests and is part of a general use of behavioural objectives for examinations. Add to this the dominance of behaviourism in audio-lingual language teaching and the temptation to identify behavioural and behaviourist is strong, especially for practising teachers without the opportunity to tease out the difference. Furthermore, some materials used frequently with Graded Objectives and Tests, especially in the first year and with less able pupils, implicitly encourage teachers to carry over from audio-lingual methodology the drilling of stimulus and response. There is a danger of which the proponents of Graded Objectives and Tests are doubtless aware.

In fact Graded Objectives and Tests literature deliberately leaves the issues of methodology to the teacher. In the introduction to one course closely associated with the movement, Buckby discusses "The teaching approach":

> It is now generally recognised that there is no single or simple key to the door of language learning, that different people teach, and learn, most effectively in different ways. Because of this, these materials suggest different ways of presenting and exploiting new language....
>
> (Buckby, 1980:5)

With respect to grammatical structures, he points that they are not the base on which the course is constructed.

> "However some understanding of key structures is clearly essential if the learners are to be able to communicate adequately and flexibly, and not merely to repeat phrases learned by heart.... The real goal is communicative competence, and grammatical principles are only explained when an explanation will help to reach this goal"
>
> (Buckby, 1980:6)

Where Language Awareness work can contribute to grammatical understanding underlying communicative competence, it can surely be excellent preparation for pupils. Buckby also describes one of the aims of the course as "to encourage an awareness of the language learning process" and this too is a point of contact. People who teach Language Awareness are wary of criticisms that their interest in grammar - albeit only one of the topics taught - is retrograde. Buckby cites H.M. Inspectorate which points out that grammatical concepts are a means to an end and not an end in themselves.

From this kind of perspective, Language Awareness work might be perceived as contradictory to the spirit of Graded Objectives and Tests. It is the purpose of this paper to identify such potential "slippage" as from behavioural to behaviourist, or from awareness of grammar as one aspect of language to teaching grammar as an end in itself.

4.1.4   In addition to the divergence in language learning theory, Language Awareness work which specifically prepares pupils for foreign language learning differs in its emphasis on attitudes towards foreign languages. Such courses assume that pupils come to foreign language learning with an ethnocentric conception of their own language and its importance. This is particularly strong in a country which has until most recently perceived itself as monolingual. Such courses set out to change attitudes towards foreign languages and to make pupils more ready for the learning process which involves a questioning of their linguistic and cultural ethnocentrism which can lead to their feeling that their self-esteem is under attack. In this respect too then, Language Awareness supports in principle teaching by Graded Objectives which aims to make pupils proficient in the foreign language.

4.1.5   The divergence in theories of language learning is an important difference and a source of mutual contradiction. In other ways, some Language Awareness aims coincide with the implicit purposes of Graded Objectives and Tests. In so far as the learning of a foreign language by whatever methods is intended to give insight into the language learning process and thus facilitate further language learning, then both concepts share common ground.

It must be remembered, however, that Language Awareness has more aims than those which centre on proficient acquisition of a foreign language for use "for realistic purposes" and the additional aims are central to the nature of Language Awareness.

4.2   Foreign Language teaching in the secondary school curriculum.

4.2.1   The most recent reflections on the place of foreign language teaching in the curriculum are to be found in the Secretaries' of State consultative paper (D.E.S., n.d.), in which incidentally there is a perhaps significant change from the term 'modern languages' to 'foreign languages'. The paper lists, under the section 'the goals of foreign language teaching', a number of aims drawn up on the basis of good practice throughout Europe:

(a) to enable pupils to understand speech at normal speed;
(b) to enable them to speak the language intelligibly;
(c) to enable them to read with ease and understanding;
(d) to enable them to express themselves in writing;
(e) to give them a knowledge of the foreign country and an insight into its civilisation and culture. (D.E.S., n.d.:5)

127

These aims require much detailed refinement and the paper stresses the need to differentiate according to ability, aptitude and duration of study, but also emphasises that schools "should concentrate more on the skills of communication particularly in the spoken form, adopting an approach more relevant to the use to which the pupil might put his learning". This emphasis is completely in tune with the purposes of teaching through Graded Objectives and Tests (cf. 4.1.2.) It shares with the implicit aims of 'traditional' teaching the notion of providing the pupil with a tool which he can put to some use. Traditionally the use was to enable pupils to read the literature written in the language and thus gain knowledge of a small part of the culture which nonetheless had high significance and status. The present-day use is to enable pupils to communicate with native speakers, especially in speaking. It remains unclear what relationship this ability has to a knowledge of the country and culture, but the latter is necessary for good communication and is doubtless worthwhile in itself. A significant difference between traditional and present-day views of aims is to be found in the recognition that native-speaker proficiency is beyond the reach of school teaching. After saying with suspicious under-statement that "mastering a foreign language is an ambitious and taxing objective", the consultative paper says later that "the proficiency enjoyed by the native speaker is not within the grasp of schools" (D.E.S., n.d.: 2,5.) Until most recent times, the implicit norm against which pupils were measured was in fact the native speaker and one who was moreover highly educated and linguistically infallible. In the understanding and production of the standard written language, this norm was reasonable although impossibly demanding. In spoken language it is quite unreasonable, yet it was implicitly carried over by teachers and examiners, even if in practice they had to recognise how unreasonable it was. Despite this change and the shift in emphasis from written to spoken language, the aims of Graded Objectives and Tests maintain the spirit of the language teaching which has exclusively stressed its purpose in terms of providing a tool. By quoting from the recent consultative paper I hope to have shown that this interpretation meets with official favour. In comparison with the aims of Language Awareness, however, the interpretation is singularly narrow.

4.2.2 Another recent statement of aims is to be found in the Report of the Working Party for French of the GCE and CSE Boards' Joint Council for 16+ National Criteria.

The aims of a course in French leading up to an examination at 16+ should be
- to develop the ability to use French effectively for purposes of practical communication,
- to form a sound base of the skills, language and attitudes required for further study, work and leisure,
- to offer insights into the culture and civilisation of French-speaking countries,

- to develop an awareness of the nature of language and language learning,
- to provide enjoyment and intellectual stimulation,
- to encourage positive attitudes to foreign language learning and to speakers of foreign languages and a sympathetic approach to other cultures and civilisations,
- to promote learning skills of a more general application (e.g. analysis, memorising, drawing of inferences).

This statement goes far beyond that of the Secretaries of State both in reference to general educational aims and with respect to the specifically linguistic contribution to pupils' education. In particular the reference to the development of "an awareness of the nature of language and language learning" will not have gone unnoticed. Thus linguistic understanding is seen as worthwhile in itself and as a useful tool in language learning. In the philosophy of Language Awareness, linguistic understanding is seen as an essential element of the individual's understanding of self and of his understanding of significant aspects of social interaction. Language Awareness provides a tool for language learning but also a tool for understanding and functioning in a polyglot world.

The contribution which foreign language teaching makes towards the pupils' awareness of language, alongside contributions from other disciplines, thus puts a different interpretation on the place of language teaching in the secondary school curriculum. The difference between this view and that of Graded Objectives and Tests is partly in scope and partly in priorities. The former is wider and points to links with other parts of the curriculum, the latter is concerned only with language teaching itself, where language learning is seen more as a means than an end. In Language Awareness the priorities are reversed. In the D.E.S. consultative paper the case for language teaching in the curriculum rests largely on arguments for usefulness and practical relevance; there are several references to trading and the European Community. In Language Awareness, the case is made above all from the view that language is a significant aspect of social and individual reality, the study of which is a valuable contribution to pupils' education.

4.3   I have argued in this final section that conceptually Language Awareness and Graded Objectives and Tests are not mutually contradictory. In respect of the processes of proficient language learning, there may in fact be important points of contact. In respect of curriculum, the one is an expansion of the other rather than a replacement or threat to it.

In earlier sections I attempted to remove the danger that Language Awareness might be perceived as a reversal of current trends both in terms of the object of study and with respect to methods. Nonetheless, there may still be a fear that "talking about" the foreign language will be detrimental to "using" or "talking in" the language. The fear might be expressed particularly with regard to the limits on time available to produce proficient users. Such fears can be answered in several ways. First, the differentiation of objectives of use ought to allow time for other worthwhile aims, including Language Awareness but not exclusive to it. Second, the recognition of the impossibility of using the native speaker as a norm ought to remove some of the unconscious pressure on teachers. Third, the recognition that Language Awareness is just as important in language teaching as developing ability in communication ought to lead to legitimation of the methods involved alongside the methods favoured for teaching for communication. This in turn must lead to serious consideration of how, in practice, the two can be used to complement each other; and there are in practice several models already in use ready to serve as a basis for development. Above all it is necessary that Language Awareness work and teaching through Graded Objectives and Tests should be recognised as complementary aspects of language teaching. Both help teacher and pupil to recognise the value of foreign language learning as a process as well as a product, as an activity which is valuable and interesting in itself as well as providing access to other people and their way of life.

References

BUCKBY, M (1980) _Action! Graded French_ Teacher's Book I. London: Nelson

DES (1977) _Modern Languages in Comprehensive Schools_ London: HMSO

DES (n.d.) _Foreign Languages in the School Curriculum, a consultative paper_ London: Department of Education and Science

GCE and CSE Boards (n.d.) _Report on the Working Party for French of the GCE and CSE Boards' Joint Council for 16+ National Criteria_

HARDING, A et al. (1980) _Graded objectives in modern languages_ London: CILT

HARRISON, A (1982) _Review of graded tests_ London: Methuen

KRASHEN, S D (1981) _Second-language acquisition and second-language learning_ Oxford: Pergamon

OMLAC (1978) New objectives in modern language teaching Sevenoaks: Hodder and Stoughton

SCHOOLS COUNCIL (1981) Graded objectives and tests for modern languages: an evaluation London: Schools Council

SOME ASPECTS OF AUSTRALIAN EXPERIENCE WITH LANGUAGE AWARENESS COURSES

T J Quinn and M Trounce

1. Introduction

A movement somewhat akin to the current interest in language awareness courses appears to have begun in Australian secondary schools
in the early seventies; it peaked in 1976, and has been in a state
of steady decline since then (at least in the statistical sense).
At first sight, it is perhaps surprising that British teachers are
addressing language awareness issues some 10 years later than their
Australian counterparts. There are, no doubt, very good reasons for
this state of affairs: the "state of the art" in language curricula
in both countries is markedly different, and this fact provides two
completely different contexts for language awareness initiatives.
We believe, nonetheless, that some reflections on the Australian
experience may be useful to British teachers in their deliberations
on this important matter. The purpose of this paper is thus to
provide an overview of certain aspects of Australian language awareness courses from about 1972 to 1983.

It is important to indicate the sources of this brief descriptive
study. One of the authors (TJQ) has been an observer (and partly
promoter) of the language awareness movement in Australia since it
began, and thus had a good deal of impressionistic knowledge of the
field. To make this study more objective, however, we undertook a
more systematic survey, deriving data from three sources:

(a) a study of all available published documentation: course
     materials, journal articles and government reports, statistics
     and analyses;
(b) a series of interviews with a wide cross-section of teachers,
     teacher trainers, researchers, curriculum consultants and
     inspectors;
(c) visits to schools still teaching language awareness
     programmes.

Our data and observations come from only two of the six Australian
States, Victoria and New South Wales, and predominantly from the
former. This limitation is less serious than might appear at first
sight, for two reasons: these two States cover some 65% of the
total school population of Australia; and the language awareness
movement has been far more predominant in Victoria than in any other
State. Finally, our data comes principally from the State education
systems - the public sector - with some limited input from Roman
Catholic schools, that part of the private sector which looks after
the education of some 20% of Australian children.

2. Terminology and definitions

The language awareness movement in Australia, like most other educational innovations, has generated a bewildering array of terms for what is essentially the same sort of curriculum. The terms most commonly encountered would include: language awareness course; introductory language programme; general language course; language and communication studies; language and culture studies; and introduction to language studies. The most common would be "introductory language programme" (ILP) and "general language course" (GLC), each representing a somewhat different emphasis. From this point on, we wish to exclude ILP, and use GLC as the most common Australian equivalent of what is called language awareness in Britain. This decision requires some explanation.

ILP has been used in Australia to cover a curricular approach that shared some of the aims of a GLC, but which differed markedly in content, even though it is sometimes difficult to decide whether a particular programme belongs in one category or the other. An ILP usually means introductory study of two or three different languages, prior to and as a means of informing a choice between these languages as the subject of subsequent more serious and sustained study. Thus, for example, in Year 7 (the first year of secondary school), a school may have, as part of the compulsory core curriculum, one term (14 weeks) of French, one term of German and one term of Indonesian. At the end of the year, the pupil would be expected to elect one of French, German or Indonesian as the language which he/she will continue in Year 8 and beyond. There are, of course, many possible variations of this approach.

We wish to distinguish a GLC quite sharply from the ILP approach, as a GLC appears to be much more closely related to the British notion of language awareness. As a starting-point, we offer the rather awkwardly expressed definition of a GLC used by the Education Department of Victoria in its annual statistical survey of school curricula: "A general language course consists mainly of culture and linguistics, without any specific language being studied for as much as one term." It is probably more enlightening to list – albeit in vague and even negative terms – four common features that seem to be shared by GLC: they tend to be similar in CONTENT, DURATION, AGE LOCATION and OBJECTIVES.

(a) CONTENT. GLCs usually include some concepts derived from general linguistics, some background cultural information about a foreign society, and some minimal exposure to the techniques of language learning.

(b) DURATION. GLCs are short-term curricular components, in that they usually last only one year, or very occasionally two years.

(c) AGE LOCATION. GLCs are offered in Years 7 or 8, i.e., at the beginning of secondary school, when pupils are 12-13 years of age.

(d) OBJECTIVES. GLCs have as their objectives something other than simply "learning a foreign language".

For the remainder of this paper we shall continue to use the terminology most common in Victorian schools, and comment almost exclusively on GLCs.

3. The growth and decline of GLCs: statistical data

The Department of Education in the State of Victoria began keeping statistical data in 1974, although such courses appear to have begun to appear some years before this. The pattern of growth, peak in 1976 and subsequent decline thereafter is illustrated clearly in Fig. 1. The actual statistics are set out in Table 1.

Table 1: Numbers of Victorian State Secondary Schools teaching GLCs, 1974-83

1974	49 schools
1975	86
1976	110
1977	107
1978	91
1979	64
1980	54
1981	49
1982	37
1983	30 (approx)

Fig.1. Victorian State Secondary Schools Teaching GLCs, 1974-83

The 1983 figure is not completely accurate, because the statistical survey was not complete at the time of writing. In addition, there is some evidence suggesting that the steady decline of the previous years in fact levelled out in 1983: while 9 schools terminated their GLC in 1983, 10 different schools initiated new GLCs.

It remains clear from the statistical data, however, that the GLC movement started with a great burst, peaked quickly, then went into steady decline. This is a situation that requires explanation.

4. Why did GLCs begin?

It is easy to give a straightforward answer to this question: somebody (in fact, several people independently) came up with an idea, and the materials to implement it, at a time when the state of foreign language teaching made the idea look attractive and relevant. We thus had a felicitous convergence of three essential components of any new movement in school curricula: the right timing, a challenging new idea, and readily usable materials promptly made available.

The time and emergence of GLCs in Australia is interesting. The movement started in the early seventies, which was a turning-point for the foreign language profession due to several factors, some of them felt world-wide, some of them peculiar to Australia. This was a time of fundamental re-thinking for the profession, as the panacea of audio-lingualism was beginning to look very shaky indeed. The Pennsylvania Project (Smith, 1970) had dashed the hopes of those who had put their faith in new methods and new machines, and Wilga Rivers' thesis (Rivers, 1964) had demonstrated that the faith was ill-founded anyway. Foreign language teachers were ready to look for new directions.

In Australia, this situation was exacerbated by several local factors. The traditional dominance of French in the foreign language curriculum – a dubious remnant of the British educational heritage – was under serious challenge. France and the French looked very remote from the Antipodes. Two new groups of languages began to look much more attractive: the languages of our Asian neighbours (Britain's "Far East" being Australia's "Near North"), and the languages of the hundreds of thousands of non-English-speaking immigrants who had made Australia their home in the great waves of post-war immigration. The Asian Studies movement and the multicultural Australia movement were looming large on the horizon. At the same time, the number of students taking the tradional foreign language (French) course was declining seriously, and "drop-out" rates were looking alarming: of those who did begin the study of French, most opted not to continue as soon as they were given the choice.

Given this state of affairs, it is not surprising that the alternative approach of GLCs began to look very attractive indeed. The course materials published at the time, and notably De Fazio's Lingvo materials (see References), address many of the issues raised in the preceding paragraph: the course is offered as an alternative to the first two years (years 7 and 8) of a traditional foreign language course; it is claimed to be more interesting and more relevant to the students; it takes account of the multilingual nature of the Australian population; it aims to dispel "anti-foreigner" feelings and to make the migrant child aware and proud of his/her non-English heritage; and the languages offered for elementary study as illustrations of points made include Greek, Italian, Turkish, Serbo-Croatian, Indonesian and Japanese.

De Fazio's materials were by far the most popular during the heyday of GLCs, and it is interesting to note their orientation, even though they are seldom used now. She described her approach as an "elementary historical linguistic" one, and called it a course in "Language Communication". The materials covered the origins of language; non-verbal communication; the history of languages; the structure of English; and comparative study of several languages, each one being accompanied with elementary cultural information about the foreign speech community, an introduction to the sound system and grammatical structure, and such activities as songs, poems, nursery rhymes, etc.

The aims of such courses were laudable indeed, and quite lofty. It is interesting to quote in full the list of aims which De Fazio drew up for her particular course (Lingvo teacher's manual, p15):

1. To increase the students' awareness of and interest in language as a means of communication.
2. To increase their range of vocabulary in their own language and their ability to structure their communication in their own language.
3. To enable students to make some simple comparisons with other languages with regard to such things as:

   a. Written – Type of script
   – Alphabets
   – Syntax
   b. Oral – Pronunciation
   – Idioms

4. To provide a background of interest and comparison from which to commence the study of a foreign language.
5. To prepare the students in the methods of foreign language learning.
6. To give the students a general backgroud on languages as one unit and give them some understanding of other lingual concepts besides their own even if they should never proceed with the study of a foreign language.

5. Why have GLCs declined in popularity?

Perhaps the simplest answer one could give to this question would be to say that they have not lived up to their stated aims, but, while that statement appears to be undoubtedly true, it tells us little. In the survey we undertook in preparing this paper, we heard many reasons why schools and teachers had tried GLCs and found them wanting, but two seemed to recur most frequently: the difficulties that teachers had with concepts and the published materials, and the difficulty experienced in justifying a GLC to the curriculum decision-makers. In addition, we were surprised to find a third common reason reported from schools with significant ESL problems. Each of these reasons requires some comment.

In retrospect, it seems clear that the kind of GLC being introduced in Australian schools some ten years ago made demands on teachers for which they were ill-prepared. On a superficial level, this could mean that a teacher might have to teach the elements of a foreign language about which he/she knew nothing except what was provided in the text and tapes of the GLC. This could work moderately well to a certain extent, but it was hazardous, and the experience made many teachers uncomfortable. And it could have comical consequences. One teacher told us of a noisy class of tough 12-year old lads being led in their unruly behaviour by a couple of boys from an Italian background. When all other attempts to restore order failed, the teacher suddenly remembered a phrase she had memorised from her GLC tape materials: "Si accommodi, prego," which had been translated as "Please sit down". So she shouted this at the rioting Italian lads, who fell about with laughter at the inappropriateness of the utterance. (It is an extremely formal and polite remark that one might address to a guest whom one has just received into one's home on a formal visit.)

But there is a far more serious side to this matter. The kinds of concepts introduced in GLCs demand a quite sophisticated familiarity with the field of general linguistics (and possibly also with comparative anthropology and sociology). Ten years ago, few Australian foreign language teachers had this sort of background, and this inadequacy revealed itself in the way they handled GLCs: linguistic concepts were distorted; "cultural" information was trivialized; and the exotic was highlighted merely for its novelty value.

Furthermore, it may well be that the issue goes much deeper than this. It may be the case that the key concepts of general linguistics are particularly difficult to popularize without distortion, even by a teacher who has had adequate tertiary training in linguistics. Perhaps linguistics is simply not a study for young minds. We have heard this claim made seriously by eminent scholars in linguistics, who have put a case for the proposition that linguistics should not be an undergraduate discipline at all. While this may sound like the special pleading of mandarins bent upon preservation of their special status, it does seem to be true that fundamental concepts of linguistics are not easy to popularize. And the same may well be true of those concepts from anthropology and sociology which formed the basis of the "cultural" components of GLCs. Whatever the reason, it is clear that many Australian teachers felt uncomfortable and inadequate in handling this sort of material in GLCs.

Many teachers reported to us that they had great difficulty in justifying a GLC to their colleagues and their school Principal. Perhaps the aims were too lofty. In many cases, the decline in serious foreign language study continued unabated, despite the claim that a GLC would stem this decline, because the students would be better prepared for serious foreign language study. When this did

137

not appear to eventuate, teachers found it difficult to point to any clearly definable outcome of a GLC. And so, in many schools, a counter-reaction set in, along the lines of "If we are going to have foreign language study anyway, why not get straight into it, instead of tinkering around for a year or two with an ill-defined GLC?" The statistical pattern we illustrated above appears to suggest that this kind of thinking has come to be adopted in many schools: a GLC is no longer acceptable as an alternative to the first year or two of foreign language study.

Finally, we found evidence of a somewhat paradoxical situation with GLCs in schools that are known as "schools of high migrant density", i.e., where large numbers of the children come from a non-English-speaking (NES) or limited English (LES) home background. In the early days GLCs seemed to be particularly appealing in such situations: the common GLC formula allowed for the possibility of using the LES children as "informants" for the class to study their home language and culture as one of the sampled illustrative components of the GLC. It was in this sense that the GLC was supposed to provide the LES child with a sense of pride in his/her cultural and linguistic heritage. We have been told, however, that things simply did not work out like this. Drawing upon a number of languages to illustrate comparative linguistic concepts was simply confusing to LES children, and schools quickly abandoned this aspect of a GLC. Direct attempts to consolidate the English competence of such children were preferred. And the modest attempts in GLCs to enhance the prestige of the NES home background soon came to appear quite tokenistic: such thinking has by now given way to far more radical talk of language rights, and to demands for programmes of bilingual education and mother tongue maintenance. Against the background of such contemporary Australian political thought about the status of non-English languages (sometimes referred to as "CLOTES"- community languages other than English), the approach of earlier GLCs appears trivial indeed.

It is interesting to establish the reasons why GLCs have survived and flourished in a small number of schools. In many ways, they are the converse of the reasons for rejection we have explained above. GLCs have prospered where an enthusiastic, well-prepared teacher has been able to demonstrate the worth of the concept, usually by pointing to a demonstrable "spin-off" in one of two areas: either in increasing student motivation to undertake and persist with foreign language learning, or in integrating the GLC with a school's commitment to multicultural policies. The teachers who were successful in these endeavours stressed to us that these achievements were slow to develop: they depended on a teacher or group of teachers remaining in a school and working at the GLC concept long enough (7-8 years) to evaluate it, modify it and adapt it to changing school needs and policies.

6. Three brief case studies of successful GLCs

As we have been fairly gloomy about the state of GLCs in Australian secondary schools, we feel we should redress the balance by giving a brief account of three successful and well-established GLCs.

Programme "A" operates in a medium-sized state secondary school in an upper middle-class suburb of Melbourne, with a predominantly English-speaking population. The one-year GLC is compulsory in Year 7 (the first year of secondary school), and is followed by a compulsory French course in Year 8. Thereafter (Years 9-12), the study of French is optional, but numbers remain high, and this fact is attributed to the success of the GLC in motivating the students for foreign language study. The GLC is taught in two weekly one-hour lessons, and the curriculum centres around 4 core topics: How Language Began; Development of Our Alphabet; Language Families; Parts of Speech. Each core topic is illustrated with concepts and illustrative examples from a wide variety of languages, and each topic is followed by a series of lessons applying the concepts of the French Language. The teacher uses a wide variety of print and non-print resources, including such things as video programmes about migration to Australia, folktales from many countries, language games and multilingual dictionaries. This is a programme with clear objectives that appears to be working very well.

Programme "B" is in a state secondary school in the western suburbs of Melbourne, in a working-class area where the majority of families are from a NES background. The GLC operates in Year 7, and is compulsory. In year 8, all students must study Greek, Italian or French. From Years 9-12, foreign language study becomes optional, and Greek and Italian are offered. The GLC has three 50-minute lessons per week throughout the school year. The course has two major components: "General Language Communication", which includes work on the origins of language, other forms of communication, the heritage of our language and the history of the English language; and "Comparative Language Studies", which covers a brief introduction to Italian, Greek, Maltese and French, dealing with such matters as geography, greetings, numbers, classroom vocabulary, family structure, the body, animals, colour terms, etc. Once again, a wide variety of books and audio-visual materials is used. This GLC is well-integrated into the innovative language teaching policy of the school.

Programme "C" operates in a very large Catholic secondary school in the northern suburbs of Melbourne, serving a decidedly multilingual feeder population, as some 80% of the children come from an NES background, dominated by Italian (about 50% of the school population), but also including significant numbers of speakers of Greek, Maltese, Arabic, Spanish and Yugoslav languages. The NES character of the feeder population is so striking that language questions and language policy have become the subject of a strong and evolving philosophy in the school. A GLC is compulsory for all students in Year 7, and is called "Multilingual and Cultural Studies". The programme's strength appears to be based on a constant use of the linguistic and cultural resources of the feeder population. After Year 7, all students must choose to do either a foreign language course (French or Italian) or a subject called "Community Language Studies". This choice is binding on all students up to and including Year 10, and even Years 11-12, Community Language Studies is available as an elective. What goes on in Community Language Studies appears to be an amalgam of mother-tongue maintenance and development for LES students, and some elementary sociolinguistic work on the status and use of non-English languages in the local community. The GLC in this school is thus of a well-developed and highly-integrated total school policy on the importance of language studies for all children. Interestingly, the teachers who originally developed the GLC had formal training in linguistics.

7. Conclusion

Even after a decade of experimentation, it is difficult to establish a balanced perspective on the Australian experience with GLCs. It would be invidious for us to suggest any lessons that may be learned from the Australian experience for our British colleagues. However, we are bold enough to conclude by suggesting three considerations that may be relevant. We offer them in no particular order of importance.

(1) GLCs - or indeed any version of "Language Awareness" - are no panacea for the serious problems that beset foreign language teaching throughout the world. Anyone undertaking language awareness work probably needs to make a fundamental decision right from the start: is this course supposed to contribute to the success of the foreign language curriculum, or is it conceived as a curricular component in its own right? It is tempting to try for both orientations, but we believe that this is neither feasible nor effective.

(2) Whatever the orientation chosen, integration with other areas of the curriculum will be both successful and difficult to achieve. Mother-tongue English is the obvious candidate for "linkage", but, in our experience it is the most difficult to establish. The early writers of GLC materials in Australia all stressed the desirability of links with English teachers and their programmes, but these never eventuated. The typical pattern with Australian GLCs was that there was very little integration with any other part of the curriculum; where there was any, it was with areas like geography, social studies, visual arts and home economics, and never with English. The traditional subject "walls" are very hard to penetrate.

(3) We believe that the question of age is crucial. Australian

GLCs have been a phenomenon of the junior secondary school, and perhaps they erred in trying to impose mature considerations on young
minds. It may be the case that language awareness is more appropriate for the later years of secondary education.

GLCs and the language awareness movement are curricular innovations
and, like all movements, they inevitably face problems of self-
definition and evolving clarification. While the GLC movement in
Australia has probably not weathered particulary well, we have
certainly seen situations where a GLC makes a strong contribution to
innovative curricular thinking. We hope that the British language
awareness movement, some ten years on from the earliest Australian
GLCs, may learn something from what went right and what went wrong
in the Australian experience.

(This paper was commissioned by the Language Awareness Working Party
of the National Congress on Languages in Education, Great Britain.
The authors are at the Horwood Language Centre, University of
Melbourne, Australia).

References

ADAMS, I (1974). "A language study syllabus for junior secondary
forms." Babel, 10, 1 (April, 1974), 23-27.

DE FAZIO, A (1974a). "A language communication course for junior
high school." Babel, 10, 1 (April, 1974), 20-22.

DE FAZIO, A (1974b). Lingvo. Melbourne: Landmark Press. (Now out
of print.) (Components: Teacher's Manual. Resource Book.
Student's Workbook. Testing Packet. Audio Tapes.)

HACKETT, T, H McLachlan and K Strong (1980). Communicate. Sydney:
Boden Books. (First published 1974).

RIVERS, W M (1964). The psychologist and the foreign language
teacher. Chicago: University of Chicago Press.

SMITH, P Jr. (1970). A comparison of the cognitive and audiolingual
approaches to foreign language instruction: the Pennsylvania
Foreign Language Project. Philadelphia: The Center for Curriculum
Development.

Section C

REPORTS OF
COURSES AND INITIATIVES
IN CORE SCHOOLS

THE ORATORY SCHOOL, READING
LOWER SIXTH PRINCIPLES OF LANGUAGE COURSE

Headmaster: Mr A.J. Snow
Assistant Master with special responsibility
for Language Awareness: Mr A.J. Tinkel

1. Description of the School

2. Selection and Academic Background of Course Members

3. Aims of the Course

4. Syllabus

5. Method

6. Description of the End of Course Examination

7. Examination Written Papers for 1983 and 1984

8. Results of 1983 and 1984 Examinations

9. Titles of Students' Extended Essays

10. Comments on the Course

    10.1 G Wiley, Esq, Moderator of the End of Course
                      Examination for the Oxford and
                      Cambridge Schools Examination Board
    10.2 J L M Trim, Esq
    10.3 M J Hampshire, Esq, Member of the 1981/2 Course

Description of the school

The Oratory School is an independent Roman Catholic school run by
laymen. It was founded in 1859 by Cardinal Newman in Birmingham and
is now situated near Reading.

The school contains 360 boys of 13 to 18 years; there are no girls.
The main entry is at 13, but there is also an 11 to 13 year old
Junior Department of 60 boys. The Sixth Form contains 150 boys and a
high proportion go on to further education. The majority of boys
are boarders; there are about 80 day boys.

The school is organised on a house system for pastoral purposes. The
academic arrangement is in traditional departments with the curriculum centred on preparation for O and A levels.

2. Selection and academic background of the course members

The Principles of Language course is offered as a minority time subject in the Lower Sixth (post-O-level year) and boys are entered for it at the suggestion of their housemaster. The course is run in conjunction with both the English and Modern Languages departments, but the students following it are by no means restricted to these departments as far as their main A level subjects are concerned. Students of Science, Mathematics, Economics, History and Geography are involved as much as English and Modern Languages.

Very few of the students do not have English as their mother- tongue when they enter the school; those that do not are expected to have a good working knowledge of the language. On the other hand a large proportion of the pupils have second language experience through family connections or residence abroad. In school all students study at least one foreign language up to O level. Most study two.

The Principles of Language course is based on a native speaker know-ledge of English, but in the context of other language experience.

3. Aims of the course

- By developing the student's awareness of what language is and how it functions, to make him more sensitive to his own and other people's use of it.

- To provide an introduction to the basic principles of linguistic study.

4. Syllabus

The course is designed to last one academic year with three sessions per week of 40 minutes each.

The course has three sections:

(a) Definition of Human Language and Communication:- natural, iconic and conventional signs - voluntary and involuntary communication beyond and alongside language - first language acquisition - animal communication - writing systems and other means of conveying language apart from speech.

The object of this section is to give the student a clearer idea of the difference between human language, human communication and animal communication, as well as to make him aware of the distinction between a human language and the variety of substances in which it may be realised.

(b) Analysis of one Particular Linguistic System - English:-

i. examination of the sounds of standard British English, leading to transcription practice in broad phonemic script - introduction to the speech mechanism and principal speech organs - intonation and stress patterns in English - comparison of English dialect sounds.

ii. the phoneme system and syllable structure in standard British English - syntactic elements of English (morphemic structure and syntactic categories) - syntactic structure (grammatical relations, transformations, embedded and compound sentences, inter-sentential reference).

The object of this section is to give an introduction to phonological and syntactic constraints in English, and through this to show that a language is both a rule-governed, social possession, as well as a possession of creative potential for each individual member of the speech community. The section is also seen as a necessary preparation for the third section of the syllabus.

(c) Examination of Change and Variety of Use in English:-

i. arbitrariness of linguistic signs and its consequences - relationship of meaning and structure - contribution of context and presupposition to meaning - other elements contributing to meaning in language use.

ii. phonological, morphological, syntactic, lexical and semantic changes in English - comparison of variations between British and American English - change in present-day British English - variety within a speech community, bilingualism/ multi-lingualism, standard language and dialectal variation, social dialect, idiolect - variety of personal usage - styles of spoken English, registers of spoken and written English and their characteristics.

The object of this section is firstly for students to examine the arbitrary nature of the linguistic sign and the variety of elements that go to make up meaning. Secondly the student will be examining the variety of his own usage and the wide variety of possible usage in English, based on geography, activity and social context.

The object of this section is firstly for students to examine the arbitrary nature of the linguistic sign and the variety of elements that go to make up meaning. Secondly the student will be examining the variety of his own usage and the wide variety of possible usage in English, based on geography, activity and social context.

5. Method

The presentation is centred as much as possible on the student's own knowledge of his mother-tongue. He is led to think about each aspect of the syllabus by exploring examples of it in use. The emphasis is on handling problems that guide the student to think for himself about the aspect of the course they are designed to highlight. The questions in the written papers of the end of course examination are examples of such problems.

6. End of course examination

At the end of the course the students sit an experimental AO level examination administered and certificated by the Oxford and Cambridge Schools Examination Board. The initial three-year trial period for the examination began in 1981/2.

The examination has two parts:

i.   an extended essay of up to 2500 words on a related topic chosen by the student and approved by the moderator;

ii.   a written paper taken under examination conditions (3 hours). In 1984 candidates will be obliged to answer at least one question on each section of the syllabus.

7. Examination written papers for 1983 and 1984

OXFORD AND CAMBRIDGE SCHOOLS EXAMINATION BOARD

GENERAL CERTIFICATE EXAMINATION

ALTERNATIVE ORDINARY LEVEL
8632/1

PRINCIPLES OF LANGUAGE

(The Oratory School) Tuesday, 14 June 1983. 3 hours

Answer four questions

1   Signs

You have received a commission from the Ministry of Public Affairs of the state of Owdnegrin to design various emblems for this new nation, which is due to gain full independence in 1984. You have been told that the new country has eight major languages, which are mutually incomprehensible, and that there is a high rate of illiteracy amongst the racially mixed population. The country has been administered up to now under a United Nations mandate. After independence it will be run as a socialist one-party state, but will be non-aligned in its relations with other countries. The economy of Owdnegrin is based on the exporting of tea and sunflower seeds for oil, but there is a deposit of diamonds in the south-west of the country and extensive fishing potential, both off-shore and in the River Owd.

What proposals would you submit for emblems in **five** of the following cases? Make a sketch drawing in each case and indicate briefly whether you consider your design to be completely arbitrary, or whether it has some pictorial link with the concept it represents. Mention any special difficulties you encounter in choosing any emblem.

   (i)   the national flag

  (ii)   the seal of state

 (iii)   the single political organisation of the state - the Party
          of the Owdnegrinan People

  (iv)   the national oil agency that has the sole right under
          Owdnegrinan law to market petrol

   (v)   the national agency controlling all imports and exports

  (vi)   the small but important state railway network

 (vii)   the national airline - AirOwd

(viii)   the tourist board set up to attract visitors from North
          America and Western Europe

  (ix)   the design on the 50 bongo note (25 bongos = £1 sterling)

   (x)   the national radio and television service

2   Communication and Language

     Answer **both** parts of the question.

     (a) Look at the following descriptions of gestures used by speakers of English, either independently or as an accompaniment of speech.

     State what meaning you would attach to each gesture and how far

149

your understanding of the gesture would depend on the context in which it is made. Explain in addition whether you consider the gesture to be an example of an indexical sign (having an automatic link with its meaning, e.g. drooping eyelids indicating tiredness), of an iconic sign (having a pictorial link with its meaning, e.g. beconing someone to come) or of an arbitrary sign (having no apparent link with its meaning).

Where the gesture could convey more than one meaning, you should consider the possible alternatives.

(i)   closed eyelids

(ii)   right index finger placed over closed lips

(iii)   the tops of the fingers and thumb of the right hand brought together, moved to the mouth, kissed then opened out as the hand is taken away

(iv)   sucking-in air through clenched teeth

(v)   raising the right index finger and keeping the other fingers and thumb against the palm of the hand

(vi)   clenching the right thumb under the right fingers

(vii)   lifting the eyebrows and narrowing the eyes

(viii) hand extended, palm downwards, and moved up and down

(ix)   making a clicking noise with the thumb and third finger

(x)   the tips of the fingers and thumb of one hand placed against those of the other hand in front of the chest

(b) State briefly how, in your opinion, the communication taking place in the examples of Part (a) of the question can be distinguished from communication that takes place through language.

3   Speech and Writing

Look at the following words of Welsh, which are pronounced like their English equivalents, and then answer the questions on them below. You may assume for the purposes of this question that there are no silent letters in written Welsh and that each sound in the language is represented by a different letter or pair of letters.

ffilm, sigaret, fforc, fôt, siop, coffi, drôr, tacsi, plismon, ambiwlans, potel, tebot, siwgr, eroplên, beic, nofel, bwced, fandal, cwcw, bws, drwm, niwclear,

(i)   Write down in phonetic script the sounds represented by 's', 'ff','c','si' (plus vowel)

(ii)   English spells 'bottle' with 'b', 'teapot' with 'p', 'bucket' with 't'. Welsh spells 'potel' with 'p', tebot with 'b', 'bwced' with 'd'. Explain, using terminology of articulatory phonetics, the connections between 'b' and 'p', 't' and 'd' that lead to these changes

(iii)   In some of the Welsh words given above the vowel 'w' occurs. In the English RP equivalents of those words three different vowels are found, e.g. in 'bus', 'drum', 'sugar', 'cuckoo', 'nuclear'. Write down the three vowels in question in phonetic script and plot their position on a vowel quadrilateral

(iv)   The diacritic ⌢ in 'fôt', 'drôr', 'eroplên', indicates lengthening of the vowels. The RP English equivalent vowels are pronounced as dipthongs. Plot the three dipthongs on a vowel quadrilateral and write them in phonetic script

(v)   Give one example from the above list of Welsh words that will fit each of the following:

(a) beginning with a voiced labio-dental fricative

(b) beginning with a voiceless velar plosive

(c) beginning with a vowel close to primary cardinal vowel 2

(d) beginning with an alveolar nasal

(vi)   The letters 'dd' at the end of 'Caerdydd' (Cardiff) represent a voiced dental fricative. Give a phonetic symbol for the sound.

4   Phonetic Transcription

Write a phonetic transcription of the following passage.
"To revert to this driving test....," said Treece.
"Well, as I say, you mustn't feel too disappointed if you don't pass first time. They throw the book at you. They failed me for not giving proper signals. I was sticking my arm out as far as the bloody thing would go. But no, they expect you to lean so damn' far out of the car that the examiner has to hold on to your feet. They just don't like passing people".

"This is only a bicycle," said Treece.
"It makes no odds, old boy," said Merrick. "They'r᷈ even worse with those things."

Malcolm Bradbury - Eating People is Wrong

5   Intonation and Stress

The following sentences have been printed with markings to indicate intonation and stress, but without any punctuation. Give a reading to each sentence that would correspond with the markings and explain your reasons.

(i)   I don't think that is what Mrs. Alsop meant

(ii)   He's bringing fifteen hundred

(iii)   Go away and think about it

(iv)   The river is rising fast

(v)   There is no need for you to worry

6   Morphemic Analysis

Answer **both** parts of the question.

(a) Look at the following prefixes and suffixes. State briefly a definition for each one, suitable for inclusion in the Oxford English Dictionary, and consider what constraints exist on their use.

--ment,   --s (plural marker),   anti--,   en--,   over--.

(b) Consider briefly what difficulties arise when analysing English from the viewpoint of the morpheme -- the minimal unit of meaning. Give examples to illustrate your answer.

7   Syntactic Elements

Answer **all** parts of the question.

(a) Look at the following expressions and say whether the underlined adjective is being used in a restrictive or non-restrictive sense.

(i)   A _lenient_ bank manager

(ii)   No _artificial_ colouring

(iii)   My _dear_ mother

(iv)   The _rare_ natterjack toad

(v)   His _favourite_ left foot

(b) Look at the following adjectives and state which, in your opinion, can be used both attributively and predicatively and which can only be used in one of these ways. Give your answers in the form of example sentences.

frequent, best, principal, afraid, pleasant, eventual, holy, red, liable, former

(c) The following adjectives have both restrictive and a non-restrictive meaning when used attributively, but the restrictive meaning only is acceptable when they are used predicatively.

perfect, poor, sheer, real, certain,

Explain this difference in meaning and illustrate your answers with example sentences.

8   Syntactic Structure

Analyse the syntactic structure of each of the following sentences.

(i)   Bonzo brought me the paper in his teeth

(ii)   I know you said you were sorry

(iii)   My next-door neighbour must have bought a new stereo

(iv)   Last night's wind blew down the fence and uprooted an elm

(v)   Stopping his pocket money has no effect nowadays

9   Syntactic and Semantic Ambiguity

Answer **both** parts of the question.

(a) Compare the following pairs of sentences. Their construction appears to be the same on the surface, but the native speaker knows instinctively that there is a different relationship between the words in each case.

Paraphrase the two sentences in each pair. Identify where the difference lies that causes these structures -- similar on the surface -- to contain different relationships between their components underneath. Ignore any question of stress.

(i)   They are running shoes
       They are running water

(ii)   It was propping up the wall
       It was growing up the wall

(iii)   The Swiss were impatient to see
       The Swiss were obvious to see

(iv)   They were bound to ask
       They were bound to trees

(v)   The girls can peas for a job
       The girls can try for a job

(b) Look at the following five sentences. They all have more than one possible reading. Briefly identify two readings for each sentence and explain the nature of the ambiguity, with particular reference to the words or structures involved. Ignore questions of stress.

(i)   He appeared to disprove the rumours

(ii)   The men were tearing up the road

(iii)   I wasn't looking at the time

(iv)   He watched the school play

(v)   They are breeding sheep

10   Regional Dialect Sounds

Consider how you would expect each of the following words to be pronounced in the speech of the region printed in brackets after it. Then plot the vowel in each of the ten words on a vowel quadrilateral.

(i)   round (Berkshire)

(ii)   call (London)

(iii)   beer (Norfolk)

(iv)   that (Bristol)

(v)   eight (South Wales)

(vi)   side (West Midlands)

(vii)   glass (Yorkshire)

(viii) bear (Liverpool)

(xi)   house (Tyneside)

(x)   man (Belfast)

11   Styles of Language Use

Answer **both** parts of the question.

(a) Mr Parnell has been plagued by carol-singers all evening. When the sixth group knock on his door, he decides not to give any more money. Write down what you consider his actual words were likely to be, when telling **five** of the following that he was not going to contribute.

(b) Arrange your five answers in order, ranging from the most formal to the most informal, and comment briefly on the lexical and syntactic changes involved. Write about 50 words in each case, to cover both Mr Parnell's words and your analysis of them.

(i)   the vicar and the church choir

(ii)   his next-door neighbour whose ladder he wants to borrow in the morning

(iii)   his other next-door neighbour who always plays his stereo too loud too late at night

(iv)   three scruffy-looking boys singing out of tune

(v)   his drinking mates from the Hat and Feathers

(vi)   uniformed nurses from the local hospital

(vii)   his wife on his way to open the door

(viii)   two young girls with a dog that is trampling on his prize
         Christmas roses

(ix)   members of a political party he would never vote for

12   Register

Read the following extracts of written English. Give a probable
context of use for **five** of them. In each case, give lexical and
syntactic reasons for the context you suggest.

(i)   They've now taken just eight points from a possible 30 over
the last ten matches, leaving the clouds over Elm Park very, very
dark indeed.

And yet, what else could you realistically expect from a Royals
side so cruelly shorn of any substantial experience or class?

With eight first-teamers sidelined due to injury, Royals manager Maurice Evans was forced to draft in no fewer than four part-
timers.

(ii)   This man, who was now travelling with us in our car, was
the same stranger whom I had seen with my father the day before in
the street. He answered politely my father's questions and from time
to time wrote down on a piece of paper different things about which
my father spoke to him.

(iii)   No interest will be charged on the amounts of purchases
repaid by the cardholder and credited to the account within 25 days
of the date of the statement of account on which those purchases
first appear. The daily balance of any such amounts outstanding at
the end of the 25 days period will be charged interest from that
statement date and will continue to be so charged until full repay-
ment is credited to the account.

(iv)   I had gained the impression that you would be prepared to
support the appeal in the financial sense, and I wonder if you are
now in a position to develop your intended gift, ideally as a Deed
of Covenant.

(v)   For the ten long years of the Gaullist regime, the workers
witnessed the impotence of the traditional reformist forms of
struggle: parliamentary skirmishes, "demonstrative" strikes, unin-
spired marches, and so on. The social crisis submitted all methods
and all doctrine to a searching and merciless examination.

(vi)   Let us adopt, tentatively, the theory of the base component sketched in Para 4.3 of Chapter 2, and continue to use the fragment of Para 3, Chapter 2, appropriately modified to exclude sub-categorization rules from the categorical component of the base, as an illustrative example of a grammar.

(vii)   No ifs. No buts. No surcharges.

(viii)   Now, largely through the recommendations of friends, over 10 million people throughout the world insist on Glittomesh.

(ix)   I do nobody no harm, I say none harm, I think none harm, but wish everybody good. And if this be not enough to keep a man alive, in good faith I long not to live.

(x)   I enclose a letter I got a little while since from Fry, one of the men you saw with me at Henley. I don't know Pegg personally but Fry has a good nose for a decent sort of chap and therefore I expect there is something in this one.

OXFORD AND CAMBRIDGE SCHOOLS EXAMINATION BOARD

GENERAL CERTIFICATE EXAMINATION

ALTERNATIVE ORDINARY LEVEL
8632/1

PRINCIPLES OF LANGUAGE

(The Oratory School) Tuesday, 12 June 1984. 3 hours

Answer four questions, one from each section and one other.

Section I

1   Signs

You have been asked by a publishing company to supply a set of designs depicting different states of the weather. The designs are to be used in a project for standardised weather forecasting in Europe.

What designs would you submit in each of the following cases?

-cloudy, showery, fog/mist, strong S.W. wind, frost, hot, humid, gentle breeze, sunny intervals, drizzle.

In each case either make a sketch drawing or give a brief description of your idea for a design. Then indicate whether you consider the design to have no apparent link with its meaning or whether you see some pictorial link existing. Mention any special difficulties you encounter in choosing a design.

You may base your answers on designs that are already familiar to you from television, printed sources or elsewhere.

2   Communication and Language

Answer all parts of the question.

(a) Describe **five** sounds made by the mouth which are gestures, not speech sounds. State a meaning for each one.

(b) Describe **five** gestures that involve use of the hands only. State a meaning for each one.

(c) Describe **five** gestures that consist only of a facial expression. State a meaning for each one.

(d) Describe **five** gestures that are made by parts of the body other than the hands and face. State a meaning for each one.

(e) With reference to the examples you have quoted above:-

  (i)   illustrate the difference in your view between iconic signs that have a pictorial link with their meanings and arbitrary signs that have no apparent link;

  (ii) consider how important context is in avoiding ambiguity;

  (iii) distinguish communication that takes place through language from communication that is taking place in examples quoted by you in Parts (a)-(d) of the question.

3   Phonetic Transcription

Write a phonetic transcription of the following passage.

'Benson, what's this about your leaving?'
'I was cross last night, Mr Basil. I couldn't ever leave

Malfrey and Mrs Sothill ought to know that. Not with the Captain away, too.'
    'Mrs Sothill was very upset.'
    'So was I, Mr Basil. You don't know what those Connollys are. They're not human.'
    'We'll find a billet for them.'
    'No one will take the Connollys in these parts. Not if they were given a hundred pounds.'
    'I have an idea I owe you some money.'
    'You do, Mr Basil. Twelve pound ten.'
    'As much as that? Time I paid it back.'
    'It is.'
    'I will, Benson.'
    'I hope so, sir, I'm sure.'

4   Intonation and Stress

Answer **all** parts of the question.

(a) A recent television commercial for beer had a dialogue consisting entirely of the word 'well', spoken with different pitch patterns to convey different meanings. Look at the ten contexts outlined below in brackets, recapturing this dialogue, and put an appropriate tonetic mark on the word 'well' for each context.

      (i) "Well." (John, Harry and David meet one another unexpectedly in the pub.)

    (ii) "Well." (John asks the others what they want to drink.)

   (iii) "Well." (David can't make up his mind.)

    (iv) "Well." (Harry wishes the others 'Good Health'.)

     (v) "Well." (John sees a pretty girl.)

    (vi) "Well." (David is surprised to see the others drink so fast.)

  (vii) "Well." (But asks them if they want another.)

 (viii) "Well." (Harry hesitates.)

   (ix) "Well." (John says, 'Why not?'.)

    (x) "Well." (After the second round they all agree it's time to be going.)

    (b) Write out the following words, marking the position of

primary and (where applicable) secondary stress in RP pronunciation:-

   -pejorative, compulsory, electrification, uncooperative, disestablishment, symposium, misled, deteriorate, reminiscence, anti-corrosive.

   (c) Give **five** examples of words that alter their stressed syllable, depending on whether they are used as a noun or a verb, as for example 'an object', but 'to object'.

Section II

5   Word Structure

   Each of the following words are made up of smaller units of meaning. State what those smaller units are, give their meaning and mention any special problems you encounter in splitting up any of these words.

   -reactivated, uncritically, privatisation, remembrances, watchmen's.

6   Word Classes

   Answer **both** parts of the question.

   (a) Look at the following sentences. Each sentence is ambiguous out of its context because a noun used in it can belong to more than one sub-class of noun. Give a brief paraphrase of two possible readings of each sentence resulting from interpreting a noun in two different ways and state the two sub-classes of noun involved in the ambiguity.

   (i) He needed the shade.

   (ii) She went into the church.

   (iii) His resolution won the day.

   (iv) I was upset by his lip.

   (v) Ruby is my favourite.

   (b) The following sentences contain the same kind of ambiguity as in Part (a), but this time involving different sub-classes of verb. Give a brief paraphrase of two possible readings of each sentence and state the sub-classes of verb involved.

(i) They are cooking.

(ii) The lamb felt cold.

(iii) Does he mix well?

(iv) He is trying.

(v) She goes to church on Sunday.

7   Syntactic Structure

Analyse the syntactic structure of the following sentences:-

(i) The waiter brought us the coffee on a tray.

(ii) We believe the man you hired is no good.

(iii) The outcome could have been different with greater planning.

(iv) The best way of conserving oil is to make better use of it.

(v) What he talks about has never really happened and never will.

8   Figures of Speech

The following sentences contain examples of oxymoron, metonymy, synecdoche, transferred epithet, pathetic fallacy, paradox, metaphor, simile, personification, assonance. Identify a figure of speech in each of these sentences and explain the special use of language that has produced it.

(i) He gets his retaliation in first.

(ii) The White House has issued a statement denying the rumour.

(iii) He switched on the box to watch the News.

(iv) Thank you for your kind letter.

(v) I'll give you a definite may-be.

(vi) The sun smiled down from a blue sky.

(vii) The deed cries out for vengeance.

(viii) My heart stirred at the word of a bird.

(ix) Someone rammed the back of my car.

(x) He has as much imagination as a cold fried egg.

Section III

9   English Dialect Sounds

Consider how you would expect each of the two words below to be pronounced in the five English accents printed in brackets after them. Then plot the different vowels in the case of each word on a vowel quadrilateral. Use at least **two** quadrilaterals - one for each word - for the sake of clarity.

(i) house   (Somerset, Berkshire, Cockney, Tyneside, Belfast)

(ii) mate   (Cockney, Yorkshire, S.Wales, RP, Southern Irish)

10   American English

Answer **all** parts of the question.

(a) Write the following in phonetic script as you would expect them to be pronounced in a General American accent:-

-clock, pass, talk, door, free, star, fed, burn, care.

(b) What words would you expect a British English speaker to use instead of the following American English ones:-

-gasoline, sneakers, two weeks, intermission, drapes, to mail, (car) trunk, subway, garbage, truck.

(c) Consider the ten words in Part (b) and state:

(i) which words you might expect to hear regularly used in British usage (leaving aside imitation) and whether they would be restricted to any particular groups of speakers;

(ii) which words you include in your own regular usage and whether they are used as replacements for or alongside the British equivalents. In the latter case do you make any distinction between the British and American words in your use of them?

11   Style of Language Use

Styles of language use are frequently measured by means of a five-point scale which range from the frozen-formal through the semi-formal, the straightforward-normal and the colloquial-familiar to the slang, as for example in the case of 'horseless carriage/ motor vehicle/car/motor/wheels or banger'.

Choose **five** words of English which have similar variants, ranging form the frozen-formal to the slang. State the variants in each of the five cases, arrange them in order from the most formal to the most informal and mention briefly any special points of note in each case.

12   Register

Read the following extracts of written English. Give a probable context of use for **five** of them. In each case give lexical and syntactic reasons for the context you suggest.

(i) The Social Service workers in Bonn working with young people were very anxious to embark on the exchange with their opposite numbers in Oxford and this seemed now to be a distinct possibility.

(ii) Should be qualified primary teachers and/or graduates in a relevant discipline. Fluency in spoken and written Gaelic essential.

(iii) This brings the best of good wishes to you
For good luck and success in all that you do.

(iv) Passing through here - very pretty with well-preserved seventeenth-century houses and buildings of various kinds. Rather touristy and v. pricey. Weather indifferent.

(v) ... and I am particularly delighted to welcome him into our midst, as I have known him for some years - when he first joined the Scouts in Basingstoke (where amongst other things I was Group Scout Leader - you didn't know that, did you!).

(vi) No club may allow any of its places in the Race to be used by any crew from another club or allow any of its own crews to row in another club's place.

(vii) He wants not friends that hath thy love
And may converse and walk with thee.

(viii) Sheared my mongrel dog Rover, and made use of his white hair in plaster for ceilings. His coat weighed four ounces. The N.E. wind makes Rover shrink.

(ix) Cash in lieu of holiday cannot be claimed.

(x) "Who the 'ell's been sleeping in my bed?" said Father Bear;
"The bleeding little nymphomaniac, Goldie Locks," wagered Mummy
Bear. "Why, the two-timing, double-crossing no-good," murmured Baby
Bear. Then they all switched over to Channel 2.

Titles of Students' Extended Essays

<u>1983</u>

Aguilera	Change in the Italian language with specific comparisons between usage of Dante and the corresponding usage in the contemporary Italian standard (Tuscan)
Avison	An outline of speech problems encountered by patients recovering from strokes
Brown	An introductory survey of deaf and dumb communication through signs
Cook	A comparison of the vowel sounds of standard British English and those of Caribbean – particularly Trinidadian – English
Davies	A review of attempts to teach primates to communicate by means of language
Greenwood	An examination of attempts to teach primates communication through language with special reference to the experiment with Koko the gorilla
Hayward	A survey of systems of communication of different animal species
Johnson	A comparison of the speech sounds of standard Dutch and standard British English
Lee	A consideration of animal communication with special reference to von Frisch's experiments with bees
O'Malley	A consideration of ways in which the human body is used to convey meaning, either consciously or unconsciously
Pover	A survey of different systems of communication used by the deaf and dumb.
Simpson	An outline survey of the usual stages by which a child acquires its first language up to the age of five
Smith	Communication between human and animal with particular reference to the experiment of Joseph Beuys
Snook	Animal communications with particular reference to experiments with dolphins

Carter	Voluntary and involuntary human communication outside language.
Cassidy	A comparison between the vowels of RP and Australian English pronunciation.
Clements	An introduction to human communication that takes place beyond the limits of language.
Groves	A survey of the development of writing systems.
Henderson	Communication techniques used in advertising.
Hopkins	A survey of Indo-European language groups.
Hely	Communication through facial expression and hand movement with particular reference to practice in South-Eastern Europe.
Lee	Runes.
Lonsdale	A comparison of the vowels of RP and West Midlands English pronunciation.
Morgan	Change in English based on a comparison between modern English usage and the language of John Donne's poems.
Olszowski	A comparison between the sounds of RP English and Castilian Spanish.
Pope	Rhyming slang.
Powell	A survey of different kinds of language games and play, either for humourous effect or with more serious intent.
Regnart	Non-linguistic and paralinguistic communication through gestures.
Sutherland	An introduction to different varieties of language use in English.
Verdon	A survey of dialect usage in the district of West Morley in Yorkshire

Oxford & Cambridge Schools Examination Board

AO Principles of Language Examination

	Number of Entries	Attempts at Questions												Grades Achieved			
		1	2	3	4	5	6	7	8	9	10	11	12	A	B	C	D/
1983	14	8	8	4	6	6	1	-	4	5	1	10	3	1	7	6	-
1984	16	13	4	6	3	4	9	3	-	-	6	6	10	2	4	7	3

10. Comments on the Course

10.1   Comment by G WILEY, Moderator of the AO examination administered and certificated by the Oxford & Cambridge Schools Examination
Board in connection with the course.

An Examinations Board, however willing it is to play its part in
encouraging innovation, approaches the examining of new courses with
some caution. Are the skills to be tested and the body of knowledge
to which they relate adequately defined and appropriate to the
students? And if they are, how should they be examined?

The overriding aim of what Tony Tinkel proposed was that the
students' own use of language and their sensitivity to the use of
language in general should be advanced. The Open University attempts
something like this and a number of polytechnics and universities
have degrees or part degrees in Linguistics. How far was it possible
to devise something which was relevant and accessible to post '0'
level students?

In the first place, it seemed sensible to have an extended piece of
work, a long essay in which the student could pursue a particular
aspect of language which interested him and which gave him scope to
utilize the knowledge and the skills acquired on the taught course.
That most students would rely on secondary sources did not seem
important.

The examination paper, which we agreed was desirable, was more
difficult. It had, of course, to examine the syllabus, which was
reasonable if ambitious, and, given the breadth of the syllabus, we
had to ensure that the questions on different areas were of more or
less comparable difficulty.

Having followed this pattern for two years, we can say that the
extended essay has worked as well as we hoped it would. The best
candidates have shown evidence of lively interest in some aspect of
language and considerable industry, producing work which would not
disgrace older students committed to more advanced study. There
have, of course, been a number of limited, if worthy, essays.

Similarly, the quality of the examination work has been generally
high. Students have obviously enjoyed mastering phonetic transcription and analysing elements of non-verbal communication, but they
have also come to terms with the linguistic complications of
different modes, of shifts in style and of the variations of
register which we encounter and use.

What is proved, I think, is that all these things can be taught at
quite an advanced level to students aged 16 to 17 and that they can
be enjoyed by them. It is also true, though some might doubt the

relevance of this, that these skills and this knowledge can be sensibly examined. The more difficult question, that of how far the students' own response to and use of language has benefited, remains more difficult to assess.

10.2 Note by J L M TRIM

I have worked together with Anthony Tinkel on the introduction of the concepts and methods of linguistics into sixth-form studies for a number of years since he followed the postgraduate course in linguistics and applied linguistics under my supervision in Cambridge in the 1970s. I have discussed the methods and materials which he has used at all stages though, of course, the responsibility for the decisions taken and the credit for the successful introduction of the course are entirely his.

I have been privileged to give a class on English intonation to his class in two successive years. I found the students alert and committed, responding quickly and easily to the conceptual content as well as the perceptual challenge. I have been glad to see that the students have maintained a high degree of motivation and enjoyment throughout the course and that the AO requirement has proved to be well within their compass. They have responded particularly well to the notion that they are engaged in an investigation of something which is already deeply imbedded in them, though not at a conscious level. It has been a voyage of inner discovery rather than an acquisition of external facts. It has also been interesting to note that the topics which they have elected to write on have in many cases been those which place language in a broader communicative framework, i.e. properties of linguistic systems in relation to other human signalling systems and animal communication systems. This seems to confirm that the narrower language awareness should be regarded in schools as part of a process of communicative awareness which may involve a number of disciplines across the curriculum.

The Oratory experiment now seems to be well-established and to be going on to the stage where the transferability of the syllabus to other schools is investigated. I look forward to the publication of Anthony Tinkel's book with its rich apparatus of self- explanatory exercises but can see no reason why other teachers should not be equally successful in introducing the subject into sixth-form work.

10.3 Comment by M J HAMPSHIRE, student of the course in 1981/2

It was with a mixture of curiosity and trepidation that our class approached the Principles of Language course for the first time. However, as we began to grasp the ideas, the 'guinea pig' feeling was replaced by the interest which invariably stems from a student's realization that he understands something new.

169

It was probably for this reason that one of the elements of the course which generated the most interest was that of phonetic script. A major criticism of the course would have to be the emphasis placed on the learning of phonetic script. Granted it is invaluable in expressing differences of pronunciation on paper, but it assumed the importance of being practically a language in its own right, with at least one question in the examination being concerned with translation into phonetic script. With all due respect, it is not difficult to obtain a good mark on this question, simply by learning a few dozen symbols. Similar criticism must be aimed at the questions on 'signs' which, given an understanding of the concept of arbitrariness, could be answered by someone with no experience of the Principles of Languages course whatsoever.

The above criticisms are largely related to the examination itself which, in fairness, it should be pointed out, copes fairly well with incorporating the multifarious aspects of the course. However, I feel that the course might have benefited from a more detailed examination of the origins of language. Placing more emphasis on such topics as the Great Vowel shift and Grimm's Law would give students a greater idea of the evolution and the foundation of the rules of language, and hence would encourage a greater sensitivity in their own use of language.

This sensitivity is the most important feature of the course, since the students came to achieve a greater awareness of register, of ambiguity, and of the use (and misuse) of language. Effectively this means the students pause to consider that which before they took for granted. To this end the elements of syntax and semantics are among the most important features of the course.

The extended essay in many ways offsets the difficulties of pre-paring a written examination paper, because it gives the student time and space to demonstrate his understanding of the principles of language, while at the same time writing about a subject of interest to him, so that he is not simply exchanging answer for question, but is able also to introduce his own views and experience.

To conclude, I would like to say that in my view the course has proved to be a successful experiment. As the course stands, the main aim - instilling in students a greater sensitivity to the use of language - has been achieved, and, despite one or two criticisms, it has been fairly effectively tailored to enable a valid examination to be set.

A NEW APPROACH TO LANGUAGE STUDY AND LANGUAGE AWARENESS IN A MULTILINGUAL SCHOOL AT NORTH WESTMINSTER COMMUNITY SCHOOL, LONDON

Head: Michael Marland CBE
Head of Languages: Sol Garson
Deputy: Cathy Pomphrey

1. The Background

    1.1 The School
    1.2 Aims of the curriculum
    1.3 Aims of language policy
    1.4 Prerequisites for a radical change of language policy

    2. The New Languages Scheme

    2.1 Mother-tongue provision
    2.2 A new approach to foreign language teaching

    2.2.1 The Language Foundation Course
    2.2.2 Development of grammatical awareness
    2.2.3 Language skills

    2.3   The World Languages Project

    2.3.1 Aims of the project

3. Outcomes

Appendix

A visitor's impressions of a lesson in the World Languages Project

1. Background

1.1 The School

North Westminster Community School was created in 1980 by amalgamating three existing schools to serve a community covering a large part of Marylebone and Paddington and beyond. It is a co-educational, non-selective school, 11 to 18, whose pupils come from a rich and diverse range of cultural backgrounds, ethnic origins, religious beliefs, social and family patterns and mother tongues. A recent count showed some 55 different languages spoken by pupils in the school. Some ten forms (300 pupils) are admitted each year at age 11, of whom 48% do not speak English at home. A high proportion of the intake qualify for remedial courses in English. Movement in and out of the area is higher than usual. The school has to cater for a large number of late entrants. Staffing is not ungenerous and a flexible policy regarding 'setting' of pupils is therefore possible.

1.2 Aims of the curriculum

From the outset the school was determined that the curriculum should reflect the diversity of the community it serves and make a positive contribution to 'exploding the ethno-centricity' which the school prospectus sees as 'the common mould of much of British education'. In the words of the prospectus: 'The curriculum should both learn from the range of cultures....represented in our area, and contribute to an understanding of them. This will mean that....topics, examples and materials studied (should be) truly representative. The curriculum will also have to be flexible, responding appropriately to changes in the composition of the communities. Every facet of the curriculum will thus be affected by our being a community school, some only modestly, but others radically, such as language (including mother tongue teaching)...'

1.3 Aims of language policy

Specifically on the language curriculum the Head of Modern Languages sets out the school's aim as follows:

'Linguists....have to begin to accept that bilingualism (in pupils) is an asset rather than a handicap. The Modern and Foreign Languages Departments of most urban secondary schools have been standing aside from this linguistic wealth, declining to make any attempt to exploit it. ....Our language department felt professionally obliged to take a very close look at its contribution... At the latest count there were over 55 different languages represented amongst our pupils. Such a multi-ethnic, multi-lingual intake is beneficial to a languages department and to all pupils...yet not many linguists have dared to allow this to interfere with the limited scope that their own language specialism and.... training have imposed on them. Our programme avoids this entrenchment by deliberately questioning some traditional educational principles'.

Mr Garson goes on to quote the senior ILEA Languages Inspector, who while stressing the need for experiments to be carefully projected and planned, believes that there is a need to challenge the following traditional, orthodox assumptions:

i.   that 5 and 8 years are required to reach acceptable standards of foreign language acquisition.

ii.   that the period of study of any subject in the curriculum must
      be continuous.
iii. that French is the language that 9 out of 10 British children
      will eventually need.
iv.   that confusion will arise from the study of the early stages
      of several languages ('The Dutch I have met do not mix their
      German, French and English').
v.   that our vast force of French teachers is capable of teaching
      only the language it has graduated or is certificated in
      (from: ILEA responses to Current Modern Language Issues,
      Modern Language Bulletin, Summer 1982).

The NWCS programme, Mr Garson stresses, 'is not a panacea'. 'Every
school is different and may well have different needs... the NWCS
experiment is only a beginning...variations and improvements...and
even more radical programmes may be taken up by schools trying to
reflect diverse intakes and exploit their own specialisms.'

1.4   Prerequisites for a radical change of language policy

If the school was to depart from a monolingual, Euro-centric language programme, Mr Garson stresses, more was needed than merely the
approval of the Head of the school and acceptance by all language
teachers.... It required the following:

i.   Total cooperation from the Director of Curriculum and the
      timetabler
ii.   Advice from and exchange of ideas with the English as a Second
      Language Department
iii. The injection of non-European literature into the library
iv.   The inclusion of clearly stated objectives in the multi-ethnic
      policy of the school
v.   The assistance of non-language specialists in passing informa-
      tion and encouraging pride in and respect for mother tongues
      and their continued study
vi.   The involvement of representatives from the community
vii. Advice and assistance from the school's monitoring and evalua-
      tion committee
viii. Ratification by the school governing body of the language
      policy

'Only if all the above accepted collective responsibility could the
inspectorate give the go-ahead to a programme as a serious educational proposition.'

2.   The New Languages Scheme

The New Languages Scheme initiated in September 1980 had three
elements:

i.   A policy for the teaching of ethnic minority mother tongues.

ii.   A new approach to the teaching of foreign languages.

iii.   A 'world languages project' as part of an 'awareness of lan-
       guages' programme.

2.1   Mother tongue provision

The school catchment area is, in the Head's words, ' a veritable
Tower of Babel'. Among the 55 languages represented in the pupil
population the most common are: Spanish and Portuguese, followed by
Greek, Italian and Serbo-Croat. Other mother tongues strongly repre-
sented are: Arabic, French, Cantonese, Bengali, Turkish, Yoruba and
Farsee.

The school's attitude towards mother-tongue provision is governed by
the belief that racism shows itself in a school's whole approach to
non-standard dialects and accents, and to the mother tongues of
minorities. It can also be seen in failure to acknowledge the needs
of bilingual pupils. There is increasing evidence that reinforcing
competence in the mother tongue assists the learning of English and
fostering of learning in general and in the development of communicative skills. The school's policy is therefore to try to give all
its bilingual pupils access to continued study of their mother
tongue. The provision of mother-tongue teaching is of three kinds:

i.   self-financing outside groups use the school premises outside
       school hours, providing their own teachers and making the
       classes available to pupils from the school. In this way
       Spanish and Portuguese are offered by the education depart-
       ments of the Spanish and Portuguese consulates and Arabic and
       Bengali by cultural bodies and parent associations.

ii.   the school directly employs language teachers under the terms
       of the Urban Aid grant. Teachers of Cantonese, Bengali and
       standard Arabic (for Moroccan children) give 4 sessions each
       outside school hours, ranging from basic literacy to advanced
       work for public examinations.

iii.   for pupils whose needs are not catered for under i. and ii.
       above the school language department offers an advisory
       service, putting pupils in touch with outside classes and
       arranging individual tuition by liaising with embassies and
       using help offered by members of the public. Guidance is also
       given on mother-tongue examinations, papers are set and
       correction is arranged.

In addition there is, in the 'World Languages Project' (see below),
a unit on mother-tongue maintenance and the Linguistic Minorities
Project video (filmed with NWCS pupils) is used as part of the
induction programme for new intakes.

Furthermore teachers of the mother tongues are involved in con-

174

tinuing discussions and interchange of ideas and in the elaboration
of schemes and materials for the teaching of languages.

For this purpose a member of the modern languages team is appointed
specially to liaise with mother-tongue teachers. This is regarded as
essential if the work is to be done properly and to have status with
the community and with outside groups whose support is needed.

2.2 A new approach to foreign language teaching

In an early discussion paper on foreign language policy the Head saw
the problem in this way:

'The major cultural and general educational arguments for the teaching of languages seem hardly to be met if there is no access to
non-European languages. Indeed the traditional concern with the
language of one of our nearest neighbours, a country which by global
comparisons is very similar to ours, could be seen as a major contribution to the existing ethno-centricity of British education...
Can we call a person educated for the 'global village' of today if
he or she has no idea at all of at least one non-European language?
In the ILEA, the Inspectorate and teachers have worked hard to break
out of the ethno-centricity of previous curriculum work by such
developments as the World History Project and integrated studies
packs. In languages the related response is surely to include some
work with a non-European language.'

But how was this to be done? The Head's initial proposal was to
introduce all pupils to four languages in their first two years in
the school, one of which would be Arabic, the others Spanish, German
and French.

After some discussion it was decided to limit the languages offered
in the 'Language Foundation Course' in the first two years to the
three European languages and to provide the 'non-European' language
experience in a quite new way, through the 'World Languages Project'
(see 2.3 below).

In the early discussions which led to this plan a key item was a
paper by the Head which set out four possible options:

Modern language provision in the school might be planned on the
following models:

i.   monolithic
      On this model a single compulsory language would be studied
      for 3 years, followed by optional courses; the commonest model
      nationally.
ii.   dual
      Two languages would be offered from the start, pupils nomin-

ally having a choice, half of the intake doing one, half the other. It is a variant of i. above. The paper cites examples at Woodberry Down School (since discontinued) and Mayfield School.

iii. multi-introductions
      Here three or four successive languages are introduced, each for (say) a half-year in the first two years, followed by concentration on a chosen language or languages. The paper cites the example of Camden School.

iv.   general course (with restricted language element) This model offers a general course, containing a small language component, mainly covering 'European Studies' which for some sets only would develop into language study proper, other pupils continuing with non-language courses.

After weighing the advantages and disadvantages of the four models the paper finds the 'multi-language' approach most convincing and most likely to serve the school aims for foreign language study which are seen as:

i.   understanding the functions of language.
ii.   helping pupils to appreciate similarities and differences between languages
iii. developing sympathetic appreciation of different cultures
iv.   enjoyment of songs, poetry, fiction, theatre, myth and humour of other cultures
v.   acquisition of useful skills for adult purposes in leisure and business or further study
vi.   paving the way for adult study of languages even when the school course does not take the pupil very far
vii. enhancing powers of precise listening
viii. giving opportunities for memory training as an essential ingredient of language learning
ix.   giving experience of a kind of learning that is unique in the curriculum

In addition the paper finds the 'multi-language' approach especially suited to the conditions at NWCS. It offers pupils and parents genuine choice after the initial introduction to several languages; late entry pupils can be more easily assimilated; a diverse team of teachers can be maintained, thus facilitating the range of languages offered later in the school course; the mix of language provision in the school can more flexibly be adjusted to changing circumstances than in the monolithic approach.

The existence in the school of a team of 15 full time specialists and three assistants, capable of teaching a wide range of languages, including French, German, Italian and Arabic with other languages at less advanced levels, obviously lent itself to the 'multi-language' approach.

2.2.1   The Language Foundation Course

The three languages chosen for the Language Foundation Course which
occupies the first two years for all pupils, were Spanish, French
and German.   These languages are taught, each for one term, the
process being repeated in the second year. (German is always taken
after the other two for reasons discussed below.)

At the end of each term two weeks are set aside for a unit of the
World Languages Project (see below) which seeks to break out of the
traditional mould and to awaken curiosity about languages and about
language itself. Although the successive language units taught each
term are entities in themselves, the courses are planned with a progressive linear thread linking the content of them all. The class is
taught throughout the year by the same teacher.   Although the teacher will probably be a specialist in only two of the languages concerned, the presentation of the third language is facilitated by
in-service training and team-teaching.

The maximum profit is drawn from comparisons between the languages,
as their patterns are explored.

Each language is given 3 lessons per week on the timetable (lessons
of 55 minutes length).

From year 3 onwards pupils concentrate on the language(s) of their
choice and prepare for the examinations of the Institute of
Linguists, and for CSE and GCE. The allocation of 3 lessons (of 55
minutes) continues in years 4 and 5. Some pupils have the opportunity to take a second or a third foreign language, and/or take
beginners' courses in Italian or Arabic.

In the 6th Form the time allocation is increased to 5 lessons per
week. Beginners and refresher courses in all the languages are
available as well as 'A' level courses.

The timetabled programme is complemented by very successful visits
and exchanges abroad as well as cultural visits related to the
courses and texts studied.

2.2.2   Development of grammatical awareness

An important aim of the course is to build up awareness of the basic
grammatical concepts through study of the contrasts between the languages studied. It had earlier been observed that some pupils who
had studied a single language for 5 years were still confused about
basic concepts such as gender and verb changes. The teachers at
North Westminster have been impressed by their pupils' ability to
make insightful contrasts between their languages as the course has
developed.

177

French, Spanish and German invite such comparisons, both with each other and with English. The discovery and discussion of grammatical differences, such as the absence of the subject pronoun in Spanish and the word order rules in German, provided that they are not so numerous or so strange as to confuse and overwhelm the pupil whose grasp is still insecure, can form a useful preparation for further language learning, by building confidence and expectations as to what learning may entail.

The accumulation of contrasts and conflicting patterns should, however, be carefully structured. For example, German is best brought in in the third term (and the sixth) since, though initially much of the vocabulary is cognate with English, grammatical aspects such as the third gender, the different plural endings and the case system can be more easily accepted by pupils who have already met two genders and plural endings of less complexity in Spanish and French.

As the class is taught for a year by the same teacher such a gradual and structured exploration of grammatical patterns becomes possible, and pupils understanding can be more sensitively monitored.

2.2.3 Language skills

Besides aiming to give pupils growing awareness of grammatical concepts on which later learning can build, the course also aims to help pupils to acquire useful skills in _using_ their languages. The degree of emphasis on each of the four skills of Speaking, Listening, Reading and Writing is not the same in all languages. In the early stages of French it is found best to concentrate on oral and listening skills, leaving writing until later, in order not to interfere with the acquisition of a good pronunciation. The difficulties of writing French can discourage pupils if this skill is overemphasised at the beginning. In Spanish and German it is possible to include more reading and writing at an earlier stage than with French. However the differences are not great. Precise listening to languages much of whose vocabulary is not very different from English, can build pupils' confidence. The small differences in writing (capital letters for nouns, punctuation in Spanish, accents in French and Spanish, with their different significance in the two languages) can sensitise pupils to the precision needed in writing foreign languages and prepare the way for exploring different alphabets and scripts in the non-European languages.

2.3 The World Languages Project

We have noted above that it had originally been proposed that, in order to avoid giving the impression that only European languages are important enough to study in school, or that all the world's languages work in similar ways to French etc. a non-European language (Arabic was mentioned) should be one of the languages learnt in the first two years in the Foundation Course. This solution was rejected because it was felt that to make Arabic one of the main languages in the Foundation Course would pose too much of a challenge. A number of complex skills and concepts would have to be learned very quickly if pupils were to progress at roughly the same rate as in the other languages. For instance the kind of writing skills required in Arabic would be very different from those needed for French, German or Spanish. The introduction of Arabic would break the continuity of approach and the possibility for across-language comparisons at the level of pupils in their first two years. This would produce a more 'bitty' foundation course. A similar argument would suggest that e.g. Russian would be less suitable as a main language in the first two years. A strong argument against Arabic (or Russian) also, is that the same teacher could not teach the complete range of main languages offered and this would mean that opportunities for a progressive and closely monitored cross-language exploration would be lost.

Rather than introduce a non-European language as a main study in the Language Foundation Course, it was decided to adopt the more radical and imaginative solution of planning a new course, called the 'World Languages Project'. This would take the form of six specially planned units, each lasting 2 weeks, to be taught at the end of each term in years one and two, by the same teacher who had taught the main languages to the class.

These short units include the following elements:

the development of speech
the history of writing
language families (language variety within the UK and across the world language map)
language borrowing
language invention and change
the Hebrew and Russian alphabets
the Arabic language
Bahasa Indonesia
Bengali
Chinese

2.3.1 Aims of the project

The World Languages Project is a deliberate attempt to break down linguistic and cultural intolerance which thrives on lack of knowledge and insecurity.

The main aim is to open pupils' minds and encourage them to be curious and receptive to new sounds, speech patterns, alphabets and through them the ways of life which languages reflect. The intention is to give pupils practice in facing new ways of expressing ideas, and the confidence to make comparisons across languages. Pupils are encouraged to bring their own linguistic experiences to contribute to the discussion.

In this discussion all pupils start equal. Linguistic diversity in the group becomes a positive advantage, not a problem to be regretted. The universals of human language (such as the everyday miracle of language acquisition by the baby in the home, and the growth of dialogue between parent and baby in the early years) become threads in the discussion that draw pupils together, and can also draw parents usefully into the work, through projects requiring parents to act as linguistic informants. The work can also most usefully involve other teachers (e.g. of Art and Drama, of Biology and History) through the wealth of projects that are suggested by the various units.

It had originally been planned that the Foundation Course, including the World Languages Project, should end with year 2, after which pupils would concentrate on one foreign language (some being allowed to start a second). It is a tribute to the success of the experiment that the school has decided to make available an additional lesson in the third year for all pupils studying one foreign language, to be devoted to 'awareness of language'. The emphasis in this lesson will be different from that of the WLP units in the first two years, with stress on developing pupils' general linguistic maturity. Three units are planned to introduce this language awareness course, building on the WLP work. These are:

i.   Study of the writing systems of the world, and the history of writing.
ii.   Bengali language and culture
iii. A unit based on a statistical survey of the mother-tongues represented at North Westminster School, led by a Maths teacher. The study will include work on numeracy and literacy and social implications.

Other units planned for the third year include:

'Uses of Bilingualism at North Westminster'
Extension of the first year work done on Arabic (cultural and literacy aspects)
Study of Creole
'Portuguese - a migrant nation'

It is significant that this extension of the work into the third year has the strong support of the Head, himself an English specialist and author of 'Language Across the Curriculum', a widely read symposium developing some of the main themes of the Bullock Report.

3. Assessment

It will be clear that this pioneering approach to the language curriculum in a school serving an urban area of great ethnic and linguistic diversity, is in its infancy. Like the school, it has clear objectives and considerable courage and tenacity. But like the school it must feel its way forward to some extent by trial and error, remaining flexible and learning by 'action research' rather than by argument. The pupils who have enjoyed the new course are only in their fourth year. Their performance in both their foreign language and in English (and in mother tongues other than English) will be carefully monitored as the scheme progresses.

Certainly all who are concerned with the language education of children in the inner city will follow this imaginative experiment with sympathy and interest.

(E W Hawkins)

Appendix

A Language Awareness lesson at NWCS - a visitor's impression
December 1983

The 20 twelve-year olds were buzzing quietly while the register was
called. There were only 20 because last night was the school play
and some had leave to come in after the break. I passed a paper to
my neighbour, a girl from Armenia, and asked her to write down for
me the countries of origin of the pupils present. This was her list
(some of her spellings amended): Bulgaria, Italy, Vietnam, Lebanon,
Yemen, Egypt, Bangladesh, Portugal, North Africa, Iran, Scotland,
England.

The lesson began briskly. The young lady teacher had no doubt whatever how things were going to go, yet she never raised her voice,
with its attractive slight Belfast accent, and her smile won the
most wary to her side. She referred to an earlier discussion about
'language families'. What was the evidence that languages belonged
to families? Several pupils gave instances from counting in the
Indo-European family.

Why did some languages spread far away from the places where they
were first used? Why had English spread so far? How far?

Deftly, without losing the thread, the teacher produced and unfolded
a large map of the world which she blue-tacked to the blackboard
behind her. A chair was placed in front of the board and volunteers
were invited to come out and find countries where English is
spoken.

So directly to the main theme planned for the lesson: another great
world language, Arabic. Where is Arabic spoken?

Pupils in the class who spoke Arabic came out in turn, got up on the
chair and found their own country of origin on the map. So, one by
one, the Lebanon, the Yemen, Iran and Algeria were located. Was
Arabic spoken in countries so far apart? What about the countries in
between? How many can you count? Let's look at it more closely.

Here the teacher produced a lesson hand-out ready cyclostyled
showing in outline the Mediterranean and the Middle East and listing
18 Arabic speaking countries. Later in the lesson pupils would work
on the hand-out.

Before we do that, can anybody tell us why Arabic spread so widely?
Was it like the spread of English, following trade and colonisation?

The teacher mentioned the use of Arabic in Muslim prayers. She used
the word 'liturgical' language and asked the class to remember the
word. Some of the pupils looked unimpressed.

When did Arabic spread so widely? The date 622 AD was written on the board. The date of Mohammed's flight from Mecca to Medina.

So Muslims got a new calendar, different from the Christian calendar. Who else uses a different calendar from the Christian one? The Jews. And who else? Of course the Chinese.

But back to our map of the Arabic language. Do Arabic speakers in all these 18 countries all speak the same form of Arabic?

Let's count to ten in Arabic. (This had been learnt in a previous lesson and many of the pupils could remember most of it.) Do all our Arabic-speaking pupils agree? No! The pupil from the Lebanon and the one from Algeria both disagreed with the teacher, but for different reasons. The pupil from the Yemen thought the teacher's Arabic numbers were OK. The teacher asked the class to compare the distance from Belfast to London. From her own experience she gave examples of differences between her own idiom, and accent, and London 'standard' forms.

Was it to be expected that over the much greater distances the forms of Arabic would differ? Again volunteers came out and identified on the map the countries referred to.

Let's go on with Arabic. When you come to a strange country what is the first thing you might want to say? 'Hello!'. Practise this in Arabic. But first an interesting contrast with English. A different address and reply for girls and boys. Again the Arabic speakers volunteered their own experience and their versions.

In many of the Arabic-speaking countries a second language was also commonly used. Examples? Volunteers mentioned French and Spanish. Why was this? The spread of these languages. Why?

Now what about the written form of Arabic. Was this different in different countries? The teacher said the written form of Arabic was spread by the Koran and the Muslim prayers. (Again the word 'liturgical' was insisted on.) At this point there was a diversion. A pupil who had been given an individual project to work on in a previous lesson wished to report. He had consulted his parents and found out why certain parts of his country of origin, the Yemen, are densely populated and others desert. He read his report carefully and it was briefly discussed.

Time was running on and now the pupils had to turn to the written task planned for the lesson. They were asked to fill in the prepared outline on the hand-out.

The discussion had been two-way, purposeful. Despite the distraction of a lot of noise from heavy traffic outside the windows which sometimes made it hard to hear the teacher or the pupils, and the pre-sence of several pupils with learning problems who might have been capable of upsetting a less professionally equipped teacher's plans, the lesson had proceeded throughout with businesslike concentration on the questions that the teacher had planned to raise with the class.

Her winning smile, her obvious rapport with the pupils and their respect for her, and her well-prepared materials, all made for an interesting and thought-provoking lesson. A marked feature was the way in which, at each stage in the discussion, the multi-lingual nature of the class, far from being a 'problem' to be overcome, was turned into an enrichment giving force and example, at the level that pupils could readily seize, to each step in the exploration. It was more like a seminar with 12 year olds taking part on level terms, than the conventional lesson.

But it was time to move next door, where a similar group of pupils, with an equally gifted teacher (like the first, a conventionally trained modern linguist who had acquired a knowledge of non-European languages partly with the help of pupils in the school) was engaged in a discussion of 'writing'. With the help of a hand-out she was exploring logographic systems, with special reference to Chinese, which the pupils were practising writing, using felt-tip pens in various colours.

DEVELOPING AWARENESS OF LANGUAGE THROUGH DIRECTED ACTIVITIES RELATED TO TEXT AT THE PRIORY SCHOOL, BARNSLEY

Head: Mr D.J. Every
Head of English: Mr Roger Beswick
Deputy Head: Mrs Jean Rogers
Head of Languages: Mr Neil Woodward

1. The School

2. Cross-curricular language policy since 1978

3. Developing Awareness of Language Through Directed Activities Related to Text

    3.1   The DARTS Course
    3.2   Staffing
    3.3   Aims of the course
    3.4   Evaluation
    3.5   Future developments

1. The School

Priory School is a co-educational non-selective 11-16 Comprehensive School drawing its intake from a Social Priority Area in Barnsley. In direct contrast to the pupils from multi-ethnic backgrounds at North Westminster, pupils at Priory are drawn from a close-knit South Yorkshire mining and industrial community. The mother tongue of all but one per cent of pupils is the regional variety of English.

Provision for language teaching is made by the English Faculty and the Faculty of World Studies which offers courses in French and German, French being taught to all first, second and third years, and German to the top set (60 pupils) in the second year, and to the top two sets (120 pupils) in the third year. After the third year German and French are available as options.

2. Cross-curricular language policy since 1978

The language policy which has evolved since 1978 is designed to meet the specific needs of pupils who bring to school a natural competence and confidence in spoken English, but for whom the written language poses serious problems. Over fifty per cent of eleven-year old pupils have a Reading Age a year below their chronological age on entry. It is for this reason that since 1978 the English department has had the collaboration of teachers across the curriculum in establishing a reading programme designed firstly, to encourage pupils' voluntary reading, and secondly, to ensure that every pupil's reading is closely monitored in a number of different ways.

The programme was made possible initially through a substantial increase in the fiction resources available, as recommended in Bullock. One thousand new books were purchased – to cater for the reading interests, needs, and abilities of first and second year pupils with reading ages from 6½ years to 13½ years. The books purchased included graded and simplified readers, as well as standard fiction; all were graded to match ten reading levels. Cross-curricular involvement was ensured by timetabling the reading programme for extended 'form' periods, and maintained through regular meetings of the teachers involved. From the start, the emphasis in the programme was on comprehension and on the development of a 'reading relationship' with each pupil in the class.

In addition, pupil progress was monitored, first through reading tests given on entry, secondly, through informal teacher-pupil interviews in which the current book, and others were discussed, and thirdly, through the pupils' own reading record – a notebook containing notes/comments on all books read.

Books were taken home, and parents were involved. They were also invited to make comments in the pupils' reading records.

It was from this initial programme that the school's current programme for developing Language Awareness through Directed Reading evolved. A further impetus for such a programme was provided by the school's involvement in the School's Council Project, Reading For Learning in the Secondary School.[1]

This involvement, initiated originally by the Deputy Head and implemented by the Head of English with the support of the Head and the Local Authority, was developed through a school-based in-service course attended by over 90% of the staff.

The outcome was two-fold:

first, an increased recognition by teachers across the curriculum of the demands made on pupils by written language, and an increased confidence in helping pupils to meet these demands in the subject areas, and secondly, an agreement to extend the reading programme to include, for all first and second year pupils, a structured course in directed reading with small group discussion. This is the course which currently provides a foundation for the development of awareness of language in English, foreign languages, and the subject areas.

186

3. Developing Awareness of Language Through Directed Activities Related to Text

3.1 The DARTS course[2]

The course involves a double period per week for all first years and a single period for all second year pupils. Classes are mixed-ability.

3.2 Staffing

The team responsible for the course consists of teachers drawn from across the curriculum, led by the Head of English. Materials for the course, originally designed by the Head of English, are discussed then tried out and evaluated by the team, with subsequent modification and supplementation.

There are regular meetings of the team, and school-based in-service training is provided for new recruits to the team.

3.3 Aims of course

The aims of the course are:

i. to develop awareness of written language varieties across the curriculum

ii. to develop awareness of the features and organisation of different types of text across the curriculum

iii. to develop confidence in studying and learning from the different types of text, and in producing them

iv. to develop awareness of the role of discussion in learning.

The specific objectives of each lesson are:

i. to introduce a text of a particular type, e.g. narrative, scientific process, physical structure, historical event or situation, theory etc.

ii. in class discussion to consider the place of the text in the curriculum, the distinctive nature of the text and the distinct types of information or linguistic features which can be found in the text

iii. to involve pupils in actively searching for information or linguistic features through an appropriate reading activity

iv. to involve pupils in collaboration and discussion in pairs, and subsequently in larger groups as they search for information

187

v. to provide pupils with models of different ways of summarising information where appropriate

vi. to involve pupils in a plenary session where the task and text are evaluated.

3.4 Evaluation

Careful long term planning and materials preparation ensures that objectives are not difficult to meet. The question of interest to the Head of English and his colleagues is, what is the value of the course?

Objective evaluation of the course using standard measures of Reading and Comprehension undertaken both within the school, and by the Reading for Learning evaluator Dr Roy Fawcett, has provided evidence of a dramatic improvement in reading each year. 1983 results are the best ever, with an average gain in Reading Age of one year eight months in a twelve month period, with the full gain of pupils who reached the ceiling in tests not being reflected in the average gain.

Nonetheless, improvement in ability to read and comprehend was only one of the aims of the course. Subjective teacher evaluation of the course as a whole reflects a wider range of concerns, and rewards. Typical of the comments of team members in the Autumn term 1983 were:

i. those expressing some disquiet about using prepared materials: e.g. "Presentation of some pieces e.g. diagrams, flow charts etc. was very poor", "Whilst the pupils who were well motivated towards learning, derived interest from all the activities, other pupils were difficult to please in many of the exercises."

ii. those which expressed an appreciation of working with a wide variety of texts: "From a teaching point of view it was exciting to find such a wide variety of exercises drawn from subject disciplines across the curriculum – the differences in the nature of the tasks ... prevented predictability and the learning of an expected response."

iii. those which showed a recognition of the need for the activities to be extended into the subject areas and pupil's own study: "I feel pupils would benefit more from their efforts in a specific subject area, rather than in form time". "The value of the Darts activities cannot be debated but there is a danger of interpreting them as segregated in nature, and I imagine their development to include activity beyond the form period into pupils' own time."

Nonetheless, for all teachers there was a recognition of <u>the value</u> <u>of the activities in developing pupil confidence, and in extending</u> <u>their</u> (and their teachers') <u>horizons.</u>

"I discovered the texts were interesting. They encouraged involvement both on an individual and group basis. [The activities] encouraged discovery, a 'need to know' - and allowed success to be proportioned equally towards the less able and through to those pupils requiring stimulation of a higher degree. Both could be challenged in group work". Furthermore the course "encouraged pupils to utilize directed reading toward the pursuit of knowledge in other aspects of their academic work."
"Much more information is retained using these methods."
"I find Darts very successful, indeed, both as a 'Form Period' (a worthwhile one) and as a preparation for work in pairs/small groups in language. ... Through discussion the pupils make the text their own."
"Broadens horizons of non-linguistic teacher."
"Darts ultimately made the pupils far more <u>aware</u> than had been hoped for previously."

3.5 Future Developments

The Darts programme is clearly well established in Priory and its value widely recognized. For the Head of English and the Head of Languages it has provided a solid foundation for the development of a more comprehensive Language Awareness programme. Experiments currently being undertaken in both departments are aimed at developing sensitivity to grammatical structure, particularly of the sentence. It is an interesting reflection that in this school, the unit of language focused on first, was the text; if it develops from that point, as it appears to be doing, to a conscious analysis of the sentence, the clause, the word and the word group it may well offer a model for studying language which sequentially, and developmentally, is radically different from the traditional one.

(F I Davies)

Footnotes

(1) Reading for Learning in the Secondary School based at Nottingham University from 1978-81, directed by Eric Lunzer and Keith Gardner.

(2) A comprehensive account of DARTS, including some developed at Priory School is available in:
LUNZER, E A and Gardner K (1983). <u>Learning from the written word</u>. Oliver and Boyd for the Schools Council.
DAVIES, F and Greene T (1983). <u>Reading for learning in the sciences</u>. Oliver and Boyd for the Schools Council.

DEVELOPING LANGUAGE AWARENESS IN HAMBROUGH MIDDLE SCHOOL, SOUTHALL

Headmistress: Mrs B Frost

1. General information about the school

2. Organisation of the school

3. Language Awareness

   Three projects

   3.4   Communication   (8-9 year olds)
   3.5   Advertising   (9-10 year olds)
   3.6   Reading   (11-12 year olds)

4. Outcomes

   4.1   Criteria
   4.2   Advertising project
   4.3   Communication project
   4.4   Reading project

1. General information about the school

1.1   Hambrough First & Middle School was opened in September 1981 as a new, purpose-built Community School located in the centre of Southall. It had been built in response to the enormous need for new schools in Southall following the London Borough of Ealing's decision to discontinue bussing of Southall children to schools in other parts of the borough.

1.2   Hambrough has a Nursery with 120 places for children from 3-4½ years old. The First School has 155 children aged 4½-7 years old with 196 children in the Middle school aged 8-12 years old. The school is open-plan throughout. The children are all drawn from the local area which is a thriving tightly-knit community, the majority of its inhabitants having originated from the Indian sub-continent. While the vast majority of the Middle School children (virtually 100 per cent) are bilingual in Punjabi and English (with some Hindi and Urdu) English is not normally the first language. Almost all of the children in the Middle School were born in England with very few children arriving as recent immigrants.

2.   Organisation of the school

2.1   The 12 Middle School staff tend to stay within the same year group and have overall responsibility for a class in addition to some specialist teaching e.g. PE, Art. Classes are, therefore, generally organised in year groups except for 3 classes where second and third year children are grouped together. These classes, therefore, have very mixed ages, abilities and language levels.

2.2   While English is the medium of instruction, the use of the children's mother-tongue is extensive in the Nursery where support is given by bilingual teachers. In the Reception Class of the First School there are 2 bilingual teachers who foster mother-tongue maintenance by telling stories, rhymes and songs in Punjabi and Hindi once a week. More recently, the Head has introduced voluntary literacy classes in Punjabi, Hindi and Urdu throughout the Middle school. These were initiated in response to parents' requests and are extremely well-attended.

2.3   Language work throughout the school is seen by the staff as central to the educational and social needs of their bilingual pupils. The children's ability in their mother-tongue is adequate but by no means comparable with the range of an English native speaker of an equivalent age and social class. Therefore, there is clearly a need for large-scale support for both the school and community languages. This is especially true of English since such development is entirely concerned with learning a second rather than a foreign language. English, in other words, is a necessary tool for all school-based learning and many out-of-school activities.

3.   Language Awareness

3.1   There has been no overt policy on developing language awareness as a discrete item on the school's timetable, since this was not considered appropriate to primary school methodology. In February 1982, however, a project to develop language awareness was initiated by a team of three lecturers from Ealing College of Higher Education (ECHE) in response to the work of the NCLE.

3.2   Initially the ECHE staff worked with teachers on an individual basis on projects whose purpose was not specifically to develop an awareness of language per se, but which aimed at developing some of the language skills which arise naturally out of content areas. This included, for example, subject-specific vocabulary in a topic on 'The Senses' for 2nd year pupils, and paragraph writing in Geography for 4th year pupils. Over the next three terms the work developed focused more centrally on the projects described in this account, which were specifically aimed at raising the children's language awareness. This work was carried out mainly by one member of the ECHE team in collaboration with Hambrough staff.

191

3.3   There were three projects:
      Communication for 1st year pupils   8- 9 year old
      Advertising   for 2nd year pupils   9-10 year old
      Reading   for 4th year pupils   11-12 year old

The projects provided teaching material from 6-12 hours each. The teachers either fitted the work into their usual "topic" slot (about 1 - 2 hours per week) or taught the material continuously over 3 afternoons. The overall aims of these projects were:

1. To start the children thinking about language, what it is for, and how it works; specifically non-verbal communication, uses of language in advertising, the uses of reading.

2. To improve the children's linguistic competence by developing appropriate language and learning skills.

3. To encourage the children to co-operate on collaborative learning tasks.

4. To teach children how to work independently.

3.4   Communication

ECHE produced materials based on "Introduction to Language" by APLIN T.R.W. et al. (Hodder & Stoughton 1981).

This was an experiment in making accessible to nine-year-olds a Secondary School course in Language Awareness by simplifying its content and adding more varied language activities. It was taught for 1¼ hours per week over 6 weeks by ECHE staff.

The aims of these materials were:

1. To develop in children an awareness of the variety in form and purpose of verbal and non-verbal communication.

2. To develop a range of communication skills so that the children's meanings become more explicit, i.e. by developing mime, design, speaking and writing skills in group and pair work.

COMMUNICATION

CLASSROOM ACTIVITIES	CLASSROOM ORGANISATION & RESOURCES	CHILDREN'S LANGUAGE DEVELOPMENT
A **ANIMAL COMMUNICATION**		
1. Introduction of topic, discussion of pets and animals, identifying how they communicate without words e.g. tail wagging, barking	T & Class	General discussion skills involving giving examples, giving reasons, speculating. Vocabulary development e.g. purr, squawk, hiss
2. Discussion of pictures of animals to demonstrate visual signs of communication	T & Class pictures	
3. Matching pictures of animals to written descriptions of ways of communication shown	Pairwork & Worksheet	Reading skills, especially skimming to develop speed initially, followed by closer reading for detail
4. Matching animal sounds on tape with pictures of animals: 5 animals given and children select appropriate answer, then children complete further 5 individually	T & Class individual & worksheet (possibility of individualised learning with listening corner and earphones)	Learning to listen carefully, lexis of animals sounds reinforced in ensuing discussion
5. Identifying purpose of animal communication e.g. to show fear	Individual/Pairwork & Worksheet	Reading and writing animal names and sounds for practising language function of expressing purpose eg. a lion roars to show it is hungry. Writing skills using vocabulary learned so far. Study skills involving filling in a chart
6. Children write/or mime a description of an animal and the way it communicates. Another child guesses the animal	Pairwork	Writing skills involving description using language above. Listening and reading for detail

CLASSROOM ACTIVITIES	CLASSROOM ORGANISATION & RESOURCES	CHILDREN'S LANGUAGE DEVELOPMENT
B NON-VERBAL COMMUNICATION		
7. Discussion of different types of non-verbal communication including facial expressions, gestures and other body language	T & Class & pictures	Lexis of body language and language to express e.g. shrug shoulders, frown, furious, embarrassed.
8. Experimentation with body language in drama lesson. Child mimes and partner guesses intention	Pair work	Asking questions, correcting, suggesting, practice in lexis above
9. Matching game using body language, speech intentions, and purpose e.g. we wave to say hello "Hello Jasbir" yellow card blue card green card	Groups of 3 children sort 15 colour coded codes into sets of 3 to form a sentence	Reading instructions of game, reading for detail language for working together – suggesting, correcting, monitoring, agreeing, disagreeing.
10. Using pictures to stimulate discussion on possible meanings in terms of body language.	T & Class Pictures on Overhead Projector	Discussing involving giving opinions, justifying, hypothesising.
11. Mapping similar sets of items already practised in Activity 9	Individual Worksheet	Consolidation of reading for detail practised with peers in matching game (i.e. preparation for individual reading task)

	CLASSROOM ACTIVITIES	CLASSROOM ORGANISATION & RESOURCES	CHILDREN'S LANGUAGE DEVELOPMENT
C	SIGNS & SYMBOLS		
12.	Describing different traffic signs and identifying their purpose. Discussing design features e.g. use of colour, shapes	T & Class Pictures of traffic signs	Lexis of traffic signs and purposes, e.g. halt, give way, use of modals for expressing obligation e.g. you must, ought, have to, should
13.	Recognising other kinds of signs and symbols e.g. consumer goods, travel signs	T & Class & pictures of signs and symbols	Vocabulary development e.g. information desk, lost property
14.	Matching signs & symbols with written description	Individual/Pairwork & worksheet	Reading for detail, involving lexis above
15.	Children bring in own examples and partner guesses product or sign from description	Pairwork	Describing colour, shape, etc. Listening for detail
16.	Child designs traffic signs and symbols for other children to guess	P & P, P & group, or P & whole class, Pictures on black- board, paper, overhead projector	Reinforcement of skills in activities 12 and 13. Discussion involving predicting, justifying, suggesting, giving opinions
17.	Using and designing secret codes.	Individual code wheels	Writing, particularly spelling, study skills involving using a key
18.	Interpreting morse code NB sending an actual message in morse code would be much better and develop listening skills very effectively.	Individual worksheet & written version	Reading and interpreting a key

3.5   Advertising

Materials planned, written and taught collaboratively by Hambrough and ECHE. The Hambrough materials on "TV & Radio Advertising" specifically focus on listening skills while developing mathematical concepts and encouraging creative activities. The section on "Printed Adverts" was then produced in direct response to the teacher's request for help with developing the children's reading and writing skills. These materials were graded in reading difficulty to facilitate group-work in this mixed-ability class.

The aims of this topic were:

1. To develop in children a sense of the purpose and means of advertising.

2. To enable children to describe and begin analysing features of advertising language.

3. To teach children to manipulate linguistic and non-linguistic features of advertisements to produce their own work.

4. To improve children's skill in listening for detail and reading, especially scanning.

ADVERTISING

CLASSROOM ACTIVITIES	CLASSROOM ORGANISATION & RESOURCES	CHILDREN'S LANGUAGE DEVELOPMENT
A	TV & RADIO ADVERTS: how do they work? What techniques do they use?		
1.	Making lists of type of adverts seen or heard	Pairwork following class discussion	Vocabulary development eg leaflet, poster, brochure
2.	Sorting videoed TV adverts by type of produce eg DIY, travel, food: timing and totalling the length of adverts	Pairwork – chart on worksheet	Language for classifying eg a kind of ..., it belongs to ... Listening for detail, study skills including reading and completing a chart, practice in use of stopwatch and concept of time
3.	Identifying techniques used in same set of TV ads, eg humour, a song, idea of luxury	Pairwork and checklist	Giving opinions, suggesting etc., listening for detail, reading and completing a checklist including scanning, vocabulary development eg slogan
4.	Classifying TV ads using criteria above	Pairwork and chart	Information transfer from checklist table
5.	Analysing radio ads for imagery	Pairwork and worksheet	Reading and underlining word fields, vocabulary development eg explosion, crash
6.	Game – child writes short advert and partner guesses product	Pairwork	Writing skills using ideas in activities above
7.	Child invents a product and writes a TV advert, with storyboard of sequence of events	Individual	Writing and design skills
8.	Making and advertising shortbread for the whole school – slogans, jingles, posters.	Groupwork	Comparing and discussing methods, design and musical skills

3.6   Reading

ECHE produced materials based on authentic texts in English used to demonstrate a variety in text type and purpose. Similar texts in different languages were also used eg Greek, German, Arabic.

Taught by Hambrough staff; a video of the materials in use was made by ECHE staff.

The aims of this topic were:

1. To develop in children a sense of the variety of purposes for which people read.

2. To help children to appreciate the range of purposes in their own daily reading.

3. To encourage children to use non-verbal clues in their reading (eg layout, type-face, pictures, etc).

4. To give practice in the skills of collecting and recording data.

3.6 READING: WHY AND WHAT WE READ

CLASSROOM ACTIVITIES	CLASSROOM ORGANISATION & RESOURCES	CHILDREN's LANGUAGE DEVELOPMENT
A TYPES OF READING TEXT & THEIR PURPOSES		
1. Making lists of text types eg adverts, signs, posters, books etc.	T & Class as introduction individual/pairwork & worksheet	Vocabulary development, developing awareness of different text types and their purposes.
2. Matching text types in foreign languages to written description of purpose eg to persuade, to find out what's on TV.	Group work using colour-coded cards and captions.)))))	Discussion involving problem solving and reading skills, especially skimming and scanning. Vocabulary development.
3. Matching parts of text in English and then classifying them according to text types eg letters, notices, adverts.	Group work using colour coded cards - text type cut into 3.))))	Developing awareness of lay-out, using contextual clue. Classifying skills. Study Skills - filling in a chart.
4. Classifying assorted text types (eg labels, menus, signs) according to purpose eg to find out how to make something, to find their way around, using a chart.	Group work using colour coded cards; and individual charts for classification.	
5. Children bring in examples of texts for other children to identify, classify etc.	Pairwork/groupwork	

3.6 READING: WHY AND WHAT WE READ

CLASSROOM ACTIVITIES	CLASSROOM ORGANISATION & RESOURCES	CHILDREN'S LANGUAGE DEVELOPMENT
B PRINTED ADS: how do they work; design and layout		
9. Matching appropriate written caption with produce; matching captions with appropriate target groups	Groupwork; assorted adverts and captions on separate cards	Skimming, completing and chart.
10. Matching difficult words with given meanings, writing out meanings	Individual/pairwork worksheet and captions and dictionary	Encouraging children to tackle difficult words independently.
11. Reading adverts to find words with "positive" meanings. Lists of positively and negatively associated words drawn up	Individual/pairwork and worksheet and dictionary	Dictionary skills involving skimming, drawing conclusions ie adverts only make use of words with positive meanings.
12. Reading adverts for specific words or word fields	Individual	Faster reading encouraged by use of scanning for specific information.
13. Matching paragraphs in longer written adverts to purpose	Individual	Reading skills, especially skimming for gist.
14. Reading adverts for specific details eg opening and closing times of an Indian exhibition, address of Indian restaurants	Adverts, London A-Z street plan, worksheet	Reading for detail, using co-ordinates on a map.
15. Designing adverts for chosen subject (after class discussion of features of effective adverts)	T & Class groups with assorted examples of adverts	Writing and design skills eg use of colour, layout, print size.

CLASSROOM ACTIVITIES	CLASSROOM ORGANISATION & RESOURCES	CHILDREN's LANGUAGE DEVELOPMENT
C. PEOPLE'S READING HABITS		
1. Making surveys of what the children themselves read in their daily lives (one day/one week) classified under headings eg spare time, entertainment, travel.	individual worksheet	Giving reasons to support opinions.
Describing personal preferences and those which are easy/difficult, interesting/necessary.		Making one's own reading needs and attitudes precise.
2. Making surveys of what classmates read Making bar graph.	group work individual worksheet	Recording data in questionnaire-form. Study skills - collecting and interpreting data in graph form. Information transfer: questionnaire bar graph.
3. Designing other questionnaires to survey differences between children/adults, men/women.		Designing a questionnaire. Study skills - collecting and classifying data, interpreting and comparing bar graphs, drawing conclusions. Developing awareness of intellectual functions of written language.

3.7   The topics outlined above are an initial attempt at developing language awareness and, it must be emphasized, do not form part of an integrated course. They do, however, reflect the kind of theme-based work which has been current throughout primary schools for several years.

In attempting to realise the overall aims of these materials (as set out in 3.3), language awareness was deliberately interpreted as a set of activities, rather than a body of knowledge to be learned. It was not seen, in other words, as another subject in the curriculum to be taught by transmission teaching. The fundamental assumption was that one of the central aims of school learning is that children should acquire a knowledge (partly or wholly conscious) of language skills, the different purposes for which we use them and the ways in which we can deploy them most efficiently. Conscious decisions were made concerning the type of activities in which the pupils were engaged. These were based on the following principles.

   i)   Children should be encouraged to bring their own interests and experience into the classroom.

  ii)   Materials used should reflect Britain's multilingual society.

 iii)   Children must be allowed to be creative and use language freely as well as in a more guided way.

  iv)   Children should be encouraged to work with peers to discuss, solve problems, suggest, make surveys, correct and otherwise generally deploy a range of natural speech functions in the classroom, ie rather than simply answering teachers' questions.

   v)   Children must be taught the necessary skills and involved in activities which will allow them to operate independently of the teacher; they need to be taught how to predict, follow instructions, read for specific information, hypothesise, ask each other questions, etc.

  iv)   The teacher is not the only audience of children's work: Children can usefully produce work which another child will use (cf writing a code, designing a new traffic sign.)

3.8   Each topic provided a different year-group with a 'taster' on language-aware curricular materials. A further stage in the project would lead to the Hambrough staff taking over responsibility for language awareness in order to develop their own materials and resources. This would necessarily entail the teachers raising their own language awareness. The kind of training in language available to Hambrough staff is of the nature of general language studies in teacher-training courses of recent years. One member of staff, however, is at present studying at the Institute of Education for an MA in "Curriculum Studies" which has developed from studying in the previous year for a Diploma in "Theory & Practice in Language (English As A Mother Tongue)".

4. Outcomes

4.1   It is difficult to assess the outcomes of such a short and incomplete project, especially one which has been initiated by an external body. What can be offered are entirely subjective views concerning the amount of interest shown by both teachers and pupils, the degree to which the children were able to perform the tasks set and to which the teachers were able to add their own materials and resources. The criteria against which the success of the materials could be measured are shown in the table below:

ASSESSING TEACHER & PUPIL REACTION

Participants	Interest in Language Awareness Project	Degree of Language Awareness
TEACHER	1. the concept	1. ability to adapt materials and resources
	2. the activities	2. ability to devise original materials, resources and activities
	3. the methodology	3. ability to foster pupils' language awareness in teaching style/classroom organisation
PUPIL	1. the topics	1. ability to perform set tasks
	2. the tasks	2. ability to 'transfer' language skills practised to other areas of school learning

I consider next each set of materials in the context of these criteria.

4.2 Advertising was probably the most successful in that collaboration by ECHE and Hambrough staff in producing materials was established from the start. The classroom teacher was very interested in the concept of Language Awareness and, although not a language specialist, had a flair for translating ideas about language development into original materials and activities. His interest in language stimulated by this work is reflected in the fact that he is currently attending an in-service diploma course at ECHE on "Teaching English as a Second Language in Multicultural Schools." The pupils in his class were encouraged to work together in groups, although some were less able to work independently because of their language difficulties.

The children appeared to enjoy the work and were on the whole fairly successful in performing the tasks set once they had become accustomed to the type of work expected and, more especially, the lay-out of work sheets used. An interesting insight into the lack of language awareness on the part of a group of poor readers was revealed in the Swap Shop task. This at first glance was seen by them as far too difficult since the page is dense with text. The children were very unwilling to examine the work more closely and were entirely unable and therefore unwilling to begin the task. By encouraging the group to predict from the title and from their own experience what the text might include they did pinpoint the underlying pattern of the text viz:

<u>What I want</u>
<u>What I can offer</u>
<u>My address</u>

When the children understood this they were far more eager to determine what was required of them and to begin thinking about the task. They in fact completed it very easily and were rather astonished to find that this was so. Thus children's confidence and ability to read can be increased by allowing them to bring their knowledge of the world as well as their knowledge of language, to the text. It was clear that even better readers were not at first prepared to look at or listen to instructions carefully enough so that they could work by themselves. It was important here for the teacher to constantly refer the child back to the text, rather than simply paraphrase the printed word for the child.

4.3 Communication was a less successful exercise in jointly produced materials. In terms of the children's work and interest, however, it was most encouraging. The materials were used with a class who were particularly poor at working either in groups or independently of the teacher. The children for example were not at all skilled in reading instructions and demanded a great deal of the teacher's attention to have a task explained. The children did not have the confidence to work in groups and constantly required confirmation from the teacher that they were doing their work correctly. This partly stems from the fact that these children were in their first year at the Middle School. They were, however, at an age where such behaviour could have been discouraged rather than reinforced.

The materials and teaching, therefore, aimed to help these pupils recognise that reading instructions was important and that recognising features of layout could help them with a written task.

They were taught to find titles, underline instructions, underline examples given, find captions and so on. This highlights an area where the teacher's own language awareness in the setting of tasks is vital. Children need to be taught the language of instructions, followed ideally by practice in giving their own instructions to other children either orally or in writing. The teacher must also be aware of the desirability of careful presentation, including clear use of instructions, titles, examples and other features of lay-out in printed materials. As mentioned in the previous section, children frequently have reading tasks paraphrased orally by the teacher, so that the child has even less opportunity to practise reading. Thus if children have difficulty in working collaboratively or independently of the teacher, the nature of the all-too-precious teacher-pupil exchange can be limited to banal "managerial" discussions on what to do next. It would have been useful to encourage the children's listening skills by having taped instructions on cassette, or Language Master which could guide the children on the selection and sequencing of activities and thereby free the teacher for one-to-one individual work.

The children did improve in their ability to work on their own and were observed using a written text far more effectively, for example by underlining and ticking words which helped them carry out a task, even though this was not suggested in the instructions.

4.4 The project on Reading contained the most multilingual resources and was interesting in that it made the children consciously reflect on the process of reading, while at the same time enhancing their actual reading performance in a more unconscious way through individual and group reading tasks. The children were again very interested in the topic and brought in examples of different text types from home. The classroom teacher suggested that the children collect texts which they could cut up themselves for other pupils to match and this was greatly enjoyed. A video made of the children working in groups revealed interesting ways in which children learn. It goes without saying that the most effective groups were those who were able to communicate effectively with each other in order to organize the way in which the task could be carried out. Groups where the members did not relate to each other and who were unwilling to explain details of the task were not able to complete the work as quickly or effectively. Most of the children, however, did manage to complete the tasks in their groups while specific individuals experiencing difficulty were given help by the class teacher.

The children were very surprised to find that they could cope with such difficult texts, especially those in foreign languages which they did not know. The classifying exercise proved to be one of the most difficult tasks and made the children reflect very carefully on the purposes of the written texts.

The production of such sophisticated materials necessarily involves a great deal of awareness by the writer of the nature and purpose of reading. This recognises that children can use rather difficult authentic written texts if the task is well-defined and pitched at the children's conceptual and linguistic level. It also recognises that there are many different types of activity associated with the reading skill; these can encourage children to reflect while they are reading, rather than merely testing their literal comprehension after reading.

4.5 Extensive research shows that most children are confused about the relationship between the four language skills, including the functions of reading and writing. An important aim common to all three sets of materials but particularly the last, was thus to make this relationship more explicit.

Assessing the children's ability to transfer the skills acquired to other areas of the curriculum is necessarily difficult since they were observed or taught using only these specific materials. I feel certain, however, that this could be more closely observed by a class teacher working with the children over a longer period of time. Judging by the way the children's performance improved over a few weeks, it would seem likely that their increasing ability to perform the tasks set would continue to grow if similar work were carried out at regular intervals. Whether such improvement is atributable, however, mainly to the content of the language topics selected remains in question. My own feeling is that the nature of the language activities was the main vehicle for overall language improvement and awareness and that the knowledge acquired about specific features of language is secondary to developing awareness of language in children of this age. It is entirely feasible to envisage language awareness courses whose aim is to draw children's attention to the ways in which they use language skills, as well as to the content of the texts.

The failure of the concept of Language Across the Curriculum to really take hold in school learning and teaching is precisely due to the fact that most teachers remain relatively unaware of the nature and function of language learning and teaching. It is vital therefore that teacher education should include initial and in-service courses covering these features so that teachers can more effectively enhance their own awareness of language and thereby that of their pupils.

I would finally like to express my thanks to the Headteacher Mrs Betty Frost and to the staff and children of Hambrough School for allowing us to work with such enjoyment in their school.

(Jean Brewster)

THE LANGUAGE AWARENESS COURSE AT THE HENRY BOX SCHOOL, WITNEY, OXFORDSHIRE

Headmaster: Mr H.E. Green
Head of Modern Languages: Mr T.R.W. Aplin

1. The School: general information

2. Internal organisation
    (English and Modern Languages)

3. The Language Awareness course

4. Outcomes

1.   The School: general information

The school is one of two mixed 11-18 comprehensive schools in Witney. There are approximately 1,000 pupils on the roll, with an entry varying between 6 and 7 forms. The social intake is reasonably well-balanced, with a defined catchment area covering town and country, although over 20% of the intake are pupils from outside this catchment area by parental choice. All pupils are native speakers of English.

In the first three years a common curriculum is followed, mainly in mixed-ability form groups, with setting in mathematics and foreign languages from year two and in sciences from year three. A guided options system operates in years four and five, each pupil taking English and mathematics and six other main subjects.

Sixth form courses are provided in conjunction with the other comprehensive school and the local technical college. Between the three institutions a wide range of A, A/O and O level courses is provided (in addition to some vocational and certificate courses). Consultation and cooperation allows for a rationalised provision between the three institutions.

2.   Internal organisation

Teaching is organised on a departmental basis. In the language subject area there is an English Department and a Modern Languages Department.

English is taught to mixed ability groups up to the end of year three. There is then some setting. While most work in the first three years is based on literature, there is in years one and two a language course which all pupils follow. It is based on Maura Heally's: <u>Your Language</u> (MacMillan) and works from the premise that pupils should study their own considerable skills at the age of 11 and 12 in order to develop those skills. Remedial help is given by withdrawal in years one to three and extra help is given to individuals in years four and five.

The foreign languages taught are French, German and Italian. After a Language Awareness course of half a term's duration all pupils start French. Setting in half year populations operates from year two. By the end of year three 95% of pupils will have followed courses in two foreign languages to an elementary level. There is no selection apart from that involved in broad setting and withdrawal for remedial help.

All lessons in the school last for 70 minutes. In years one to five English has three periods per week (two in year three). All modern languages teaching is given within three periods weekly in years one to three and two periods per language per week in years four and five. The division of time in years one to 3 will take the form of:

a) equal time for FL1 and FL2 throughout the year
b) one term of FL1, one term of FL2 (or vice-versa) with mix in third term
c) one half year of FL1 followed by one half year of FL2.

Formal contact between English and Modern Language teaching consists of an exchange of syllabuses and discussion with regard to approaches to language work in the early years, especially with regard to the Language Awareness course.

3. The Language Awareness course

The course started in the mid-1970's and was conceived by former members of the Modern Languages Department. The present staff continue to contribute to the development of the course.

All pupils at 11+ entry follow the course for half a term in three 70 minute periods weekly. It is taught entirely by teachers in the Modern Languages Department who will teach French in those periods after the first half term.

3.1 Aims

The overall aims of the course are
(a) to create an awareness of the phenomenon of language and to arouse an interest in this vital aspect of human development,

209

(b)   to lay a foundation for foreign language learning by showing
      how language works, by training pupils in careful listening and
      by placing languages in their broader context, and

(c)   to promote a positive relationship between teacher and pupil in
      the latter's mother tongue before embarking on foreign language
      learning.

Thus the purpose is to introduce a pupil to language learning by
indicating certain basic study skills, by fostering a greater understanding of the processes involved as well as awakening an interest
in the nature of language itself and specifically directing attention towards the foreign language study on the curriculum.

3.2   Major stages of the course

a)   Language as communication

      Pupils are asked to consider why humans need language, and
      study production of speech and its arrangement into agreed
      patterns of words and phrases. The idea of language as a code
      understood by messenger, sender and recipient is firmly
      planted. Animal communication and the relationship between
      verbal and non-verbal language, visual and aural signs and
      signals and varying degrees of complexity in artificial codes
      are areas which are touched on.

b)   How language is created

      Group work allows exploration of possible origins of language
      and a primitive simulation exercise shows the need to under-
      stand the codes of neighbouring communities. Consideration is
      given to the historical development of languages and their
      relationship to communicative means in terms especially of
      lexis. The influence of the mass media in effecting rapid
      change is discussed and some attempts to create artificial lan-
      guages are examined.

c)   How babies learn to talk

      With anecdotal and cassette evidence the linguistic development
      of young children is briefly considered with a strong parallel
      being drawn between the baby's position and that of the learner
      of foreign languages. Various specific study skills can be
      shown to be useful and possible for all to adopt arising from
      the experience of learning one's mother tongue.

(d)   The families of languages

      The major groupings of the world's languages are referred to and an example given of one language family e.g. hamito-semitic. Consideration is given to the variety and number of existing languages and their distribution. Discussion of the relative international importance of certain languages leads to classification of the languages of western Europe and detailed comparison of some items eg numbers, identical messages. The connection between nationality and language is touched on briefly.

(e)   The anatomy of language

Pupils are introduced to certain basic concepts of language structure that they will encounter in their learning. The ideas of word order and words performing tasks are examined in English with the possibility of looking at examples if necessary. The concept of languages having patterns and rules, the existence of gender, the importance of recognising kinds of words are all dealt with briefly.

(f)   The golden rules

The final lesson of the course attempts to draw all these elements together, with the aim of synthesising the lessons to be drawn for the pupil in learning a foreign language.

3.3   Materials and methods

The course materials were developed by present and former members of staff and are now in published form: Introduction to Language T.R.W. Aplin, J.W. Crawshaw, E.A. Roselman, A.L. Williams (Hodder and Stoughton 1981). The published version contains material additional to that used in the first year course but the shape reflects the needs of the school. Little use has therefore been made of other published materials but teachers are always looking for extra examples and resources, some of which are brought to the course by the pupils themselves.

There is no prescribed method but the syllabus is agreed. Classes react in quite different ways to the material and at this stage in their learning childrens' enthusiasm and interest deserves the response of a flexible approach. There are individual and group assignments built into the course which combines oral, listening, reading, writing skills in the mother tongue as well as allowing the investigative approach for those who show a special interest. Some lessons are taught by more than one member of staff.

4.   Outcomes

There is no formal course assessment nor is any planned. It is felt among the staff in the department that pupils begin study of a foreign language in a more secure position. They are 'aware' of the significance and uses of language and languages and have an appreciation of the study skills that will be useful to them in learning. They have settled into the school and have a relationship with their foreign language teacher in English. They are definitely no less interested! By the end of the first year they have covered as much ground as pupils would normally be expected to do from September.

The course has certainly created interest among the staff as a whole and among parents. The subjective reaction of a group of pupils asked to complete a questionnaire two and a half years later was altogether favourable. A selection of their comments appears below:

"Really anybody who doesn't begin their language by having this book or taking a similar course would be at a great disadvantage as it tells you meaning and uses for words".

"It helped me see how language lives and how complicated a language is to learn".

"I think the list of golden rules is useful and accurate".

"I do think it covers too much. It should cover the basics in more detail and forget about the irrelevant bits".

"It is good for younger children just starting a new language because it is best to know what's in a language before going straight on to it".

"I think maybe the other [chapters] are too humorous and take out the seriousness of learning and being able to speak a foreign language".

From a newcomer in year three:

"All in all I don't think much more can be done to improve this book"! If I'd had it in the first year it would have improved my foreign languages no end (but add more colour!!!)".

(T.R.W. APLIN)

212

THE INTRODUCTION TO LANGUAGE COURSE AT FARRINGDON SCHOOL, SUNDERLAND

Headmistress: Mrs D.J. Hale
Head of Modern Languages: Mrs L. Powell

1.   The School

1.1 Intake and structure.

- Farringdon is a co-educational, 8-form entry comprehensive school with pupils from 11 to 18.
- The pupils come from a wide range of socio-economic backgrounds; the school serves a large council estate, an established private housing estate and two new private development areas.
- There are approximately 1,300 pupils on roll, with some 70 staff.
- There are very few immigrant pupils in the school.

213

1.2 Foreign-language teaching.

- Pupils are taught, as in all subjects, in mixed ability groups in Year 1. From Year 2 banding is introduced. For Years 2 – 3, half the year-group learns French and half German. The 4th Year Options system produces groups in French, German, French Studies and German Studies.
- In Year 1, all pupils have 4 x 35 minutes per week on a course "Introduction to Language"; remedial pupils are however withdrawn from all these lessons.

1.3 Curricular policy with respect to language teaching.

- Some co-operation between the F.L. department and the Remedial Department in the planning of the Introduction to Language course.
- Present Head of English and Head of Languages are discussing future co-operation.
- Head teacher requires a curricular statement from each department.

2.   Introduction to Language Course

2.1 Origin and rationale.

- The course originated in a departmental workshop, attended also by members of the Remedial Department, in July 1981.
- The workshop's main aim was to review and discuss the most effective ways of achieving departmental aims. Two aims of seven identified, were not being fully achieved: getting as many pupils as possible to examination level and introducing pupils to the cultural content of the language(s) they learn. The second aim, and others of the original seven, it was decided, should be given particular emphasis in Year 1. It was agreed that remedial children benefit from language teaching, particularly by acquiring an "awareness of language". It was hoped that remedial pupils and staff of the remedial department would be integrated into the new course. This did not in fact take place, but the presence of the Remedial teachers was a valuable factor in the original conception and planning. A further source of inspiration was the BBC series on Modern Language teaching, in particular the programme on Archbishop Michael Ramsey School, London.
- The reasons for introducing the course were:

(a) The cultural background element should help to dispel prejudice, showing that 'different' does not mean 'inferior' (the geographic distance of Sunderland from continental Europe often creates lack of interest in languages).
(b) Exposure to two or three languages in the first year will allow a guided choice for further study from the second year.

214

(c) All classes will be taught by a number of teachers, allowing a more even exposure to teachers' teaching strengths and obviating difficulties caused, for example, by prolonged absence of a member of staff.

(d) General motivation should improve through a more varied approach.

- At this stage the course was to include the following elements: French, German, Spanish, Geography, History of Languages, Cultural Studies, Testing, elementary linguistics and grammar and word games.

2.2 Development of the course.

- The first workshop was followed by meetings to consider the 'mechanics' of the course and to plan course content.

The course began in September 1981, on the decision of the Head of Modern Languages after consulting the Headteacher.

The course was visited in November 1981 by an HMI, who expressed general satisfaction with what he had seen. This reassured the Headteacher who had expressed some doubt about the course.

Parental reaction was fairly encouraging.

Modifications were made during the first two years. After the first year one aspect of the course, Spanish, was dropped due to staffing problems. "History of Language", "Linguistics" and "Grammar" became "Language Families" and "Grammar Games", and a module running throughout the year, "Language Awareness", was introduced. The department became aware of parallel developments elsewhere through the link established by the Language Awareness Working Party.

2.3 The course from September 1983.

2.3.1 Aims

(a) To enable pupils to see how language has evolved, how it is acquired, and how it is used.

(b) To help pupils see that human language is something unique and changing.

(c) To give pupils an understanding of what is common to most languages.

(d) To give pupils an awareness of the skills which combine to form language behaviour.

(e) To give an understanding of grammatical concepts in both English and the two foreign languages to be studied.

(f) To promote an interest and enjoyment in language.

(g) To enable pupils to make a guided choice between French and German in Year 2 by exposing them to both languages.

(h) To show that "different" does not mean "inferior" and to
     encourage an unprejudiced approach to other cultures and
     civilisations, thereby contributing to the formation of a more
     tolerant society.
(i) To put the foreign languages to be studied into their geogra-
     phical context.

2.3.2 Structure

- 4 x 35 minute periods per week during Year 1, taught in
  mixed-ability groups.
- Units distributed as follows

> ### Term 1
>
> Geography of Europe - 2 periods
> Language Families   - 1 period
> Language Awareness   - 1 period
>
> ### Term 2
>
> German   - 2 periods
> Cultural Studies   - 1 period
> Language Awareness - 1 period
>
> ### Term 3
>
> French   - 2 periods
> Grammar/Games   - 1 period
> Language Awareness - 1 period

2.3.3 The Modules.

(a) Geography of Europe

The aim: "To make the pupils aware of the differences and similarities between the peoples of Europe." The work is done largely with
maps, dealing with physical geography, political and linguistic
frontiers, communications, products and exports, trade and military/
political groups.

Discussion of, for example, the different names in three or four
languages for Germany, or of the divergence of political from linguistic frontiers create the awareness of language and geography
which is the main purpose. Collection of articles widely imported
into Britain and discussion of the trade groupings produce an understanding of the interdependence of the countries of Europe, including Britain. The syllabus gives some information and suggests
approaches but is deliberately not exhaustive.

216

(b) Families of Languages

The approach to this unit is thematic, with the intention that more or less time can be spent on each theme as the teacher and class prefer.

The themes are:

(a) What is a Family?
   - The notion of human family tree is used to explain relation-ships between languages.
(b) How many languages? How many people?
   - "large" and "small" languages are compared through bar-charts and maps.
(c) It sounds similar and it looks similar,
   - the point is made through comparison of words across some Indo-European languages; pupils have to listen to recordings and thus begin to appreciate the importance of listening in language learning.
(d) Sort them out for yourselves!
   - pupils see and hear short texts in French, Spanish and Italian, and then in German, English and Dutch, to compare and contrast Romance and Germanic languages.
(e) How the split began,
   - a brief account of the effects of the invasion of the Roman Empire and the Völkerwanderung on the linguistic map of Europe.
(f) The families move out,
   - an account of the effects of colonialisation and the distribu-tion of English, Spanish, French and German into the rest of the world.

(c) Language Awareness

The aim: To encourage children to discuss and create language in all its many forms, in order that they might begin to understand and enjoy it in its various guises. (It is hoped that they might also begin to use it more effectively themselves as a result of their experience).

The syllabus suggests a list of topics and some ideas and approaches:

How we make sounds, Language acquisition, Foreign 'loan' words, Names, The changing nature of language (responding to technological developments), Nonsense language (à la Stanley Unwin et al), Register, Slang, Accent, Dialect, Learning to listen (phoneme dis-crimination games), Reading (learning to read, different scripts), Punctuation. Experience has shown that with respect to methodology, it is important to involve pupils in doing things rather than telling about them; for example taping each other's dialect, inventing new words, and allowing them to take an active part in deciding the course of any discussion.

(d) French and German

The two modules are similar and are based on a series of "survival" situations, supplemented by skills in counting, telling the time and using foreign currency. The French module is based on the BBC "Dès le début"; the German module is home-made.

This part of the course will be familiar to most language teachers.

(e) Cultural Studies

The topics covered in this module will also be familiar to most teachers, as will the methods. The significance here is that for each topic – for example food and drink or schools – the cultures of three countries are compared and contrasted: France, Germany, and Britain.

This is in accordance with the principle of the course that the emphasis should be on languages and cultures, rather than one language. It also creates a more open approach instead of contrasting one culture with the "superior" home product.

Topics covered are: Currency, food and drink, sport, schools, festivals and holidays, prejudices.

(f) Grammar

Aim: This part of the course is not intended to be an exhaustive grammatical analysis of each language. It is intended to introduce some concepts which are of major importance in the learning of a foreign language.

After a brief revision of what pupils know of English grammar – primarily an ability to identify a verb, a noun, an article, a pronoun and an adjective – the following concepts are taught: plurality, gender, nouns and pronouns, infinitives, word order, tense.

In each case the concept is taught with one eye on future language-learning. The concept is examined first in English, and then in French and German. For example, the subject pronoun system in English is established through substitution of nouns in sentences, and then the relationship between singular and plural pronouns established. This is then compared and contrasted with the French and German systems. For this and other concepts, much of the teaching is done through games and activities.

2.3.4 The Materials

- Geography: the ideas are home-made, the materials used are outline maps and atlases borrowed from the geography department.

  Families of Languages: the themes are home-made, some illustrative material is used from T.R. Aplin et al: Introduction to Language.

- Language Awareness: the following books were used in compiling the list of topics and suggestions for work:

M. Raleigh: The Languages Book   ILEA
T.R. Aplin et al: Introduction to Language Hodder and Stoughton
C. Jenkins: Language Links Harrap
S. Potter: Our Language   Penguin
Locally Speaking - accompanying pamphlet to a BBC series.

Some further input was provided from the local university School of Education.

- German: home-made: "survival language"
- French: based on BBC Dès le Début
- Cultural studies: the selection of topics and materials used are those familiar to language teachers.
- Grammar: home-made, with ideas for games developed mainly in the department.

2.4   Outcomes

- Subjective evaluation by the teachers involved suggests a high degree of interest and motivation in both pupils and teachers. It is particularly important that there is an opportunity for the teachers to create good classroom relationships. This comes first from the opportunity to speak English with the pupils rather than feeling obliged to use the foreign language and, second, from the fact that pupils can contribute to the knowledge created in the classroom from their own experience, rather than being limited to accepting the knowledge of the foreign language which only the teacher has.

- It is not intended that any psycho metric evaluation should take place, as this would not do justice to all the aims of the course.

2.5   Staff

Some but not all of the staff teaching the course have studied linguistics at degree level. One teacher had been introduced to the notion of language awareness courses during the PGCE year.

The course was planned and developed entirely within the school,
almost exclusively by language teachers but with some help initially
from Remedial Department teachers. The system of rotation of classes
through teachers allows each to concentrate on two or three modules
and the re-writing of the course in Spring 1983 was done by alloca-
ting modules to individual teachers.

2.6   Reactions to the course and plans for the future.

Interest in the course has been expressed by the new Head of
English.

Parental Response.
Initially, due to lack of familiarity with the aims and methods of
this type of course, some parents expressed reservations. Now, most
parents are both sympathetic and encouraging in their response.

Response from other departments.
There has been considerable interest and support from the Humanities
Faculty.

It is hoped to continue running the course, with some possible modifications and perhaps the involvement of the English Department.

3.   An afternoon of Introduction to Language
       (report by an external observer)

The first term modules are Geography of Europe, Language Families
and Language Awareness. A visit on one Wednesday afternoon in
November allowed me to see examples of all three modules. I am
grateful to the pupils and teachers involved for an interesting
experience.

The first lesson, under the title Language Awareness, treated the
topic of loan words. After the pupils had settled down and the
visitor - who had come to watch "like the Dutch visitors a few weeks
ago" - had been introduced the teacher reminded them how last week
they had talked about languages changing, how some languages die,
how others, like Welsh, almost died. When a language is revived,
explained the teacher, it often needs new words for modern inven-
tions, new ideas. Welsh which almost died when English settlers went
to Wales, was revived and needed to borrow words from English. So
now we are going to listen to a bit of Welsh and pick out the
English words. (The pupils were not at all surprised by this introduction of Welsh; the teacher has in fact a Welsh-speaking husband
who has been an invaluable resource). So listen to the tape and see
how many of the 31 loan words you can hear; some will sound like
English, others will be less easily recognisable.

We got out our paper and pen and listened. My neighbour, on the first attempt at the tape which lasted about two minutes, got about 12 words, whereas I only managed 6, including 'rugby' and 'school'. At the second attempt, after the teacher had got a show of hands to determine how many pupils were hearing, my neighbour got more than 20. Then we heard the same story, - of two boys leaving school and having a quick game before arriving home to tea, - in English. Finally we heard the speaker read out the 31 loan-words in Welsh and in English, and we ticked our lists. The final show of hands demonstrated that 4 - 5 pupils had heard more than 20, 4 - 5 had less than 10, and the other 12 - 15 had recognised about half the words. In the final minutes of the lesson the teacher explained how people in Wales had wanted to revive the language in order to maintain the culture, how English had been forced on school pupils in the nineteenth century, and how they were punished for speaking Welsh.

For homework, we have to make a list of 15 words which our ancestors in 1660 would not have known. And so the bell rang and we went to the next 35 minute lesson on 'Language Families'.

The second lesson began with a reminder, by question and answer, of how last week in this lesson we had established two groups of languages from listening to and then seeing the spelling of the numbers 1 - 10 in French, Spanish, Italian, German, Dutch and English. The teacher had prepared for the lesson by writing the first lines of the Lord's Prayer on the board in French, Italian and Spanish. The main part of the lesson consisted of looking and noticing similarities in the three versions. The teacher's main problem in the lesson was stemming the tide of enthusiasm. Pupils volunteered their observations more than readily and the teacher then numbered the words in each version which looked similar. There was disappointment when he stopped them after 12. To complete the activity, the teacher asked what they had seen from these comparisons and one of the pupils reviewed their observations of the connections between the three languages last week and this.

At this point the teacher rolled up the board and produced versions of the Lord's Prayer in German and Dutch. He dictated the English version and the pupils copied the other two. This revealed the range of language ability in the class, where some pupils had difficulty with the dictation and yet those same pupils had been contributing accurately to the earlier observations and would probably be able to handle the homework: to number the similarities in the same way in the three Germanic versions.

The last lesson, after break, lasted 70 minutes and was 'Geography of Europe' with a different group of pupils. For homework, pupils had been asked to discover the meaning of EFTA and which countries belong to it. This provided the first stage of the lesson, as the list was checked and corrected in exercise books. The next stage was to introduce the label Comecon and to establish from pupil suggestions the list of member countries. Then pupils were given outline maps and shaded in the three trade areas – the EEC list had been done last week. When one pupil asked how they were to know which countries were which, others smiled because <u>they</u> knew, and the teacher reminded them of the other maps they had in their exercise books.

While they were doing this, I had an interesting conversation with two girls sitting in my corner. Some of the questions produced the following responses.

They like the Introduction to Language "because it's easy – and so is the homework". Their parents think it is a good idea, and so do they, "because we learn about the countries first". When discussing whether they would learn French or German next year, one said French "because it's the second most important language" but she was interrupted by the other: "It isn't really, we did a graph and it didn't come in the first 10 most spoken languages in the world." The second said she would wait and see which language she liked best (of French and German in the language modules) before deciding. She said she didn't mind waiting until after Christmas before starting a language.

After everyone had finished their maps, the teacher moved them on from trade alliances to military alliances and asked "Which countries belong to the Warsaw Pact?" but then when there was no reply "Where is Warsaw?". "In Russia" said one pupil, thus demonstrating the need for some elementary geography, despite the effect of news reports. The rest of the lesson was spent on establishing the meaning of the abbreviation N.A.T.O. and the names of member countries. Just before the bell went, they were given the homework task of finding out the names of the Warsaw Pact members and off they went.

(M S Byram)

THE LANGUAGE EXPERIENCE AND AWARENESS PROJECT (LEAP) AT VILLIERS HIGH SCHOOL, SOUTHALL

Headmaster: Mr L.W. Baker
Head of English: Mr M. Harrison

1.   The School

2.   The LEAP project: background

3.   Planning the project

4.   Progress to date

5.   Results

6.   The way forward

1.   The School

1.1   Intake and structure

Villiers High School is situated in the centre of Southall, in the London Borough of Ealing. It was founded as a County School in 1907 and continued as a Grammar School until 1974, when it became a 12-18 years Comprehensive High School. It is situated in the area of Southall which houses the majority of the local Asian community, and after the 1974 change in status and selection policy the percentage of ethnic minority pupils rose from the 30% of 1973 to 60%. Such pupils now account for almost the entire school population.

Under the strong leadership of the headmaster, Mr L Baker, who was appointed to take the school through the reorganisation of 1973-4, Villiers has dealt creatively with its problems and has maintained high academic standards in spite of the changes through which it has passed. It has continued to be a popular and highly-regarded school. This report deals with work within the school on language, but this is only one area of a diverse programme of both pastoral and curricular development. The school's achievements have been documented in a Schools' Council report (Hider, 1981).

1.2   Curricular policy with regard to language

The concern at Villiers with language has centred on the English and ESL Departments as they have developed to deal with the changes of the last ten years. One of initiatives was the two-year Language across the Curriculum project, which started in 1978. This formalised and focused work already underway on the school's language policy and, as a cooperative venture, also established the continuing link between the school and the Division of EFL/ESL at the nearby Ealing College of Higher Education (hereafter ECHE) (See 2.1 below). The project has been documented in a College report (ECHE, 1980).

2. The Leap Project: background

2.1 Origin and participants

For some time, a group of teachers at Villiers have been working very specifically on increasing staff links between Villiers and its feeder middle schools. In 1982 this group decided to formalise and focus this work around the area of language.

A small project team was formed consisting of the heads of the Biology, English, ESL and Geography departments, plus the head of the Humanities Faculty at Villiers and myself from the EFL/ESL Division at ECHE. Several, including myself, had been involved in the previous Language across the Curriculum project at the school. We chose to work with two local middle schools, who already had well-established links with Villiers.

2.2 Assumptions

Members of the LEAP group, having already established links with feeder middle schools, had gained the impression that while there was a 'language gap' of sorts experienced by pupils as they transferred from one school to the next, its nature was not necessarily predictable. Maybe it did not invariably constitute a progress but rather a regression. We tested this idea informally by collecting early second-year written work at Villiers across a range of subjects and found a large amount of blackboard copying and written answers to closed questions. This was in contrast to the more varied and creative types of writing seemingly required by many middle schools.[1] The project has therefore proceeded on the assumption that while there presumably is a 'language gap', its nature is complex and not necessarily determined by a transition from the 'easy' to the 'difficult'.

---

1   This may be one facet of F Davies' assertion, developed in another of these papers, that 'more time is spent on language study in primary schools than in secondary'.

2.3 Aims

2.3.1 To examine the difference in demands made on pupils in their receptive and productive use of language between the last year of their middle school and their first year at Villiers High School. (We have called this the 'language gap', hence LEAP.)

2.3.2 To look at this language gap with particular reference to English, Geography and Science.

2.3.3 In connection with 1 and 2, to look particularly at pupils' writing.

2.3.4 In the light of the understanding gained, to discuss, encourage and develop relevant changes in classroom methodology.

2.3.5 By implication, to contribute to the working of the language policy at Villiers, to the strengthening of links with its feeder schools and in general to foster the professional development of the teachers involved in the project.

2.4 Rationale

We do not see LEAP as the type of research project which can be defined in terms of aims and product or described in terms of a statistically measurable result. This may be regrettable on one level but we believe our work has a value which, even if difficult to quantify, is nevertheless real.

Our aims are directly related to the language policy of Villiers High School, current work there on teacher development, the establishment of closer links with feeder schools and the implementation of changes in the second-year (the 'new intake' year) curriculum. Thus our desire to keep LEAP within properly planned boundaries is balanced by developments within the school. Every so often it becomes apparent that we, as a group of sort of language 'experts', can contribute more effectively to these developments by making modifications to the Project. We believe that LEAP exists to serve the schools in which it operates rather than as a rigorous academic study. It would not in any case be possible to organise such a study, given that the project team, as busy practising teachers, have neither sufficient expertise nor time to do so. Their skills and responsibilities lie elsewhere. Thus we have to be honest and realistic about our ability to produce a study with definably valid 'findings' and to do the best we can with very limited resources and very small samples.

The main value of the Project is to the participants. The experience of reflecting on one's teaching, in an organised way and with colleagues, can only be beneficial, both to individuals and to schools.[1] The interest of more staff, the dissemination of findings around the school and our involvement in another area of staff development (see 3.2.1. below) bear this out. At a time when resources and support for new initiatives in education are severely limited, we believe that a study of this kind, by teachers who are working with other teachers, is, in spite of the problems it poses, of great practical value.

3. Planning the Project

3.1 Collection of Data

In preparation for the summer and autumn terms of 1983, we made the following decisions:

- to observe at least two final-year English, Geography and Science sessions in each of the two feeder schools and to make video recordings of these whenever possible.
- to do likewise early in the autumn term at Villiers.
- to choose, from each of the two feeder schools, three 'middle-range' pupils due to start at Villiers in September 1983 as subjects for individual study. A range of their summer term writing to be collected ready for comparison with their early second-year work at Villiers. Their early progress there, in terms of the project's interests, to be monitored and compared with their summer term's work in the middle school.

3.2 Describing the Data

3.2.1 Classroom Observation

The LEAP group discussed a number of approaches to classroom observation, both published and locally developed, e.g. at ECHE for the training of EFL/ESL teachers. We produced an experimental observation framework for members of the group to use on visits to the feeder schools.

Meanwhile however, the Language across the Curriculum group at Villiers started to make video recordings of certain classes. When these were played back to interested teachers, LEAP people who were present noticed that the audience, not being accustomed either to looking at such recordings or making an assessment of classroom teaching in terms of language, found it impossible to describe usefully what was going on in the recordings.

---

[1]   See G Donmall's comments on acquiring the capacity for classroom observation in: Some Implications of Language Awareness Work for Teacher Training.

This new framework consisted of a simple report sheet enabling the observer to record chronologically the progress of the lesson and to note the language and study activities to which each stage gives rise.

3.2.2 Describing and assessing written work

Only in the case of the six feeder school children mentioned in 3.1 do we intend to look in detail at the writing which is required of and produced by pupils across 'the language gap'. We have therefore drawn up a series of headings under which teachers can describe and assess, in a minimum of time, these pupils' written work.

We are obviously interested in the writing of all the children whose classes we record, but this is in a more general sense and will be reported on in the context of the overall observations.

4. Progress to date

4.1 Data from the feeder schools

We observed and video-recorded one or two middle school classes at the end of the summer term, but not nearly as many as we had planned. This was largely because the bulk of our data collection occurs just at two times in the school year when teachers are particularly busy, namely the beginning and the end. This affects both the LEAP observers and the teachers they are trying to work with.

4.2 Data from Villiers Second-year

We have succeeded much better with observing classes and collecting work at Villiers, since most of the project group are based there and are themselves working with the pupils concerned.

5. Results

Since we are still collecting information, it is not possible to give a final report on our findings. We have however gained a number of impressions about the 'language gap' and these are described below.

5.1 Classroom organisation

In the four subject areas of English, ESL, Geography and Science, early second-year lessons are not so far removed from those in late middle school. They contain a high proportion of activity-based tasks where the learning derives from what pupils are doing just as much as what the teacher is saying.

227

5.2   Written work

The writing tasks required of pupils in these four areas showed variety in terms of opportunity for creativity and of text type. This too mirrored what we had seen of the work in the two middle schools, where we were impressed by the level and variety in both style and content of pupil's writing. On the other variables concerned with our study of written work, we are not yet able to comment.

5.3   Interpretation

What we appear to have observed may have arisen for a number of reasons. For example, the teachers concerned are making a conscious effort to continue at least temporarily what they consider to be middle school learning patterns, or, this is naturally how they would introduce their subjects to this year group, or, they have thought about the copy-writing we discovered last year (see 2.2.).

It also has to be borne in mind that we have only been working with two middle schools and with a small group of teachers. It may well be that teachers who agreed to work on LEAP teach in a particular way. All we can say at present is that we are not yet in a position to judge the reasons for our impressions.

6.   The way forward

6.1   Problems

6.1.1   The main problem for the teachers working on LEAP has been time, particularly since several are already involved in other developmental work. Classroom observation, collecting pupils' work from other colleagues, describing, collating and reporting on findings, arranging for your own teaching to be covered in order to spend a morning in another school, these are all time-consuming activities for people who already have heavy commitments.

6.1.2   A secondary problem arose from the need to collect data from different schools. Coordination sometimes proved difficult to achieve.

6.2   Possible solutions

What is needed is a research assistant who can collect the data and coordinate the work actually on-site. In the present climate this is of course a pious hope, although it is always worth pressing for such assistance.

We are considering involving students on teaching practice, by asking them to observe the classes in which we are interested and to collect up the writing of the LEAP pupils. This would also have an advantage for them by providing a structured framework for reporting on some of their school experience.

6.3 Hopes

6.3.1 The language gap between middle and secondary school is clearly a matter of great interest for many teachers. It is a matter of regret that because of our slender resources, we have not yet discovered as much about it as we would have liked. However, as this academic year progresses we shall continue to observe and record second-year classes at Villiers and to monitor the written work of the six chosen pupils (see 3.1 above). We also hope to strengthen the links with the two feeder schools so that they can participate more fully in the data collection required in the summer term of 1984.

6.3.2 Through our efforts to increase language awareness among teachers we hope to continue to contribute to the programme of classroom observation among colleagues at Villiers and thus to the ongoing programme of curricular and professional development in the school. We also hope to increase the fruitful contact between secondary and middle school teachers.

(Alison Piper)

References

Ealing College of Higher Education, Division of EFL/ESL, (1980), Language across the curriculum: Progress Report, E.C.H.E., (mimeo).

Hider, A T. (1981), A School facing change: a case study in staff development, Schools Council.

230

Appendix A

BIBLIOGRAPHY

FOREWORD

During the course of the work of the Language Awareness Working party, it became clear that there was a need for an interim bibliography to guide teachers, thinking of introducing 'language awareness' courses in their schools and colleges. This has indeed proved to be welcome and several hundred copies have been purchased in the last few months.

A number of additions and corrections have been suggested by those who have read the interim bibliography in detail and these have now been incorporated into this edition produced for the Assembly of the National Congress on Languages in Education held at York in July 1984.

I am grateful to the Centre for Information on Language Teaching and Research for the preparation of the original short bibliography which served as a basis for this work; to my colleagues on the Working Party for their contributions to it, especially Richard Aplin who has edited the material into publishable form and to Peter Downes for producing and distributing the bibliography.

John Sinclair
Chairman

CONTENTS

The bibliography was published in July, 1984. It is hoped to keep it up-to-date with amended versions from time to time. Suggestions for additions should be sent to Mr T R W Aplin, Head of Dept. of Modern Languages, Henry Box School, Witney, Oxfordshire.

A: Sources of materials for use by pupils

The numbers at the end of each annotation indicate the age-range of
pupils for whom the items are suitable.

ALGEO, John: <u>Problems in the origins and development of the English
language</u>. Harcourt Brace Jovanovich, second edition 1972. (See also
PYLES, Thomas in Section C).

16 - 18

ALLINGTON, R and K Krull: <u>Listening; Reading; Talking; Writing</u>
(Beginning to Learn About...series; four books) Blackwell Raintree,
1981.

A useful and lively introduction for children in primary schools.
Simple questions and clear illustrations encourage the children to
think about and discuss a range of text types and their purposes in
reading, writing etc. The four basic language skills are placed very
firmly in the context of both school and everyday life.

6 - 10

APLIN, T R W and others: <u>Introduction to language</u> Hodder and
Stoughton, 1981, revised edition due March 1985; Teacher's notes
from: P J Downes, 42, Huntingdon Road, Brampton, Huntingdon, Cambs
PE18 8PA.

Seeks to provide pupils with an awareness of language; suitable for
use before foreign language learning is started; jargon-free style
to explain basic words of language structure. Deals with: language
as communication, origin of languages, how a baby learns to speak,
language families, history of European languages, writing, animal
language.

11 - 13

ASTLEY, Helen: <u>Get the message!</u> (Awareness of language series)
Cambridge University Press, 1983.

Deals with means of communication without the written or spoken word
- animal communication, the language of symbols, signs, uniforms,
flags, mathematics, music, computers, braille etc.

11 - 14

ASTLEY, Helen and Eric Hawkins: <u>Using language</u> (Awareness of language series) Cambridge University Press, 1984.

Looks at the different ways in which language is used. Explores
special ways of using words, e.g. puns and proverbs, slang and swear
words. Pupils are encouraged to find out about and use language
tools such as dictionaries.

11 - 14

BROWN, B: <u>Outlook Europe: people and languages</u>. (Outlook Europe series) Macdonald, 1979.

An illustrated topic book on the peoples and languages of Europe, with sections on 'feeling foreign', language borrowings, countries with more than one language, dialect, language families, cultural mixing, European colonisation, minority languages, and the need for communication in the modern world.

11 - 16

CLOSE, R A: <u>A university grammar of English workbook</u>. London, 1974.

16 - 18

CRIPWELL, Kenneth: <u>Man and language</u>. Harrap, 1979.

A topic book in the Harrap World History programme on uses of languages in history: how they spread, how they are related, how they are recorded, why some are more successful than others and the problems which arise out of the existence of different languages.

11 - 16

DARTON, Nicholas: <u>Europe in the world</u>. Harrap, 1981.

A topic book in the Harrap European Studies course, Part One. Unit 6 provides an introduction to European languages with questions and activities.

13 - 16

DIXON, M: <u>In communication</u>. Wayland, 1982.

A comprehensive and practical picture of communications in the world today. It begins with simple experiments using light bulbs to flash Morse code and ends with an introduction to the new microchip communication systems.

9 - 12

DOUGHTY, Peter, John Pearce and Geoffrey Thornton: <u>Language in use</u>. Edward Arnold, 1971.

A comprehensive set of resources from which the teacher chooses and arranges a programme adujsted to local interests, needs and speed. Part of the Schools Council Programme in Linguistics and English Teaching.

DRUMMOND, J: <u>Living history</u>. Holmes McDougall, 1973, out of print. Includes a short chapter on the development of languages.

11 - 14

ELDON, K and M: <u>Tom-tom to television</u>. Wayland, 1977, out of print.

9 - 12

FITZGERALD, Barry: <u>Working with language</u>. Heinemann, 1982.

Looks at the history and development of language, providing tasks, games, and details of further resources. Chapters on animal language, origins of language, varieties of English, children and language, our changing language.

13 - 16

FLETCHER, H J: <u>Secret Codes</u>. Franklin Watts, 1980.   8 - 11

FORSYTH, Ian J and Kathleen Wood: <u>Language and communication</u>. Longman, 1980.

A three-part English language course for the early years of secondary school; teaches all the language skills of reading, writing, listening and talking by taking a close look at language itself, and examines how language has developed as a form of communication and how this relates to our use, enjoyment and understanding of language in everyday life.

11 - 14

GOLDENBERG, Steve and others: <u>Language</u>. Hutchinson, 1983.

Examines the power of language as a force in everyday life and in all forms of communication. Includes treatment of standard English, dialects and accents, rules, spoken and written language, the importance of reading and writing. Exercises and activities for pupils. This book also accompanies the Thames Television series <u>Language 2</u>.

14 - 16

HAWKINS, Eric: <u>Spoken and written language</u> (Awareness of Language series). Cambridge University Press, 1983.

Looks at how we acquire skills of speaking and writing and then traces development of writing, showing how the modern alphabet developed. Other alphabets, e.g. Russian and Chinese, are introduced.

11 - 14

HAWKINS, Eric (ed.): <u>How do we learn languages?</u> (Awareness of Language series). Cambridge University Press, 1984.

The baby learning its mother tongue and how we learn foreign languages. The differences between the two processes are discussed and pupils are encouraged to discover pointers and helpful rules for their foreign language learning.

11 - 14

HEALY, Maura: <u>Your language</u>. Macmillan, 1981, three books.

An English course in three parts for secondary pupils which explores the ways in which we communicate with each other. Investigates communication through words, gesture, sign, symbol and expression. Emphasises the expertise of pupils as users of language and their diversity of language and dialect.

11 - 14

HOWARD, S: <u>Communications machines</u>. Blackwell Raintree, 1980.

10 - 12

HUGHES, Arthur and Peter Trudgill: <u>English accents and dialects</u>. Edward Arnold, 1979 (tape available).

16 - 18

JENKINS, Clive: <u>Language links: the European family of languages</u>. Harrap, 1980.

An introduction to the history of language development. Drawing its examples mainly from English, it covers dialects, the Indo-European family of languages, Greek and Latin roots, the mechanisms of language change, the history of language in the British Isles (including the Celtic languages) and artificial languages; also suggests possible future trends.

11 - 16

JONES, Barry: <u>How language works</u> (Awareness of Language series). Cambridge University Press, 1984.

Shows how to discover 'patterns' in language and how to work out rules, how to describe them, finding names for different parts of speech and ways to learn what a word means and how it gets its meaning.

11 - 14

KING, B: <u>Instants: people talking, Europe and language</u>. Somerset Resources for Learning Project, 1976.

A four-page broadsheet presenting the concept of language in a most stimulating way. Raises ideas on what language is, language families, the history of English and language development.

11 - 16

McNEIL, Frank and Neil Mercer: <u>Here I am; Language around us; Talking and feeling</u> (The Primary language project). A & C Black, 1982 (tape available).

In three separate books, the course makes children aware of their own language, the dialects and languages around them, and the different ways they can use language. Includes sections on bilingualism and the language of school.

8 - 11

MAY, J: <u>Britain in Europe</u>. Clearway Press, 1973.

Contains a short chapter on language groups in Europe.

11 - 14

NEWBY, Michael: <u>Making language</u>. Oxford University Press, 1982.

A three-book course for lower and middle secondary students designed to enable pupils to discover how the English language works in speed and in writing. Each book focuses on three main levels of language: sound, meaning and structure. Includes topics for research on dialect and the history and international use of English. Offers a heuristic approach to grammar in which the pupil has to discover the rules.

11 - 14

OLIVER, Gregory: <u>Oxford Junior English 5: Our language</u>. Oxford University Press, 1979.

Part of an English course, this book follows the theme of our language with a variety of exercises. Includes history of English, signs and symbols, picture-writing, gestures, etc.

9 - 11

OSMOND, L: <u>People in Europe</u>. Allen and Unwin, 1977.

Has a brief chapter on language families.

11 - 16

PENMAN, Tony and Al Wolff: <u>Web of language</u>. Oxford University Press, 1981.

Linked with the BBC series of the same name, but can be used independently. Twelve thematic chapters (with cassette and exercises) including dialect, slang, accents, origins of names, development of English.

8 - 13

PITT, V: <u>Signals</u>. Franklin Watts, 1973.

8 - 11

POMPHREY, Cathy: <u>Language varieties and change</u> (Awareness of language series). Cambridge University Press, forthcoming 1985.

Covers the families of world languages, looks at the pattern across Europe and at the linguistic varieties within British society, drawing on the resources of the multi-cultural community in the classroom of many schools. Some discussion of dialect and language change.

11 - 14

PROUDFOOT, L: <u>Keep in touch</u>. Mary Glasgow, 1976

Includes four pages on languages in Europe.

11 - 16

RALEIGH, Mike: <u>The languages book</u>. ILEA English Centre, 1981. Pupil's book, teacher's book and cassette also available. Available from ILEA English Centre, Sutherland Street, London SW1.

Covers: different languages, dialects and attitudes to them, young children learning to speak, what languages share, playing with words, inventing words, the history of English, slang and special ways of talking, writing and speaking, giving names to people and places, games with words, language and situations.

RICHMOND, John and Helen Savva: <u>Investigating our language</u>. Edward Arnold, 1983.

Core-book for English classes, with five main topics: origins of language and the birth of writing, how babies learn to talk, varieties of English, history of the language in England, and the historical and political reason for the world importance of English. Makes use of extracts from literature from a wide range of sources.

14 - 16

SHOWERS, P: <u>The listening walk</u>. A & C Black, 1973.

7 - 9

STRANGE, Derek: <u>Language and languages</u>. Oxford University Press, 1982.

For pupils about to start on the study of a foreign language. Aims to develop their awareness of language, increase their understanding of English and stimulate their interest in other languages. Includes analysis of the sounds, scripts, structure and the use of language and practical uses of learning a foreign language.

10 - 12

WALLWORK, J F: <u>Language and linguistics</u>. Heinemann, 1969.

An introduction to the study of Linguistics, designed primarily for Sixth-formers and students in colleges of education. The workbook contains exercies and subjects for discussion.

16 - 18

WELLS, J C: <u>Accents of English</u>. Vol.1: An introduction; Vol.2: The British Isles; Vol.3: Beyond the British Isles. Cambridge University Press, 1982 (tape available).

Other materials which are suitable for use by pupils but which are not commercially available are:
ALPINE (Awareness of Language Project in Norfolk Education)
    R E Whiley, Coordinator of French in the Middle Years,
    Central Area Education Office,
    28, St Giles Street, Norwich NR2 1TQ

Language Awareness (Nottinghamshire Curriculum Development Unit)
    Miss M Squire,
    Chaumont,
    Willow Way,
    Burton Joyce, Notts.

These materials are available for inspection only at CILT.

B: Sources of materials for use by teachers

BARBER, C L: The story of language. Pan, revised edition, 1982.

A useful source book, easy to read, including essential concepts of phonology, accidence, etymology and semantics.

CARTER, Karen: Proposals for teaching 'background' topics (French – Level 1). West Sussex County Council, 1980. Teacher's handbook available for reference, but not for sale, at CILT

CRUTTENDEN, Alan: Language in infancy and childhood. Manchester University Press, 1979.

DE VILLIERS, Peter A and Jill G De Villiers: Early language. Fontana/Open Books, 1979.

ELLIOTT, R W V: Runes. Manchester University Press, 1959

FAST, Julius: Body language. Pan, 1971.

FREEMAN, P: Europe today and tomorrow. Longman, 1977.

One chapter examines the nature of the ethnic and linguistic barriers to harmony in Europe, and considers the role which various forms of communication can play in overcoming them.

FREEMAN, Roger D and others: Can't your child hear? Croom Helm, 1981.

Intended for the parents of hearing-impaired children, this book has useful sections on the signing systems used by the deaf.

GEIZEL, J: The Europeans. Longman, 1969, out of print.

A survey of the ethnic origins and languages of the peoples of Europe.

GELLING, Margaret: Signposts to the past: Place names and the history of England. J M Dent, 1978.

HALL, Edware T: The silent language. Doubleday/Anchor, 1973.

HAWKINS, Eric: Awareness of language: an introductory guide for teachers. Cambridge University Press, 1984.

A practical background book for teaching language awareness which also expands and supplements materials in the Awareness of Language series topic books. The accompanying cassette provides examples for the topic books and illustrations for the introductory guide.

HOULTON, David: All our languages: A handbook for the multilingual classroom. Edward Arnold, forthcoming 1985.

This handbook for primary school teachers in multi-cultural areas presents practical classroom ideas for supporting the bilingualism of ethnic minority children and introducing all children to linguistic diversity. Includes information about cultural diversity and gives sources for help and further research.

JAMES, C V (ed.): The older mother tongues of the United Kingdom. Centre for Information on Language Teaching and Research, 1978.

JORDAN, Terry G: The European culture area: a systematic geography. Harper and Row, 1973.

The book treats Europe as a culture area and emphasises human geography, and it contains one chapter about the geography of languages in Europe, with a map.

KATZNER, K: The languages of the world. Routledge & Kegan Paul, 1977.

A compendium of information on 500 living languages. It has a chart of the world's language families, passages in the native scripts of 200 languages, together with an English translation, and a country-by-country survey listing every country in the world along with latest information about the principal languages spoken, and the number and distribution of speakers.

KING, Charles: Hieroglyphs to alphabets. Fred Muller (no date known).

KLEIN, G: <u>Resources for multi-cultural education: an introduction</u>.
Longman, 1982.

KOSINSKI, L: <u>The population of Europe</u>. Longman, 1970, out-of-print.

A study of European demography which provides information on the
effects of migration on languages and on the relation between ethnic
groups.

LINDEN, Eugene: <u>Apes, men and language</u>. Pelican, expanded edition,
1981.

MIDDLESEX POLYTECHNIC: <u>Reading materials for minority groups</u>.
Reports and materials from Ms J Ingham, Middlesex Polytechnic, All
Saints' Site, White Hart Lane, London, N17 8HR.

MILLER, Jane: <u>Many voices: bilingualism, culture and education</u>.
Routledge and Kegan Paul, 1983.

On the basis of transcripts of conversations with bilingual children, this book discusses the problems and advantages of bilingualism, especially relevant for inner-city schools. Chapters 7 and 8
refer to the language awareness that bilinguals have and the educational implications thereof, with practical examples from London
schools.

MORRIS, Desmond, and others: <u>Gestures: their origin and distribu-
tion</u>. Cape, 1979.

A highly amusing and readable book on man's use of gesture to communicate, and on the differences in use of gesture in twenty-five
European countries.

PATTERSON, Francine and Eugene Linden: <u>The education of Koko</u>. Andre
Deutsch, 1982.

THORPE, W H: <u>Animal nature and human nature</u>. Methuen, 1974.

VON FRISCH, Karl: <u>Bees: their vision, chemical senses and language</u>.
Oxford University press, 1960, Jonathan Cape, 1968.

WELLS, Gordon: <u>Language development in the pre-school years</u>.
Cambridge University Press, forthcoming March 1985.

WILLIAMS, Raymond (ed.): <u>Contact: human communication and its
history</u>. Thames and Hudson, 1981.

C: Works of reference for teachers

I. GENERAL EDUCATION AND LANGUAGE TEACHING

BARNES, Douglas R: From communication to curriculum. Penguin, 1976.

BARNES, Douglas R and others: Language, the learner and the school: a research report. Penguin, revised edition, 1971 (Penguin papers in education).

CARTER, Ronald (ed.): Linguistics and the teacher. Routledge & Kegan Paul, 1982.

CILT: The Space between: English and foreign languages at school. Centre for Information on Language Teaching and Research CILT Reports and papers 10, 1984.

A language for life: report of the Committee of Inquiry appointed by the Secretary of State for Education and Science under the the chairmanship of Sir Alan Bullock FBA. HMSO, 1975.

See especially Part Four.

DES: Aspects of secondary education in England: a survey by H.M. Inspectors of schools. Department of Education and Science, HMSO, 1979.

See especially Chapter 6.

DONALDSON, Margaret: Children's minds. Fontana, 1978.

DOUGHTY, Peter: English and the curriculum. Edward Arnold, 1974.

DOUGHTY, Peter, and others: Exploring language. Edward Arnold, 1972.

DOUGHTY, Peter and Geoffrey Thornton: Language study, the teacher and the learner. Edward Arnold, 1973.

FALK, Julia S: Language and linguistics: bases for a curriculum prepared by ERIC Clearinghouse on Languages and Linguistics, Center for Applied Linguistics, Arlington, Virginia, 1979, (Language in Education: Theory & Practice 10).

GANNON, Peter and Pam Czerniewska: Using linguistics: an educational focus. Edward Arnold, 1980.

GATHERER, W A: A study of English. Heinemann, 1980.

GATHERER, W A and R B Jeffs: Language skills through the secondary curriculum. Holmes McDougall, 1980.

GRAVES, D H (ed.): Writing: Teachers and children at work. Heinemann, 1983.

HAWKINS, E W: "Language as a curriculum study" in The mother tongue and other languages in education. CILT, 1979 (NCLE Papers and Reports 2)

See also other papers in this and the companion volumes.

HAWKINS, Eric: Modern Languages in the Curriculum. Cambridge University Press, 1981.

H M Inspectorate of Schools: Curriculum 11-16: Modern languages, a working paper, July 1978. DES Information Division, 1978.

H M Inspectorate of Schools: Primary Education in England: A survey by H M Inspectors. HMSO, 1978.

HMSO: Language performance in Schools: Primary survey.
Report No. 1, HMSO, 1981
Report No. 2, HMSO, 1982

HMSO: Language Performance in Schools: Secondary survey.
Report No. 1, HMSO, 1982
Report No. 2, HMSO, 1982

KROLL, B and G Wells (Eds.): Explorations in the development of writing: theory and research. John Wiley, 1983.

LITTLE, A and R Willey: Multi-ethnic education: the way forward. Schools Council, 1981.

LUNGER, E A and others: Learning from the written word. Oliver and Boyd, 1984.

MERCER, Neil (ed.): Language in school and community. Edward Arnold, 1981.

NUTTON, Allan E: Language awareness and the place of Esperanto. Esperanto Teachers' Association, 140, Holland Park Avenue, London W11 4UF.

PERERA, K: The language demands of school learning. Open University Supplementary Reading Course no. 232 (Language Development) Open University Press, 1979.

RICHARDS, J: Classroom language: what sort? Unwin, 1978.

ROSEN, Harold and Tony Burgess: Languages and dialects of London schoolchildren: an investigation. Ward Lock Educational, 1980.

STEVICK, Earl W: Teaching and learning languages. Cambridge University Press, 1982.

STUBBS, Michael and Hilary Hillier (eds.): Readings in language, schools and classrooms. Methuen, 1983.

SUTTON, Clive (ed.): Communicating in the classroom. Hodder and Stoughton, 1981.

THORNTON, Geoffrey: Language experience and school. Edward Arnold, 1974.

TINKEL, A J: "The relationship between the study of language and the teaching of languages" in Issues in Language Education. CILT, 1981 (NCLE Papers and Reports 3).

See also other papers in this and the companion volumes.

TORBE, M and P Medway: Language teaching and learning: the climate for learning. Ward Lock Educational, 1981.

WILKINS, David: Linguistics in language teaching. Edward Arnold, 1972.

WILKINSON, Andrew: Language and education. Oxford University Press, 1975.

II. LANGUAGE AND LINGUISTIC THEORY

In this section, the works marked with an asterisk have also been found to be of use to older pupils in secondary schools, e.g. Sixth Formers taking a course in Principles of Language or a General Studies course in Communications/Linguistics.

*AITCHISON, Jean: The articulate mammal; an introduction to psycholinguistics. Hutchinson, 1976.

AITCHISON, J: Language change; progress or decay? Fontana, 1981.

BAETENS-BEARDSMORE, H: Bilingualism: basic principles. Tieto Ltd., 1982.

BAUGH, A C and T Cable: A history of the English language. Routledge & Kegan Paul, revised edition, 1978.

BOLINGER, D and D A Sears: Aspects of language. Harcourt Brace Jovanovich, revised edition 1981.

*BRADLEY, Henry (revised by Simeon Potter): The making of English. Macmillan, revised edition, 1968.

*BROOK, G L: Varieties of English. Macmillan.

BURCHFIELD, Robert: The Spoken Word: A BBC Guide. BBC, 1981.

*BURGESS, Anthony: Language made plain. Fontana/Collins, revised edition, 1975.

COOK, V J: Young children and language. Edward Arnold, 1979.

CORDER, S P: Introducing applied linguistics. Penguin, 1973.

CORNER, John and Jeremy Hawthorn: Communication studies: an introductory reader. Edward Arnold, 1982.

CRYSTAL, David: Linguistics. Penguin, 1971.

CRYSTAL, David: Child language, learning and linguistics. Edward Arnold.

CRYSTAL, David: What is linguistics? Edward Arnold, 1974.

CULLER, Jonathan: Saussure. Fontana, 1976.

*FOSTER, Brian: The changing English language. Macmillan, 1968, Penguin, 1970.

*FROMKIN, Victoria and Robert Rodman: An introduction to language. Holt, Rinehart and Winston, 1974.

*GIMSON, A C: An introduction to the pronunciation of English. Edward Arnold, second edition 1974.

*GIMSON, A C: A practical course of English pronunciation. Edward Arnold, 1975.

HALLIDAY, M A K: "The functional basis of language" in Class, codes and control (Bernstein, B (ed.) Vol 2.) Routledge & Kegan Paul, 1973.

HALLIDAY, M A K: Language and social man. Longman, 1974.

HALLIDAY, M A K: Learning how to mean. Edward Arnold, 1975.

HUDSON, Kenneth: Dictionary of diseased english. Macmillan, 1977.

246

*JESPERSEN, Otto: Growth and structure of the English language. Basil Blackwell, 1946.

KRASHEN, Stephen D: Second language acquisition and learning. Pergamon, 1981.

*LADEFOGED, Peter: Elements of acoustic phonetics. University of Chicago Press, 1962.

*LEECH, Geoffrey: Semantics. Pelican, 1974.

LEECH, G and others: English grammar for today. Macmillan, 1982.

LYONS, J: New horizons in linguistics. Penguin, 1970, (Pelican Original).

MINNIS, N: Linguistics at large. Collancz, 1971.

*MOSS, Norman: What's the difference? Hutchinson.

*O'CONNOR, J D: Phonetics. Pelican, 1973.

*O'CONNOR, J D and G F Arnold: Intonation of colloquial English. Longman, second edition, 1973.

*O'DONNELL, W R and Loreto Todd: Variety in contemporary English. George Allen and Unwin, 1980.

*PALMER, F: Grammar. Pelican, 1971.

*PALMER, F R: Semantics: a new outline. Cambridge University Press, 1976.

*PEI, Mario: The story of the English language. George Allen and Unwin, 1968.

POTTER, S: Our language. Penguin, revised edition, 1966, (Pelican).

PUGH, A K and others (eds.): Language and language use. Open University course E263 set book. Heinemann, 1980.

*PYLES, Thomas: The origins and development of the English language. Harcourt Brace Jovanovich, second edition, 1971.

*PYLES, Thomas and John Algeo: English: an introduction to language. Harcourt Brace Jovanovich, undated.

*QUIRK, Randolph: The use of English. Longman, second edition, 1968.

ROBINSON, Ian: The survival of English. Cambridge University Press, 1973.

STUBBS, Michael. Language and literacy. Routledge & Kegan Paul, 1980.

TRUDGILL, P: Accent, dialect and the school. Edward Arnold, 1975.

*TRUDGILL, Peter: Sociolinguistics: an introduction. Pelican, 1974.

*ULLMANN, Stephen: Semantics: an introduction to the science of meaning. Basil Blackwell, 1962.

WADE, Barrie (ed.): Language perspectives: papers from 'The Educational Review'. Heinemann, 1982.

*WAKELIN, Martyn F: English dialects: an introduction. Athlone Press, revised edition, 1977.

WALLWORK, J F: Language and people. Heinemann, 1978.

III. JOURNAL AND NEWSPAPER ARTICLES

Where an article has been summarised in Language Teaching (formerly Language Teaching and Linguistics: Abstracts) a reference starting LTLA is given. The number that follows refers to the year in which the abstract appeared, e.g. 75-271 = 1975, abstract no. 271.

ALPIN, T R W: "An introduction to language". British Journal of Language Teaching, vol 19 no.2, summer 1981.

BLOOR, Thomas: "Learning about language: the language studies issue in secondary schools". English in Education, vol 13 no.3, autumn 1979, pp 18-22.

BRUMFIT, C J and K F Reeder: "The role language study in teacher education". Educational Review (Birmingham) vol 26 no.3, 1974, pp251-9. LTLA: 75-271.

GARDNER, R A and B T Gardner: "Teaching sign language to a chimpanzee". Science, 165, August 1979.

HALLIDAY, M A K: "Relevant models of language". Educational Review, Vol. 22 no.1 pp 26-50.

HAWKINS, Eric: "Awareness of Language". Times Educational Supplement, no.3310, 16.11.79, pp34-5.

HENRICI, Gert: "The framework for linguistics as a school subject." Linguistik und Didaktik, vol 5 no.3, 1974, pp182-193. LTLA: 75-112.

PREMACK, Anne J and David Premack: "Teaching language to an ape." Scientific American, October 1972.

STORK, F C and others:" Language study in secondary education". English in Education, vol 14 no.1, spring 1980, pp23-34
                          no.2, summer 1980, pp18-29.

TINKEL, Tony: "A proposal for the teaching of linguistics at the secondary level". MALS Journal (Birmingham), vol 4 spring 1979, pp79-100. LTLA: 80-133.

TINKEL, Tony: "Language study in the sixth form". Nottingham Linguistic Circular, vol 10, no.2, December 1981.

WEEKS, Valerie: "Language awareness: a new approach to teaching English". Times Educational Supplement, no.3487, 29.4.83, pp52-53.

D: Class reference books

ADDISON, N: Understanding English place names. Futura, 1979.

ADDISON, N: Understanding English surnames. Batsford, 1978.

BRUN, T: International dictionary of sign language. Wolfe, 1969.

CAMERON, K: English place names. Batsford, 1978.

FOWLER, H W: A dictionary of modern English usage: Oxford University Press, 1926.

GLENDENNING, P J T: Teach yourself to learn a language. English Universities Press (now Hodder and Stoughton,) 1965.

GOWERS, Sir Ernest: The complete plain words. HMSO, 1954.

NEWNHAM, R and Tan Lin-Tung: About Chinese. Penguin, 1971.

QUIRK, Randolph and Sidney Greenbaum: A university grammar of English. Longman 1973 (See also R A Close in Section A).

REANEY, P H: The origin of English place names. Routledge & Kegan Paul, 1960.

REANEY, PH: The origin of English surnames. Routledge & Kegan Paul, 1967, paperback, 1980.

Appendix B

A MAP OF
LANGUAGE AWARENESS
ACTIVITIES

The map above and those on the next page indicate, according to Local Education Authority, those parts of the country in which any Language Awareness work is taking place.

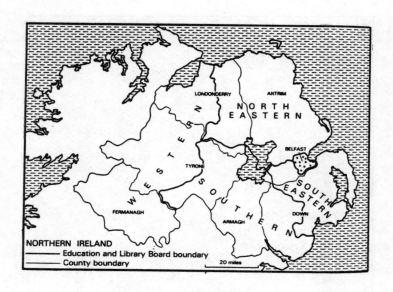

NORTHERN IRELAND
— Education and Library Board boundary
— County boundary

LONDONDERRY
ANTRIM
NORTH EASTERN
WESTERN
BELFAST
TYRONE
SOUTHERN
SOUTH EASTERN
FERMANAGH
ARMAGH
DOWN

20 miles

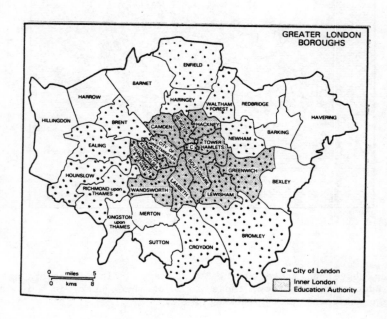

GREATER LONDON BOROUGHS

ENFIELD
BARNET
HARROW
HARINGEY
WALTHAM FOREST
REDBRIDGE
HILLINGDON
BRENT
CAMDEN
ISLINGTON
HACKNEY
HAVERING
EALING
CITY OF WESTMINSTER
TOWER HAMLETS
NEWHAM
BARKING
KENSINGTON & CHELSEA
HAMMERSMITH
C
SOUTHWARK
GREENWICH
HOUNSLOW
WANDSWORTH
LAMBETH
BEXLEY
RICHMOND upon THAMES
LEWISHAM
KINGSTON upon THAMES
MERTON
SUTTON
CROYDON
BROMLEY

miles 0 5
kms 0 8

C = City of London

Inner London
Education Authority

254

Appendix C

A LIST OF SCHOOLS CARRYING OUT LANGUAGE AWARENESS WORK

Schools active in the field of Language Awareness

Numbers relate to type of activity as listed below, where known.

1)   A course for 11-13 year olds, to create awareness of and interest in "language" as a preparation for foreign language learning.

2)   A Language Awareness or linguistics element in Humanities or English for 11-13 year olds.

3)   A course in the language development of children as part of a Child Care, Preparation for Parenthood or Social Studies course in fourth or fifth years.

4)   Introduction to linguistics in the sixth form (possibly as part of General Studies.)

Avon

Whitefield Fishponds School, Bristol (1, 2 and 3)
Backwell School, Bristol (2)
St. Mark's School, Bath (2)
Hayesfield School, Bath (3)
St. Mary Redcliffe and Temple School, Bristol (1 and 2)
Hartcliffe School, Bristol (3)
Patchway High School, Bristol (3)
Nailsea School, Nailsea
Broadoak School, Weston-Super-Mare (2 and 3)
Norton Hill School, Midsomer Norton (2 and 4)
Chipping Sodbury School, Bristol (2)
Broadlands School, Keynsham (3)
Mangotsfield School, Bristol
Monks Park School, Bristol (2 and 3)
Brislington School, Bristol (2)

Barnsley

St. Helen's School (2)
Darton High School (4)
Milefield Middle School (3)
Wombwell High School (4)
Holgate School (2)
Honeywell School (3)
The Priory School (3)

Bedfordshire

Beech Hill High School, Luton

Belfast

Orangefield Boys' Secondary School (1)
St. Gabriel's Secondary School (1)

Birmingham

St. Paul's RC Girls' School (4)
Baverstock School (1)
Bishop Challoner RC Secondary School (1)
Washwood Heath School (1)
Holte School (2)
Holyhead School (2)
Cadbury College (4)
Bordesley Green Girls' School (1)
Four Dwellings School (1)
Hodge Hill School (1)
Moseley School (1)
Perry Common Comprehensive School (1)
Queensbridge School

Bolton

Sharples School

Bradford

Lidget Green Middle School (1)
Thornbury Middle School (1 and 2)
Tyersal Middle School (1 and 2)
Nab Wood Middle School (1 and 2)
Hainsworth Moor Middle School (1 and 2)
Burley Middle School (1 and 2)
Priestman Middle School (2)
Delf Hill Middle School (1 and 2)
Stoney Lee Middle School (1 and 2)
Tong Upper School (3)
Hanson Upper School (3)
Belle Vue Boys Upper School (1 and 3)
Greenland Upper School (1)

Brent

William Galdstone High School (1 and 3)

Bromley

Bullers Wood School for Girls (1)

Buckinghamshire

Lord Grey School

Cambridgeshire

Hichingbrooke School, Huntingdon (4)

Clwyd

Ysgol Evvirys op Iwan School, Abergele (1 and 4)

Coventry

Foxford School (1)

Croydon

Monks Hill High School (1)

Derbyshire

Sinfin School, Derby (1)
Ripley Mill Hill School
Hadfield School (1)

Devon

Okehampton School and Community College (2)
Estoner Comprehensive School, Plymouth (1)

Dorset

The Woodroffe School, Lyme Regis (4)
Bournemouth Grammar School for Girls (4)
Fosters School, Sherborne (1)

Durham

St. Bede's RC Comprehensive School, Lanchester (1)

Ealing

Villiers High School
Hambrough Combined School
Acton High School

East Sussex

Varndean Sixth Form College

Enfield

Winchmore School (2)
St. Angela's School (4)
Albany School (4)
Ambrose Fleming School (4)
Aylward School (4)
Bullsmoor School (4)
Enfield Chace School (4)
Kingsmead School (4)
Minchenden School (4)
Salisbury East School (4)

Essex

SE Essex Sixth Form College (4)

Haringey

Somerset School (1)

Hereford - Worcester

Christopher Whitehead High School
Wolverley High School (4 and 1)
The Dyson Perrins C of E High School (1)
The Abbey High School (4)
Alvechurch C.E. Middle School
Haywood High School (1)

Hertfordshire

Tring Secondary School (1)
The Highfield School, Letchworth (4)
St. Angela's RC School Stevenage (4)
Heathcote School, Stevenage (4)
Collenswood School, Stevenage (4)
Bedwell School, Stevenage (4)
Sir Frederic Osborne School, Welwyn Garden City (4)
Holy Trinity RC School, Welwyn Garden City (4)
Hatfield School (4)
Bishop's Hatfield Girls' School (4)
St. Audrey's School, Hatfield (4)
Nicholas Hawksmoor School, Boreham Wood (4)
Mount Grace School, Potters Bar (4)
Owen's School, Potters Bar (4)
Francis Bacon School, St. Albans (4)
Townsend School, St. Albans (4)
Margaret Dane School, Bishop's Stortford (4)
The Sele School, Hertford (4)

The John Warner School, Hoddesdon (4)
Cardinal Bourne School, Broxbourne (4)
Hemel Hempstead School (4)
Adeyfield School, Hemel Hempstead (4)
The Highfield School, Letchworth (4)
Ashlyns School, Berkhamsted (4)
Queens' School, Bushey (4)
Bushey Meads School, Bushey (4)
William Penn School, Rickmansworth (4)
St. Joan of Arc RC School, Rickmansworth (4)
Westfield School, Watford (4)

Hounslow

Hounslow Manor Comprehensive School (1)
Longford Comprehensive School (1)

Humberside

Brumby Comprehensive School, Scunthorpe (planning 1)
Snaith School (planning 1)

ILEA

North Westminster Community School (1)
Archbishop Michael Ramsey School (1)
Quinton Kynaston School (1)
Parliament Hill School (2)
Stoke Newington School (1)
Clissold Park Comprehensive School

Isle of Man

Douglas High School (2)
Ballakermeen Junior High School, Douglas (2)
Castle Rushen High School, Castletown (2)
Queen Elizabeth II High School, Peel (2)
Ramsey Grammar School (2)
College of FE (Nursery Nurse course)

Kent

Aylesford School, Maidstone (1)
Charles Dickens School, Broadstairs (3)
The Eden Valley School, Edenbridge
Hillview Secondary School for Girls, Tonbridge

Leeds

15 primary schools are engaged in a project based on awareness in language.

Lothian

A long-term project is starting in Primary schools in 1984-85 which is to be continued eventually into the Secondary stage.

Manchester

Parrs Wood High School (1)
Ducie Central High School (2)
St. Alban's High School (2)
Whalley Range High School (4)

Newcastle-upon-Tyne

Gosforth High School (3)

Sunderland

Farringdon School (1)
Ryhope School (1)

Surrey

Weydon County Secondary School, Farnham (1)
Thamesmead School, Shepperton (1)
St. Andrews RC School, Leatherhead (1)
The authority is planning a substantial initiative next year in middle schools.

Trafford

Delahays Secondary School for Girls, Altrincham (1)
Great Stone Secondary School, Stretford.

Walsall

Alumwell Comprehensive School (1 and 3)
Brownhills Comprehensive School (3)
Blue Coat C.E. Comprehensive School (2 and 4)
Darlaston Comprehensive School (2)
Joseph Leckie Comprehensive School (3)
Manor Farm Comprehensive School (1,2 and 3)
Pelsall Comprehensive School (2 and 4)
Pool Hayes Comprehensive School (2)

Queen Mary's High School (4)
Shire Oak Comprehensive School (3)
Sneyd Comprehensive School (3)
St. Francis of Assissi RC Comprehensive School (2 and 3)
Streetly High School (2 and 3)
Willenhall Comprehensive School (3)
Blackwood Middle School (1)

Newham

Little Ilford School (1)
Rokesby School (1)

Norfolk

Alpine Materials (A Language Project in Norfolk Education) have been provided to 10 High Schools (11/12 - 16/18), 30 Middle Schools (8/12) and 32 Primary Schools (5/9 - 11) in the County of Norfolk. Evaluation of the project is proceeding. The adviser, Mr R E Whiley has requested that no direct approach for information be made to the schools; they are therefore not listed here. Further information should be sought from Mr Whiley himself.

Northamptonshire

Northampton Trinity School, Northampton (1)
Kingsthorpe Upper School, Northampton (1)
Chenderit School, Banbury (1)

North Tyneside

Valley Gardens Middle School, Whitley Bay

Nottingham

The Manning School (1)

Oxon

The Henry Box School, Witney (1,3)
Banbury School (1)
Faringdon School, Faringdon (1)
Milham Ford School, Oxford
Bayswater Middle School, Oxford (1)
Cooper School, Bicester (1)
Larkmead School, Abingdon (3)
Peers School, Littlemore (1)
Lord Williams School, Thame (1)
Wood Green School, Witney (1,3 and 4)

Richmond

Orleans Park School (3)

Salford

Broughton High School
Clarendon Park High School
Irwell Valley High School
Kersal High School

Sheffield

Carter Lodge School (1)
High Green School (1)

Staffordshire

Holmcroft Middle School (1)

Stockport

Hazel Grove High School (1)

Suffolk

Reydon High School, Southwold (1)

Waltham Forest

Rush Croft High School (3)
Highams Park Senior High School (2)
Tom Hood Senior High School (2)
Leyton Senior High School for Girls (3)
William Morris Senior High School (2)
Walthamstow Senior High School for Girls (2)
Cardinal Wiseman Senior High School (2)

West Glamorgan

Bishopston Junior School
Rhos Primary School
Rhyd-y-fro Primary School
Glanafan Comprehensive School, Port Talbot (2 and 4)

Wigan

Shevington High School (1)

Independent Schools

The Oratory School, Woodcote

The following authorities/schools have indicated interest in
beginning or developing Language Awareness work further:

Authorities

Birmingham
Bolton
Dumfries
Manchester
Rotherham
Sheffield
Wakefield
Wigan

The London Boroughs of:

Barking and Dagenham
Havering
Merton

Bedfordshire
Central Regional Council
Clwyd
Kirklees
Mid-Glamorgan
North Yorkshire
Powys
South Tyneside
Tameside
Warwickshire
Western Isles Islands

Schools

Culverham School, Bath
Chase Cross School, Romford
Marshalls Park School, Romford
Areley Kings, The Windmill School, Stourport-on-Severn
The John Masefield High School, Ledbury
Vale Wood Primary School, Liverpool
Hillside High School, Bootle
Kingsfield School, Bristol

The above list was compiled primarily from responses to questionnaires sent to Local Education Authorities in 1982 and 1984. It
should be noted that several authorities replied to the request for
information indicating that they knew that Language Awareness
featured as an aspect of courses in their schools, but were unable
to be more specific. A number of schools are also involved in
Language Across the Curriculum projects. The Working Party would
like to express its appreciation of the responses, including those
where a 'nil' finding was indicated!